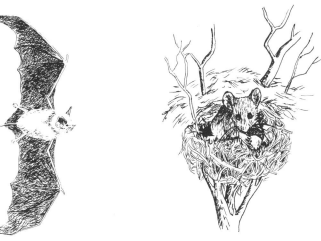

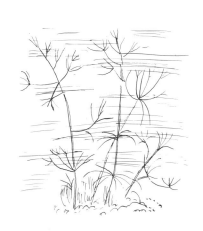

God's Marvelous Works

Book Two

God's

Marvelous

Works

Book Two

Rod and Staff Publishers, Inc.
Crockett, Kentucky 41413

Telephone (606) 522-4348

Acknowledgments

To the God of heaven and earth we give thanks for His grace that enabled vessels to prepare this textbook. As the book is used in many schools it is our sincere desire that it will continue to bring glory and honor to His Name.

We extend a special thanks to Rosa Kurtz Mullet for her vision, perseverance, and willingness to spend hours of labor in writing this book. The following persons also contributed much to this project: the editor, Isaac D. Martin; the artist, Michelle Coon; the reviewers, Clyde Beidler and Nelson L. Baer. Many of the Rod and Staff personnel labored to complete the book in its final form.

The Bible was used for direction in presenting the material contained in this book. Other books, including encyclopedias, concordances, dictionaries, other texts, handbooks, and field guides, were searched and checked to maintain accuracy in this text. Presented in a readable style which will produce student interest and cause them to marvel at God's creation, it is also factual.

We are grateful to the Harold M. Lambert company for granting permission for most of the photographs in this book. Permission for the photograph on page 220 was granted by H. Armstrong Roberts.

We appreciate the prayers and financial support which made this work possible. Our prayer is that these studies may bring forth fruit unto everlasting life. May His Name be praised.

—The Publishers

Contents

Unit 3 Sponges, Mollusks, Sea Worms, and Sea Jellies

Unit 4 Amphibians

1. Algae and Fungi

The Fungi Whisper . . .

We are the soil builders.
We are the plant feeders,
Everywhere fulfilling God's Word.

Hour after hour,
Night and day,
Summer and winter,
Above ground and underground,
Silently we work.

In cold and heat,
Darkness and light,
Moisture and drought,
We break down each plant and animal body
On every prairie,
By swamps and rivers,
Through lakes and oceans,
Deserts and mountains,
In all the forests of the world.

*"All are of the dust, and all
turn to dust again." Ecclesiastes 3:20*

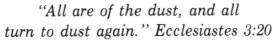

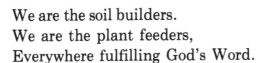

1. Mushrooms With Gills

A great many of our most delicious and nutritious foods are found in the plant kingdom. When God created the first man and woman He told them, "Behold, I have given you every herb bearing seed, which is upon the face of all the earth, and every tree, in the which is the fruit of a tree yielding seed; to you it shall be for meat" (Genesis 1:29).

Most plants of God's creation multiply by seeds. A seed is a very small inactive plant in a protective coating. Sometimes the coating also holds food for the developing new sprout. The tasty fleshy parts of cherries, peaches, plums, apples, pears, and various berries cover the seeds. Nuts, grains, peas, and beans are among the seeds that God has given to mankind for food.

About one-third of the plants that God has made reproduce by forming

Some individual spore-bearing cells

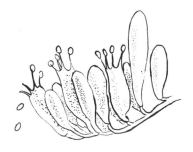

Cells like these grow on the surfaces of mushroom gills. Each cell usually has four prongs.

spores. Ferns, mosses, mushrooms, and certain plantlike animals produce single-celled spores in great numbers. In suitable conditions these spores divide to make two cells. As the cells continue to multiply the new plant or animal grows larger. Most spores are so small that they cannot be seen without a microscope. Clumps of spores resemble dust.

Look at a piece of moldy bread. Do you see the tiny white threads that are growing through the bread and on its surface? Each of these is a hypha ('hī-fə). The first hypha of this mold appeared when an invisible spore landed on the bread, burst its wall, and sent out the thin thread. There are so many hyphae ('hī-fē) now that they look like a flat, cottony film. This mass of hyphae is called the mycelium (mī-'sē-lē-əm). The mycelium is the main body of the mold and is composed of only one kind of cell. It spreads and grows as long as there is anything on which it can feed. The rootlike hyphae digest tiny particles of bread and absorb them, staining the bread and producing a characteristic odor.

After the mycelium has grown for a while, tiny white spore cases appear. These spore cases hold reproductive cells that become black as they mature. Each cell is able to begin another mycelium. The spore case bursts. Spores appear by the millions. Air currents carry them everywhere. But favorable conditions are necessary before the spores will send out hyphae.

Just as bread mold grows upon bread, so various mycelia live on wood or soil. Most spores do not find good growing places and are wasted.

If a tree has been injured so that the bark is broken, the wind will often carry some spores to that place. The spores will push hyphae into the wood, dissolving and absorbing it. In time a hard wind may complete the work of destruction by breaking it at the weakened spot.

To prevent further damage of an injured tree, remove any loose bark or splinters, leaving a flat sloping surface from which rain water will drain. Cover the wound with pruning balm. This is a substance especially made to aid the

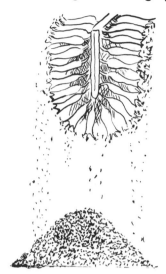

Mushroom gills are covered with microscopic cells. Spores rain from prongs on the cells, forming visible ridges.

healing of live trees. It may be found in nurseries selling shrubs and trees. Spores cannot take root where cuts are sealed.

The black spore cases of the bread mold are like mushrooms. Both are spore holders springing from mature mycelia. The mushrooms of woods and fields carry the reproductive spores that will begin a new network of hyphae wherever food is present in warm, moist conditions.

The plants which produce mushrooms may have been spreading underground for months or even years. Sometimes the mat of threads has had an equal rate of growth in all directions from its starting point. When the mushrooms push to the surface during favorable weather they appear all along the border of the underground mycelium. Such a circle of mushrooms is

A mushroom mycelium grows underground for weeks, months, or even years before it sends up the fruiting bodies that we know as mushrooms.

12

known as a fairy ring.

Gilled mushrooms have three main parts—the stem, the cap, and the gills. Various species have differently shaped caps. The gills are thin blades fastened to the underside of the cap by their upper edges, and growing from the stem to the margin. Shorter gills begin at the margin of the cap and extend toward the stalk, filling in the spaces left at the rim. Mushrooms usually drop white, pink, rusty-brown, purple, or black spores; but there may be other colors of spores, too.

The stems of some mushrooms have a ring, the tatters left when the inner veil breaks loose as the cap opens. Some stems rise out of a cup or volva.

Probably the mushroom we know best is the one we have eaten in soup or bought on the market, the meadow mushroom. This delicious mushroom grows wild in the United States and Europe and is also cultivated as a food. If during July, August, or September we should find it in the fields or pastures, we would see a dry white cap from 1½ to 4 inches across with pink gills that become chocolate colored as the mushroom matures. The spores are brown. The stem is short, perhaps only 2 or 3 inches high. The cap expands, somewhat as a folded umbrella opens, until it is nearly flat. A ring left by the inner veil clings to the stem when the plant is young. This mushroom does not grow in thick woods, but in grassy places, such as pastures or lawns or where manure is found.

Another good-tasting mushroom is named delicious *Lactarius* (lak-'ta-rē-əs). An orange-colored milk oozes from the plant when it is broken. The flesh at the break slowly turns green. Delicious *Lactarius* grows on the ground in pine woods, hardwood forests, and mossy swamps. It may be as large as 5 inches across. The stem grows from 1 to 4 inches long. The spores are white. When the cap becomes mature it is sometimes funnel shaped, colored with rings of deeper yellow on a paler ground. The gills are orange. This species is found from July to October.

The beautiful orange-yellow jack-o'-lantern, found in forests at the same

The edible or meadow mushroom is the species most commonly eaten.

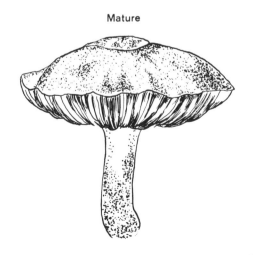
Mature

Young

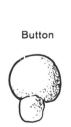
Button

The delicious Lactarius has an orange-colored juice. It is often found in pine woods and mossy swamps.

time of the year as the delicious *Lactarius,* is poisonous when eaten. It grows in tufts on decaying woods such as logs, stumps, or buried roots. The cap is 2 to 5 inches across and the stem may grow to a length of 7 inches. The gills extend down the stem and shed round, white spores. The cap is nearly flat. It may have a slight hollow with a knob in the center. The jack-o'-lantern glows brightly in the dark and can be easily recognized by this characteristic.

A delicate little mushroom is the glistening inkcap which grows on the ground or on decaying wood from May to November. This tan or brownish spore shedder is only 1 or 2 inches across, bell shaped, thin, and marked with narrow ribs that extend part of the way from the margin toward the center. The center is smooth and sometimes has small glistening particles on it. The margin is often notched and splits when the cap expands. The spores are brown and fall from gills that are whitish at

first, soon change to pink, then become black or brown, and turn to a dripping liquid. The ink making may begin only a few hours after the cap opens. Sometimes in dry weather the spores do not melt at all. The species is common in cities along sidewalks where trees have been cut down.

Perhaps you remember the story of the angel which God sent through all the coasts of Israel to destroy the people after King David had disobeyed the instructions given to Moses years before about numbering the men of war (Exodus 30:11-16; 1 Chronicles 21:11-15; 2 Samuel 24:15-17). Seventy thousand men lost their lives by the destroying angel.

One of the gilled mushrooms has received the name destroying angel

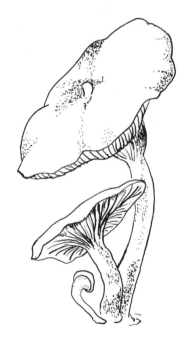

The jack-o'-lantern is a rich-yellow color and gives off a glowing light in the dark. It grows in clusters.

This glistening inkcap, only an inch or two across, is a very common mushroom.

are good to eat. They all grow from cups that are sometimes hidden under the soil. Over 90 percent of the fatal mushroom poisonings are due to eating *Amanitas.* Dr. W. Thomas Stevens reports that in New York City as many as thirty persons in a single year have died from this cause.

The destroying angel, appearing from July to October, is usually white with white spores. However, various species of poisonous *Amanitas* are buff or tan, greenish or yellow, orange or red, reddish-brown or blackish. The inner veil leaves a ring on the stem. Often specks of the outer veil form warts on the cap. The fly *Amanita* has a red cap with white warts. This mushroom family usually grows in open woods.

Never eat a mushroom with a stem enclosed in a cup. It is also dangerous to

because it brings death to the people who eat it. One small mushroom can be fatal if eaten, because usually there is no discomfort for 12 or more hours. By that time the poison has reached the liver, the heart, the lungs, and the kidneys.

The Amanita (ˌam-ə-ˈnīd-ə) group has five poisonous species and two that

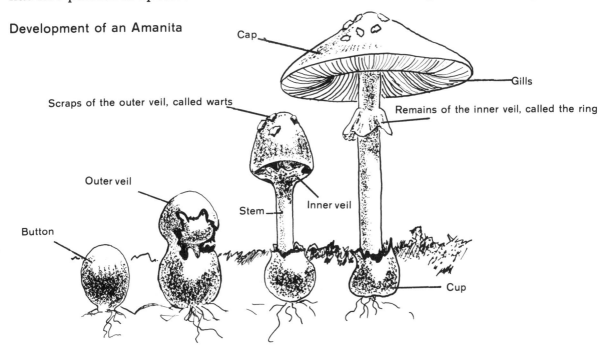

Development of an Amanita

Cap

Gills

Scraps of the outer veil, called warts

Remains of the inner veil, called the ring

Outer veil

Stem

Inner veil

Button

Cup

The Amanita, like most other gilled mushrooms, begins as a button. It grows to 6 inches tall, always with a cup at the base of the stem. The cup is often hidden underground.

eat a wild unknown mushroom in the button stage or one broken off above the ground, because it might possibly be an *Amanita*.

The *Amanita* is not the only poisonous mushroom. Some mushrooms that are poisonous have no cup at the base of the stem. There is no one characteristic possessed by all the poisonous mushrooms. To be safe eat only mushrooms collected by one who has had experience and positively recognizes the species.

God has designed many gilled mushrooms that display beauty of form and color. But this loveliness is delicate. It is gone in a very short time. Add enjoyment to your nature walks by becoming a mushroom hunter.

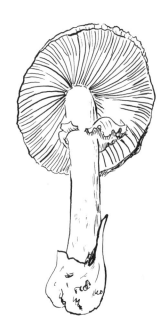

Gill arrangement
Mushroom gills stretch like the ribs of an umbrella from the stem to the margin of the cap. Shorter gills run partway from the outer edge toward the stem, filling in the wider spaces near the rim.

Class Project

Collect various gilled mushrooms. Cut the stems very short. Prepare squares of dark and light cardboard by smearing them on one side with a thin layer of egg white or a mixture of water and mucilage. Dark-spored varieties may be placed over light cardboard and light-spored species over dark cardboard.

Push several toothpicks into the side of the cap and rest them on small chips of wood so that the gills are held $\frac{1}{8}$ inch above the sticky paper. Cover with a turned-over bowl. Allow the spores to drop for a full day.

Lift the bowl. Allow the print to dry.

Art stores carry a product called fixatif used to prevent pastel and charcoal drawings from smudging. Spray your print with fixatif. Dry again.

Identify the species if possible. Label with the species name, the date, and the place where it was found.

Questions

1. What did God give to the human race for food?

2. God has created (all the plants, two-thirds of the plants, one-third of the plants) to bear seeds.

3. The main part of a plant that bears mushrooms is called the (stem, crown, mycelium, root).

4. Why does breaking the bark on a tree often seriously damage the tree?

5. How can a wounded tree be preserved?

6. Name two mushrooms that are good to eat.

7. Name a bright orange mushroom that can be seen at night.

8. What common mushroom has spores that melt?

9. Most cases of mushroom poisoning occur when people eat mushrooms of the ——— group.

10. Poisonous mushrooms (are, are not) easily recognized.

11. Which rules are safe to follow in selecting mushrooms to eat?
    (a) Eat mushrooms gathered by someone with experience and knowledge in collecting edible species.
    (b) Eat mushrooms carefully checked to be sure that there were no cups around the base of the stems.
    (c) Eat cultivated mushrooms.
    (d) Eat mushrooms that do not have white spores.

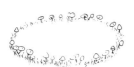
"Stand still, and consider the wondrous works of God." Job 37:14

2.   Mushrooms Without Gills

God has not created every mushroom with gills. He has planned other spore-shedding forms, too. Some of these are very curious indeed. If you knew nothing about spores you could not guess the purpose of these unusual shapes. We will become acquainted with a number of them as we go along. Every new bit of knowledge about God's world adds to our enjoyment of it.

Pore mushrooms have many small pores or tubes opening downward under the cap. Spores are formed inside and are shed from the tubes. This group is named polypore, meaning "many pores."

The pine cone mushroom is shaped much like a small meadow mushroom but has a longer stem. Tufts on the blackish cap look like pine cone scales. The stem is rough and dark and the whitish tubes become nearly black with

A pine cone mushroom. Bumps like pine cone scales cover the cap of this pore mushroom. It grows to 4 inches across.

age. You may find this common mushroom in the woods during July and August. It does not have a very good flavor.

While fleshy, gilled mushrooms grow and drop spores in a few hours or days, pore mushrooms may produce spores occasionally for months or even years. Many of them are leathery, woody, or papery. A few are fleshy and soon decay.

Artist's fungus ('fəŋ-gəs) grows as a bracket on oak or beech trees. It is from 2 to 8 inches across or even as wide as 2 feet. Brown or grayish, it is sometimes covered with rusty-brown spores. Each year a ring of new growth adds to the width and thickness. The tubes from which the spores fall are pure white, but when they are injured they turn dark. A picture may be drawn on the underside of the artist's fungus just by pressing with a pointed stick. Heavy pressure will leave a dark-brown line. Tracing lightly will make a pale-brown line. As the mushroom dries, the picture will become permanent. Already-dried artist's fungus will not develop color under pressure.

One home chose an attractive feature for its guest rooms. On the walls of each was displayed a specimen of this mushroom with a Bible verse written on it.

Artist's fungus has pure-white tubes that turn brown when pressed. Pictures may be drawn upon it. This polypore occasionally grows to a width of 2 feet.

The rusty-hoof *Fomes* ('fō-mēz) is another pore mushroom. It grows on beech, birch, and a few other hardwood trees, and may live as long as 35 years. Its form and habits of growth are similar to artist's fungus. Rusty-hoof *Fomes* were commonly used as tinder and punk in former days. Had you been a child living in colonial times you might have been sent to the forest to collect these pored fungi (ˌfən-'jī) to be carried along to kindle campfires. If your own fire had died during the night, perhaps you might have scampered over hard, frozen, snowy ground to a neighbor's house to bring back a smoking piece of this mushroom to light a fire in your own fireplace.

The white or buff *Hydnum repandum* (ˌhid-nəm rē-ˌpan-dum) has a spore scatterer of still another shape. The smooth cap grows as wide as 8 inches across. The stem is off center and is less than 2 inches long. The *Hydnum repandum* has many brittle, white teeth from which the spores rain.

The mushrooms of the *Hydnum* group grow both on the ground and on wood. Some species have teeth which hang from ascending branches. Other

Cross section   Top view

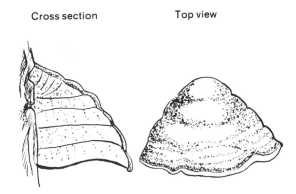

In the days before matches, rusty-hoof Fomes were used for punk and tinder. Growing like a shelf on beech and birch tree trunks, this mushroom may reach a width of 12 inches.

What Happens When . . .

Look at beech, birch, and other hardwood trees for rusty-hoof *Fomes*. Hold a lighted match under the thin edge of the mushroom. Place the smoldering piece in an enclosed spot such as an empty tin can. When does the smoke stop rising? How long afterward can the piece be used for starting fires?

The Hydnum repandum sheds its spores from straight, brittle, white teeth. This very short stemmed species has a cap 1 to 8 inches broad.

species have teeth which project down from the undersurfaces of dead wood. Most *Hydnums* are good to eat.

Puffballs have their spore-producing organs covered by a tough, sometimes papery covering. Giant puffballs often grow to 20 inches across. One that was 6 feet across and weighed 61 pounds was reported from Ohio in 1933. Another giant from New York was recorded as being $5\frac{1}{4}$ feet long, $4\frac{1}{2}$ feet wide, with a wall $9\frac{1}{2}$ inches thick. Since a puffball weighing a little over 5 pounds is estimated to produce 7 trillion spores, one as large as this would contain a higher number than we could even imagine. Some are too small to be seen individually with the naked eye. A cloud of spores looks like smoke.

If each of the 7 trillion spores grew and produced a puffball likewise weighing 5 pounds and each of these puffballs also produced 7 trillion spores that grew into 5-pound puffballs, there would be a mass of puffballs eight hundred times the size of our planet Earth. How wise God is to plan that

The giant puffball may grow to 20 inches across and weigh 10 pounds.

The gem-studded puffball may grow as much as 2 inches across. It has a warty, white surface.

most of the spores produced never live or grow.

When the spores of a puffball are mature, the papery covering tears. Every disturbance sends up clouds, resembling small jets of smoke. An animal stepping upon a puffball can carry spores away. When rain strikes, they rise and float off.

When puffballs are young and solid they are often used for food. Only a few species are unfit to eat.

The gem-studded puffball grows in thick clusters on rotten wood or on the ground. It has a round white surface 1 to 2 inches across covered with warts. The top slopes to a broad stem.

One interesting puffball, growing on decayed wood, is named bird's nest fungus. The tan, cup-shaped lower part, as much as $\frac{1}{2}$ inch wide, holds several white egglike spore balls. Each of these is fastened to the cup by a thread.

Growing on bare soil is the rough, dark-gray, water-measuring earthstar. Pointed papery segments from seven to twenty in number fold around the 1- to 2-inch dry center ball. In a damp atmosphere these segments relax and spread away from the middle. When moisture is low, the points contract and cover it again. As the humidity changes they curl inward or bend outward, indicating the amount of water in the air. Finally the spores mature and float through a small hole in the top.

Some earthstars have four outer sections that reach down and lift the ball up more than 3 inches. In this position this fungus resembles a human figure standing erect with long arms hanging to the ground. The spore container on its short stem looks like a head and neck.

Besides pore mushrooms, toothed mushrooms, and puffballs there are various other forms that you will notice when you begin to observe mushrooms. Unusual shapes and soft beautiful colors belong to the mushrooms without gills.

These tiny, tan-colored cups $\frac{1}{4}$ to $\frac{1}{2}$ inch in diameter hold a number of miniature puffballs, each on its own thread. They are called bird's nest fungi.

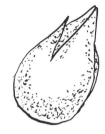

Wide open,
wet and very humid

Partly open,
rather damp

Closed, dry air,
little moisture

An earthstar measuring moisture
The water-measuring earthstar, a fairly reliable gauge of humidity.

Class Project

Walk in the woods and damp fields. Find as many of the mushrooms in this lesson as you can. Test the "smoke-making" qualities of the various puffballs. Draw a picture on the flat tube surface of the artist's fungus.

Questions

1. Every mushroom (has, does not have) thin soft velvety plates called gills.

2. Pore mushrooms shed spores from (tubes, plates, scales, stems).

3. In the early days of this country what use was made of rusty-hoof *Fomes?*

4. What mushroom has pure-white tubes that turn brown when pressed so that pictures can be drawn upon them?

5. The *Hydnum repandum* scatters spores from (branches, leaves, white teeth, balls).

6. Puffballs have (a few dozen, many thousands, billions and trillions) of spores.

7. Full-sized giant puffballs are (no larger than a baseball, no larger than a basketball, the size of a big pumpkin or larger).

8. Spores coming from a puffball look like (clouds of smoke, drops of water, grains of sand, bits of wood).

9. Water-measuring earthstars are (1 to 2 inches high, 3 to 4 inches high, 5 to 6 inches high, 7 to 8 inches high, fleshy, gritty, woody, papery, slimy, jellylike, wet, dry, red, yellow, gray, black [choose four]).

10. Bird's nest fungus belongs to the (gilled, toothed, pore, puffball) group.

11. Individual spores are (as fine as dust, as small as grains of sand, about the size of a radish seed).

"Blessed be the Lord God, . . . who only doeth wondrous things." Psalm 72:18

3. Wide Water Pastures

"And God saw every thing that he had made, and, behold, it was very good" (Genesis 1:31). Ever since that time man has been living among the countless wonders of God's creation. Each sunrise opens a new day and its opportunity to behold God's works and to see that they are good.

The living things on God's earth are found in two kingdoms, the animal kingdom and the plant kingdom. What is the difference between a plant and an animal? One answer might be that plants are green and animals are not. However, many plants are not green, either. Another answer might be that animals move about from one place to another by their own power and plants do not. But there are plants that are rather active during some part of their growth, and there are animals that move very little.

Most animals large enough to be seen move easily from place to place throughout their lives. They are not green. Most plants move of their own accord only when they are growing or shedding seeds. But quite a few species living in salt or fresh water and others too small to see without a miscroscope are not green. Scientists sometimes find it hard to decide whether a certain living form belongs to the plant kingdom or to the animal kingdom.

In the plant kingdom we find life that is very simple and life that is very complex. Have you ever thought of all the different materials in a tree? Look at the dogwood tree. It has bark, roots, and root hairs. It has heartwood, sapwood, flowers, pollen, nectar, leaves, leaf stems, twigs, and berries. Each is composed of a different sort of cell.

There are also plants so simple that they have very few kinds of cells. These simple plants belong to the division known as thallophytes ('thal-ə-ˌfīts). About eighty thousand species, almost one-third of the known plants, belong to this division. Algae ('al-jē) are thallophytes.

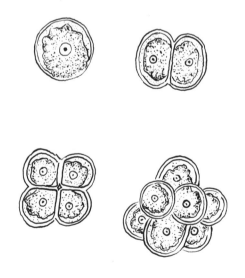

A single-celled green alga
This green alga multiplies by cell division. It is commonly found on trees, stones, and fences in moist shady places.

Most algae have one type of cell that forms the main body, or thallus ('thal-əs). Other kinds of cells develop only during reproduction. Some algae appear to have roots, stems, and leaves; but these parts do not perform as true roots, stems, and leaves do. Thallophytes have no tubes through which sap moves.

Algal ('al-gəl) plants contain the green coloring matter named chlorophyll ('klōr-ə-ˌfil). Sunlight or indirect light enables chlorophyll to combine carbon dioxide from the air with water and minerals, thus producing food for the plant. This food-making operation is called photosynthesis (fōd-ō-'sin-thə-səs), which means "to put together in light." Because they need light, algae grow in shallow water or in the upper layers of deep water.

Some algal plants have only one cell. But this single cell is alive. It can take in its own food. It can multiply to form another living individual. Many algal cells are covered with thin gelatinlike layers. Separate plants often form sheets and clumps because their outer walls cling together.

Algae, numbering thousands of species, are divided into four classes according to their color. Each class has plants of various sizes and shapes. The colors are blue-green, green, brown, and red.

The blue-green algae, found in both salt and fresh water, can be seen only with a very powerful microscope. They can endure heat close to 200 degrees, drying, and below-freezing temperatures. Certain species when dried were alive even after 70 years. Plants of this family live and grow on land if they have a supply of water. Some of the rock terraces and basins at Yellowstone National Park are colored by algae. Many simple blue-green and green algae increase by cell division. Each cell divides, grows larger, and divides again. Colonies form, break apart, and continue to multiply.

Almost all the fresh water of the world is home to one or more species from the three main groups of green fresh-water algae. Many thallophytes from these three groups likewise thrive in warm salt water. Common names for these plants are water moss and pond scums. The smallest kinds of algae are found among the desmids ('dez-məds), which coat sticks, shells, and other objects.

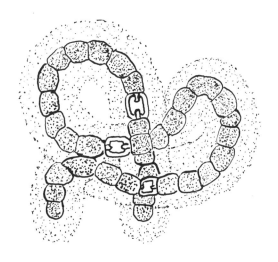

A blue-green algal plant. Notice the gelatinous sheath and the dead colorless cells. The filament will break into pieces at these points. This plant has no holdfasts.

From a clear sunlit pond or lake take ½ cup of water. Use a hand lens and try to see crescent-shaped desmids. Sometimes so many desmids are present that the water is colored green.

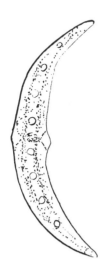

This desmid can often be seen with a hand lens.

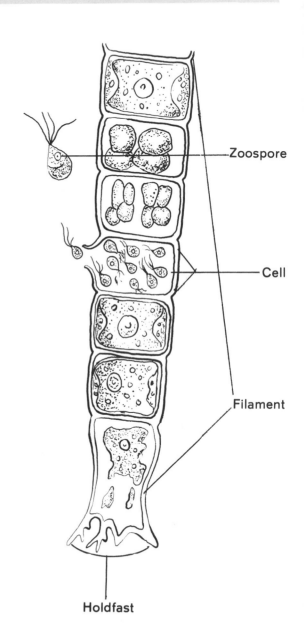

An algal filament often multiplies by zoospores. Notice the four short hairs by which the zoospore swims.

If you have ever seen a bright-green hairy growth in water tanks or streams, you were looking at one of the thread-like algae. This plant does not branch. It often grows to be an inch long and is anchored by means of a single cell called a holdfast. The holdfast may have rootlike fingers, but these do not absorb food or moisture as roots do. They simply prevent the filament ('fil-ə-mənt) from floating away.

When the algae is mature some of its cells form little free-swimming bodies which leave the parent plant. They are called zoospores because they move

Chara

Nitella

Stoneworts are also called candelabra plants.

around as animals do. These little zoospores swim off by means of four little hairs growing from one end. They find a small crack in some underwater object, attach themselves, and begin to grow. Soon another green filament is waving downstream.

The third group of green fresh-water algae is named stonewort. One stonewort is *Chara* ('Ka-rə), which grows in ponds found in limy soil. It secretes lime which forms a crust on the surface of the plant. *Chara* has fruiting organs like brightly colored oranges. These can be seen at the bases of the branches with a hand lens.

Nitella (nī-'tel-ə) has a more delicate form than *Chara* and usually lacks the limy covering. Both *Chara* and *Nitella* are known as the candelabra plant. Stoneworts, like other algae,

lack true roots, stems, and leaves; but they are shaped much like plants that do have these parts.

Another kind of green algae grows on the shaded side of trees, rocks, buildings, and other places having enough dampness and light. Many of these plants are so small that 625 side by side would stretch only the width of a pencil. Some species of algae living on land multiply by spores that are carried along by air currents to a new place.

The film of golden brown on plants, stones, and water creatures is a layer of tiny one-celled algae. These are called diatoms ('dīə-ˌtämz). Diatoms are the most abundant of all living things in salt water or fresh. They are too small to be seen with the naked eye. Most other fresh-water algae are green or blue-green.

27

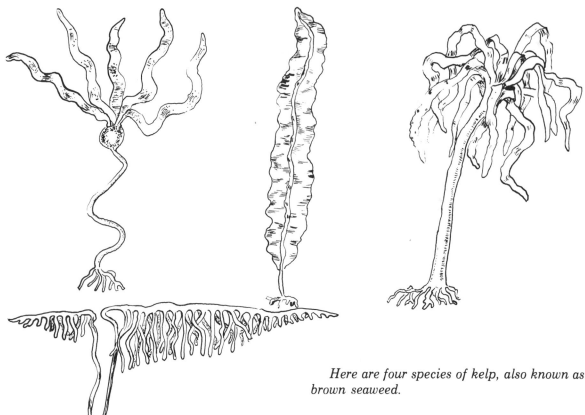

Here are four species of kelp, also known as brown seaweed.

The brown algae live mostly in the ocean or on rocky seashores between the low and high tide marks. Their green chlorophyll is often completely covered by purplish-brown or golden-brown coloring. The largest brown seaweed is kelp that may grow to a length of 200 feet. The leaflike fronds and stalks of some species have small air-filled floats that keep them near the surface of the water.

A tropical seaweed named sargassum (sär-ˈgas-əm), or gulfweed, is found in the North Atlantic Ocean. The Gulf Stream flows north from the Gulf of Mexico and along the Atlantic coast, swinging to the east in a clock-wise motion. Other ocean currents sweep south past Europe and the northern part of Africa. In the center of these swirling currents lies a large calm of warm, salty water with an area of 2 million square miles. Sargassum, torn

Sargassum weed. Notice the berrylike air-filled floats.

Many legends have been told about the dangers of the Sargasso Sea.

loose from the rocks where it grows, drifts out of the currents into this quiet water called the Sargasso Sea. Some students think that perhaps 10 million tons of the algae are floating here, providing homes for hosts of crabs, shrimps, small fishes, and various animals.

The weed does not grow thickly enough to hinder sailing vessels, but mariners in the old days heard and told tales of ships being trapped in the Sargasso Sea until they rotted away in the hot sun.

Another brown seaweed is known as rockweed. True to its name, it grows on rocky shores and sometimes forms a thick cover. This leathery plant is about a foot long and usually has two

branches, each with its floats. Brown algae grow only in salt water.

The red algae are always found in ocean waters, too. They like warm temperate or tropical seas and grow at a lower depth than the brown seaweeds.

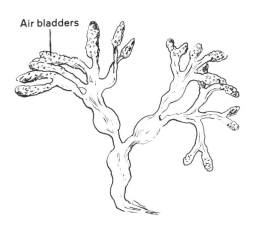

Here is another brown seaweed which grows on rocky shores and is named rockweed.

This red alga grows 2 to 9 inches long and is found in tropical waters.

Many of these are finely branched and feathery. The green color of their chlorophyll is covered by bright red or purple, or shades of violet and rose. They are very beautiful.

Algae are eaten by many tiny water animals that in turn are swallowed by fishes which man uses for food. Lobsters, crabs, clams, and oysters eat algae, too.

Are algae of any value to people? Japan, China, and Hawaii use more than one hundred different kinds of seaweeds as food. In Japan desirable algae are cultivated in beds covering perhaps 1,000 acres and harvested 3 or 4 months later. Goiter and leprosy are treated with the products of algae. Iodine is prepared from kelp.

In this country agar-agar, from a seaweed, is used to thicken soups and sauces, ice cream, desserts, and pastries. Canned fish is improved by adding agar-agar.

Those who study food problems have become acquainted with the algae *Chlorella* (klə-ˈrel-ə). *Chlorella* when dried tastes like raw pumpkin or raw lima beans. High in vitamin value, it is more than 50 percent easily digested protein. Perhaps food shortages in the future may be partly relieved by growing *Chlorella,* either for human use or to feed meat animals. Sometime we may eat algae as often as we now eat wheat or potatoes.

Class Project

Find algae on trees, rocks, and the shaded sides of buildings. Visit a pond or stream and find as many species of algae in the water as you can. If convenient, go to an ocean beach and study various forms of seaweeds.

Questions

1. Thallophytes are (plants without roots, stem, leaves, or flowers; plants with true roots, stems, leaves, and flowers; a class of animals).

2. Algae are (animals too small to be seen except with a microscope, thallophytes that make their own food, thallophytes that cannot make their own food).

3. Chlorophyll is (red coloring, green coloring, yellow coloring) in leaves and stems.

4. Chlorophyll makes food (in the light, in the darkness, when it is cold).

5. Photosynthesis is (the growth of a plant, the reproduction of a plant, the food-making processes of a plant).

6. Algae are grouped according to (size, the place where they are found, color, habits of growth).

7. What are the four classes of algae?

8. Which of the following are *not* true of blue-green algae?
   (a) too small to be seen without a microscope
   (b) live and grow even in hot water
   (c) can be dried for years without dying
   (d) live and grow in both salt and fresh water
   (e) can be frozen without being killed
   (f) always large enough to be seen with the naked eye
   (g) can endure being frozen, but die when exposed to hot water

9. Algae growing in water are often covered with (sharp scratchy teeth, a gelatinous covering, poisonous spines, heavy rocky lumps).

10. Algae are used by man for (clothing, food, shelter).

11. Algae multiply by (seeds, cell division, spores, roots, zoospores [choose three]).

12. What is the Sargasso Sea?

"Sing unto him . . . . : talk ye of all his wondrous works." Psalm 105:2

4. The Toughest Plants

Lichens are among the most remarkable plants that God has created to live on this earth. They are found throughout the world. Some are on the highest mountains; others grow at sea level along lake and ocean beaches. Lichens cover the branches of jungle trees in warm countries as well as flourish on frozen ground in the Arctic. These thallophytes take hold and grow where most plants could not even sprout. Only in places covered with water are lichens absent.

God has designed that certain species live together in a relationship called symbiosis (ˌsim-bī-ˈō-səs). Two plants or two animals may live together in this way. The combination is often a plant and an animal. This symbiotic (ˌsim-bī-ˈät-ik) relationship helps both partners.

The yucca (ˌyək-ə) moth and the yucca plant live in symbiosis. The yucca moth is the only insect that pollinates the yucca plant. Yucca plant seeds are the only food of the yucca moth larvae. The yucca moth lays her eggs and pollinates in a single visit to the yucca flower.

Something to Do

With a hand lens search your own backyard or the school ground for lichens. Look on bare soil around foundations and under shrubs. The bark of trees, old weathered siding, rocks, and pebbles may hold lichens. How many different species do you find? Name the various colors.

A lichen (ˈlī-kən) is algae with fungi for a partner. Both algae and fungi are thallophytes. Most lichens are fungi and algae combinations. The same alga that lives with a fungus in lichen form is sometimes found alone.

A small piece of lichen that was magnified to show the mycelium of the fungus holding the algal cells.

But the fungus cannot live without the alga.

The fungus forms a frame in which the algal cells are held. The fungus absorbs moisture and minerals for the alga. The alga makes food for both by the action of its chlorophyll.

How do lichens multiply? As other thallophytes do, they form spores. However, these spores must find the right kind of algae in a favorable place before they can begin growing. Probably few multiply in this way.

A large animal may walk over or rub against lichens and crush them. Falling trees and tumbling rocks grind others loose. The wind can spread these pieces far and wide. Each scrap already contains both algal and fungal cells. These form new plants.

The spores of a thallophyte and the plant parts that hold them are called fruit. The spore cases of mold are known as fruiting bodies because the reproductive spores are formed there. Likewise, mushrooms are the fruiting bodies of underground mycelia. The fruiting bodies of lichens sometimes appear as small round dots. After the spores are gone tiny hollows or holes remain.

There are three groups of lichens. Some are crustlike, tightly fastened or even embedded in rocks, tree trunks, or soil. Others are leaflike, usually with rootlike parts below that hold them to rocks or trees. Those of the third group are shrublike or branching. These may be found on soil, rail fences, old rotten tree trunks or logs.

Lichens can endure extreme drying

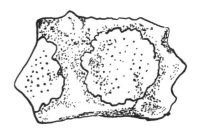

The pitted lichen grows on limestone, leaving many small pits in its surface.

and cold and revive when moisture and warmth are again present. They always grow with blue-green or green algae. These thallophytes are found all over the world. As many as sixteen thousand species have been named, two thousand of them in North America.

Some of these tough plants attach themselves to the barest rocks. Acids formed by both living and decaying thalluses gradually crumble the surface. Larger lichens and mosses are then able to gain a place. Each species that lives and dies, decays and leaves a small amount of plant food behind. Soil builds up.

Pitted lichen grows everywhere on limestone. Its grayish-white thallus has many small black fruiting bodies. This crustlike thallophyte sinks into the surface of the limestone. When it dies, an arrangement of holes is left behind where the fruiting bodies had grown. The limestone is pitted.

The clot lichen, flat gray or greenish-gray, is found around the world in the Northern Hemisphere. The cracked, warty crust is sometimes as large as 5 inches across. The fruiting bodies are shiny black dots, blood red underneath.

The clot lichen grows on evergreens and on high mountain rocks.

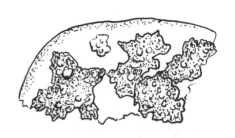

The toad skin lichen is thickly sprinkled with hollow warts.

Smooth rock tripe has a brown oval thallus that is black underneath. This leafy lichen grows on rocks in the mountains of eastern North America. When cooked, the 2- to 12-inch plant has some food value and may be eaten if nothing else is available.

The toad skin is commonly found east of the Rocky Mountains. The leaflike dark-colored thallus appears to have been dented from below. Each bump on the upper surface is hollow underneath. The fruiting bodies are black. This stiff, 4-inch plant belongs to the rock tripe lichen group.

Anywhere in eastern North America the red crest lichen may be found growing on old rail fences, decayed wood, or on the ground itself. Gray-greenish scales cover its sides. The fruiting bodies are red balls at the tips of the branched thallus. British soldiers is another name given to it, probably because the British soldier's uniform is scarlet.

The pale-green goblet lichen is

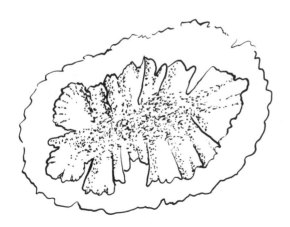

The smooth rock tripe holds to rocks by a single cord.

The 1-inch red crest lichen is greenish gray with red tips.

The 1-inch goblet lichen has many species that grow in North America.

shaped like a scaly stem with a cup on the top. When the fruiting disks form, they perch on the rim of the cup or at the tips of little branches that grow from the goblet's lip. The disks are brown, and the entire plant is only an inch high.

One leaflike fungus-bacteria (bak-'tir-ē-ə) combination is named the red blanket "lichen." Real lichens have algal cells, but the red blanket has a purple bacteria. This beautiful red plant grows on trees along the Gulf of Mexico and farther south.

Great areas of arctic and other northern regions are home to the branching lichens called reindeer moss that grow to a length of several inches. Musk ox, caribou, and domesticated reindeer feed on reindeer moss.

Old man's beard is a hanging lichen. It is often seen on trees in the cool, cone-bearing evergreen forests of the North. High mountains are likewise suited to its growth.

The northern parula warbler chooses to nest in old man's beard. The southern parula warbler in the warm, humid South nests in Spanish moss that

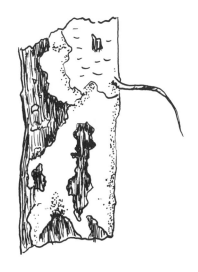

The red blanket "lichen," a bacteria-fungus combination, is common on trees in Florida and farther south.

looks like old man's beard but is not a lichen at all.

Some people think that lichens draw food from trees and injure them. But lichens have no true roots. They simply cling to the tree as they do to rocks or the soil.

Reindeer moss is an important food for northern animals such as musk oxen, caribou, and reindeer.

People who live in Iceland gather Iceland moss and use its starchy thallus in breadmaking. Some lichens are poisonous, however, and are unfit to eat.

Do people use these plants in any other way? Lichens produce colors used in dyeing. Lichens are also used in the manufacture of litmus paper, medicines, and perfume.

If you look closely you will find these tough plants in many unexpected places. They belong in the Creator's web of life.

Old man's beard is a greenish-gray or dark-gray hanging lichen that grows in the North. Notice the disklike cups in which the reproductive cells are formed.

Class Project

Make a collection of lichens, gathering them in the fruiting form if possible. Dry under light pressure so as to preserve the shape. Label each with the place and the date found. If you are able to identify them, label them with the species name. If not, state whether the specimen belongs to the crustlike, leaflike, or shrublike group.

Questions

1. Lichens are (large, small, tough, tender, common, rare, animals, plants [choose four]).

2. Lichens grow (in warm countries only, in cold countries only, all over the world, underwater).

3. Symbiosis is (two species living together without either helping or harming each other, two species living together for the good of only one species, two species living together for the good of both of

them).

4. Lichens are (plants with true roots, stems, leaves, and flowers; algae and fungi combinations; dwarf trees).

5. Lichens are grouped according to (size, color, where found, shape).

6. Name the three groups of lichens.

7. Pitted lichen leaves (black marks, bumps, small holes) on limestone.

8. The clot lichen (grows all around in the Northern Hemisphere, is a crusty lichen, is a branched lichen, grows in the tropics only [choose two]).

9. If you were stranded in the wilderness, what lichen would be fit to cook to eat?

10. The toad skin lichen is (smooth and pale orange, a hanging lichen, dark and bumpy like a toad's skin, found most often in California).

11. The red crest lichen is also named (red top, scarlet crown, British soldiers, crimson cover).

12. The pale-green goblet lichen is shaped like a (glob of mud, stem with a cup on top, a barrel, a straight-sided tank).

13. The red blanket "lichen" (grows on trees in warm countries, grows on rocks in cold countries, has many algal cells, is a bacteria-fungus combination, is leaflike, is red [choose four]).

14. Reindeer moss (grows in the Arctic, grows in the tropics, is a crustlike form embedded in rocks, is an important food for animals, is never eaten [choose two]).

15. Which statement is true?
    (a) Old man's beard looks like Spanish moss.
    (b) Old man's beard and Spanish moss are both hanging lichens.
    (c) Old man's beard and Spanish moss are the same plant.

16. Various species of lichens are used by people for (food, drink, shingles, glue making, dye making, pasteboard, litmus paper, flavorings, perfumes, medicines [choose five]).

17. Lichens multiply by (pieces being broken off and growing at another place, seeds, roots).

18. Lichens often (grow on trees without harming them, grow on trees and kill them).

"O Lord, . . . I will shew forth all thy marvellous works." Psalm 9:1

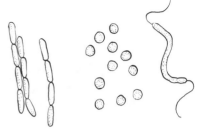

5. Year-round Soil Makers

"Look," the dusty ragged men said, pulling the old sacks from the shoulders of the animals. Untying the strings, they reached inside. Before the eyes of the army captain they lifted out pieces of very old bread. "This bread was hot when we began our journey. You see it is dry and moldy now. Look at these torn wine bottles. Our shoes and our garments are worn out because of the long journey."

The bread *was* dry and moldy. Surely it must have been carried a long distance. So Joshua and the elders of Israel made an agreement of peace. They did not know that these men from only 20 miles away had *begun* the journey perhaps only 3 days before with

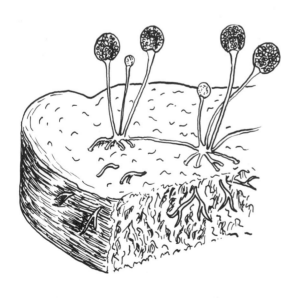

Bread mold is a very common fungus.

worn-out clothing, battered shoes, old sacks, torn wine bottles, and dry moldy bread.

God had told Moses at Sinai (Exodus 23:31-33) that Israel should make no agreement of peace with any city in Canaan. After the truth was discovered Joshua decided to make the men of the Gibeonite cities *Nethinims* (Ezra 7:24; Nehemiah 10:28, 29), a word meaning "given." They were given to the service of the tabernacle (Joshua 9:27). They helped the Levites, who were the first given ones (Numbers 3:9; 8:19).

Gibeon became one of the headquarters for the high priest's family (Joshua 21:17), and in the time of David and Solomon the tabernacle was set up there (1 Chronicles 21:29, 30; 2 Chronicles 1:3). In this way the men of Gibeon became closely associated with the worship of the true God (Psalm 84:10).

The mold on the bread that the Gibeonites brought was a fungus. Probably all of us have seen how old bread becomes moldy. Molds are very common fungi. They live on leather, paper, and many other materials.

Fungi are far more important to man than algae are. Algae can make their own food. Fungi do not have chlorophyll and cannot carry on photosynthesis.

Fungi obtain their food in two different ways and are classified according to this characteristic. Dead animals and plants are eaten by one fungal ('fəŋ-gəl) group known as saprophytes ('sap-rə-ˌfīts). The other group feeds in or on another living animal or plant.

For what purpose did God create the saprophytes? Are they of any value? Without saprophytes every tree, plant, and animal that has ever died would still be in the world except those eaten by scavengers, predators, and man. As years would pass, the earth would be covered with dead materials. Forests would be clogged and the soil buried, so that no new plants could root. More and more food materials would be locked in the still-fresh dead bodies. Occasionally lightning would strike and set afire the huge wood pile. The terrible heat would destroy the ground. Without saprophytes no new soil would form. More and more of the earth would become a desert.

God has designed that dead plants and animals be changed by saprophytes into carbon dioxide and simple materials that enrich the land. Living plants use carbon dioxide, water, and soil for growth. Animals and man eat plants, and after death saprophytic ('sap-rə-ˌfid-ik) fungi change each body into simple elements.

This process completes what is called a food chain. Green-leaved plants are usually at the beginning of the food chain, and fungi are the last link. Most food chains have no more than five links, and many times they have only two.

Plants produce by photosynthesis such foods as bark, nuts, seeds, leaves, bulbs, fronds, fruit, buds, and twigs. Creatures eating plant parts may be insects, moles, millipedes, turtles, lizards, deer, porcupines, birds, squirrels, rabbits, shrews, and mice. These animals are the second links in the food chain. Bears, raccoons, hawks, owls, foxes, bobcats, opossums, and skunks live on the small plant-eaters. Except for hawks, owls, and bobcats, plant food is taken by this group as well. When these animals die, fly larvae, beetles,

Something to Do

Divide a slice of bread into four pieces. Moisten two of them with applesauce or fruit juice. Place each on a saucer. Collect dust from the furniture with a clean cloth or a feather and sprinkle it upon each piece of bread. Cover the four saucers with four glasses. Place a dry and a moist specimen in a sunny place. Set the two remaining saucers in a warm dark spot. Which of the four pieces of bread shows mold first?

vultures, and others may dispose of their bodies. But sooner or later the fungi will change these materials into forms that plants can use again. Bacteria, yeasts, and molds are all fungi. Bacteria are the smallest fungi of all and cannot be seen with the naked eye. Some fungi multiply by tiny reproductive bodies called spores that are present nearly everywhere.

Look at the mold on an orange. This blue and green powder is composed of large numbers of spores, any one of which will begin a new colony of mold if it is in a favorable place. Some of the most valuable of all fungi are found in this group.

In 1929 Alexander Fleming, working in a British hospital, found clumps of mold on the plates in his laboratory. He identified this fungus as a relative of the mold on oranges.

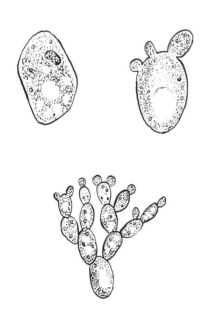

Yeast plants reproduce by budding.

During World War II doctors were looking for substances to treat wound infections. They worked with Alexander Fleming. From the mold discovered before by Mr. Fleming, they developed the antibiotic (ˌan-tē-ˌbī-'ät-ik) penicillin (ˌpen-ə-'sil-ən).

From organisms first found in the soil, various other antibiotics have been produced. Tuberculosis, whooping cough, and other diseases are controlled by these medicines.

Yeasts are common, one-celled fungi. Yeasts live mostly on sugar solutions, making alcohol and carbon dioxide. This process is called fermentation (ˌfər-mən-'tā-shən). The yeast cakes sold in stores are yeast cells held in a starchy material. They do not multiply when cool and dry. But if they are damp and warm, they will begin to ferment (ˌfər-'ment).

Yeast is used to produce alcohol in wine making. Many evils go with drinking (Proverbs 23:29-32; Ephesians 5:18). Drinking strong drink even affects man's standing with God. Heaven is closed to every drunkard. "They which do such things shall not inherit the kingdom of God" (Galatians 5:21; 1 Corinthians 6:10).

Yeast is also used by bakers. Bubbles of carbon dioxide, developing during the growth of the yeast, lift bread dough and make it light. The carbon dioxide and alcohol are lost in the baking process. Jesus spoke of how the leaven placed in flour goes through the total mass (Luke 13:21). The apostle Paul wrote to the Christians at

Corinth that sin allowed in the church affects the entire group as leaven penetrates the whole lump of dough (1 Corinthians 5:6).

Vinegar results from the action of both yeasts and bacteria. Fermentation

Various milk products—yogurt, buttermilk, butter, and others—acquire their odor and taste through the work of one-celled plants. Cheese manufacturers grow various molds and add them at certain times in the processing

What Happens When . . .

Take ½ cup of warm water (100-110 degrees) and dissolve ½ teaspoon of sugar in it. Add 1 teaspoon of baker's yeast. After 10 minutes what do you see?

occurs when yeasts change the sugar in cider to alcohol and carbon dioxide. Vinegar bacteria and oxygen in the air then turn the alcohol to vinegar.

Sauerkraut is grated cabbage, salted and kept until it ferments and bacteria have developed the desired flavor.

of their cheeses. During the aging time the mold grows throughout the cheese. Many kinds of bacteria also develop the various characteristic flavors.

The preparation of some textile fibers and the tanning of leather are completed with the help of fungi.

Foods made by bacterial action

Vinegar, cheese, yeast bread, and sauerkraut are made with the help of fungi.

The work of fungi is usually taken for granted. Bread leavened with yeast rises. Food exposed to warmth and air becomes unfit to eat. Plant and animal bodies decay.

Fungi are an important part in God's well-ordered world. It is hard to imagine this earth without them. Small though they are, even too small to be seen with the naked eye, they fulfill God's plan in an outstanding way.

Class Project

Before class submerge two bowls and two saucers in a pan of water, and boil. Drain the water off. Avoid touching the inside surfaces of the bowls and the saucers.

Soften $\frac{1}{2}$ teaspoon of plain gelatin in $\frac{1}{2}$ teaspoon of cold water. Pour $\frac{1}{3}$ cup of boiling water over the softened gelatin. Dissolve the gelatin. Divide the mixture between the two saucers. Cover with the bowls and tape together. Allow to cool.

In class uncover one saucer and select the dirtiest hand present. Press the tips of two soiled fingers against the gelatin surface. Hold them there for a few seconds. Mark the areas on the outside of the bowl. Retape the bowl over the saucer.

Wash the hands thoroughly with soap. Repeat by holding the tips of all the clean fingers against the other gelatin. Tape the second bowl over its saucer so that no dust can enter. Place both saucers in a warm dark spot.

Three days later look at both saucers. See the cloudy growth where the dirty fingers touched the gelatin. Fungi are multiplying in these spots. See if any fungi are growing in the spots touched by the washed fingers.

Questions

1. Joshua and the elders of Israel thought that the Gibeonites had traveled a long distance because of the (fungi, algae, lichens) growing on their bread.

2. The Gibeonites were given work in the (fields, army, tabernacle).

3. Thallophytes that cannot make their own food are called (algae, fungi, kelp). (Hint: A previous lesson can help you answer this.)

4. Fungi are grouped according to (size, the place where they are found, color, the way that they get

their food).

5. Plant and animal matter that is not living provides food for the class of fungi known as (algae, parasites, saprophytes, seaweed).

6. Each individual fungus has at least (one cell, one thousand cells, a body large enough to be seen without a microscope).

7. Fungi spores are found (in very few places, nearly everywhere, in water only, in soil only, in air only).

8. What is the most important work of saprophytic fungi?

9. Which statement is correct?
   (a) A food chain is the relationship of an animal to its food items and to its predators.
   (b) A food chain is the relationship between an animal and its food.
   (c) A food chain is the relationship between an animal and the creatures that eat it.

10. Molds and yeasts are (flowering plants, very tiny animals, thallophytes).

11. Yeasts and molds grow fastest in a (warm moist place, warm dry place, cold moist place, cold dry place).

12. The apostle Paul compared sin in the church to the action of what fungi?

13. In what important way does man use a certain blue-green mold?

14. What foods depend upon certain fungi for flavor and/or texture?

15. What harmful products does man produce by using yeast?

16. Antibiotics, which are produced by using fungi, are (valuable foods, vitamins, medicines).

"Dost thou know . . . the wondrous works of him which is perfect in knowledge?" Job 37:16

6. Parasites and Nitrogen Traps

Fungi are thallophytes, plants without true roots, stems, or leaves. A fungus that lives on dead animal or plant matter is a saprophyte. Most of the gilled mushrooms that we see are saprophytes. Nearly every gilled mushroom is found growing on the ground, on logs, on stumps, or on dead limbs of living trees. Because they grow on materials that are not alive they are plainly saprophytes. Less than one in twenty mushroom species grows on living wood.

The fungi that build soil are also saprophytes. They change dead plant and animal bodies to carbon dioxide and simple elements. Fungi are divided into two groups because not all of them feed on dead materials. Fungi that grow on living plants or animals are called parasites ('par-ə-ˌsīts).

Fungi are not the only parasites. Any plant or animal that grows on another living species and hinders it by taking food, water, or shelter is known as a parasite. When each one helps the other, the relationship is called symbiosis. When one is helped and the other harmed it is a parasitic (ˌpar-ə-'sit-ik) relationship. The one helped is the parasite. The one harmed is known as the host.

Man is often a host to parasites. Ringworm and athlete's foot are parasitic fungi that grow on man. One-celled fungi called bacteria often live in man's body and multiply, causing cholera, diphtheria, dysentery, pneumonia, scarlet fever, and various other diseases.

Mildews, smuts, rusts, blights, and wilts are fungi. Mildew is a whitish or grayish fungus seen on the leaves of roses, lilacs, and other plants. Some mildews do not greatly hinder the plant on which they live. Others do much damage. When the Hebrews were unfaithful to God, He punished them by sending mildew on their crops (Amos 4:9; Haggai 2:17).

Another fungus that grows on plants

The gray cells of this corn smut will shed millions of spores when they become ripe and dry.

is called smut. Perhaps you have seen ears of sweet corn with clumps of gray swollen cells. These cells hold millions of black spores that spread, blow, and remain in the soil to infect young plants the next season. Wheat, barley, and corn are all food for smuts.

develops. Black spores cannot infect wheat plants as red spores do. The black spores, however, grow on the common barberry. Here they form tiny cups on the undersides of the leaves. In the spring more spores are released. These spring spores are red, and they

Something to See

Look at an ear of corn or other grain infected by smut. Keep it until the spores are dry enough to rise like puffs of smoke when the cells are broken open.

Rusts destroy wheat, oats, barley, and other cereal grains. The red spore stage causes an appearance like rust. The stem and leaves of a wheat plant become red in the spring. During late summer and fall the black stage

grow on wheat plants. If all the wild barberry plants were removed from a given area, the wheat rust would largely disappear.

Other fungi also grow on two plants in turn. The white pine blister rust

Wheat rust on wheat stems
This fungus called rust grows on the stems of wheat, oats, barley, and other cereal grains.

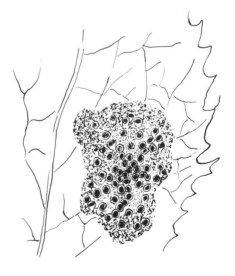

Black spores from wheat rust grow on the underside of this common barberry leaf. The leaf will shed red spores to live on next season's wheat crop.

A cedar "apple" that has shed some spores

This white pine bark is a host to the white pine blister rust.

This red cedar twig holds a brown spore case from which jellylike orange tongues are hanging. Spores from the tongues will drift to any nearby apple trees and grow on the leaves.

infects the white pine and the wild currant bushes. The cedar-apple rust lives on the red cedar part of the time and on apples trees during the remainder of the year.

Among the most useful bacteria are those living in the soil. One student states that there may be as many as 300,000 bacteria in a single ounce of surface soil. How are they important to man?

All living things must have nitrogen in some form. Where nitrogen is absent, life is impossible. About 80 percent of

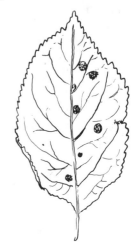

White pine blister rust is growing on this wild currant leaf.

The spots on this apple leaf are caused by the cedar-apple rust.

the atmosphere is nitrogen; but most plants, animals, and man cannot use the nitrogen in the air. How has God planned that this plentiful source of nitrogen be changed so that plants and animals can use it?

Just as algae and fungi live together in a symbiotic relationship in lichens, so certain bacteria have a symbiotic relationship with lentils, clover, vetch, soybeans, cowpeas, and similar plants. These important bacteria grow on the young roots, taking from them food and water. The bacteria draw nitrogen from the air in the soil and mix it with oxygen and other elements to form a solid food used by the plant. Knots of nitrogen called nodules ('näj-ˌüls) are produced. Later the roots and nodules decay, dissolve in water, and nourish other

Alfalfa

Cow vetch

Lespedeza

Clover

Hay and nitrogen-producing plants
Lespedeza, cow vetch, clover, and alfalfa provide hay for the farmer and enrich the soil as well.

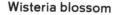
Wisteria blossom

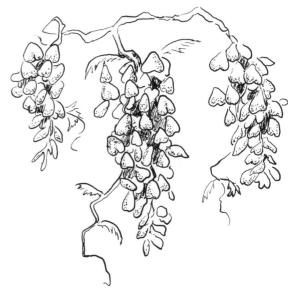

These bean roots show nitrogen nodules as do the roots of many peas, beans, and clovers that trap nitrogen from the air.

The wisteria, with its purple or white pea-blossom-shaped blooms, is a woody vine in the nitrogen-trapping group.

herbs or trees which in turn benefit animals or man.

Other soil bacteria that do not grow on plant roots do a similar work. This process is called fixation (fik-ˈsā shən) of nitrogen. Fixation of nitrogen by soil bacteria is God's way of providing plants, animals, and man with the necessary food elements.

Most fungi are not large and easily seen as are the flowering plants. But life as God has planned it here on earth would be impossible without them.

Class Project

Visit a field of lentils, clover, vetch, soybeans, or cowpeas. Pull up a plant and study the nodules of nitrogen on the roots.

Questions

1. Most gilled mushrooms are (saprophytes; parasites; plants with true roots, stems, and leaves).

2. (All, Most, Some) mushrooms are parasites.

3. Which of the following is true?
   (a) Parasitic fungi have chlorophyll and make their own food.
   (b) Parasitic fungi have no chlorophyll. They feed on dead plant and animal bodies.
   (c) Parasitic fungi have no chlorophyll. They feed on living plants and animals.

4. Which of the following is true?
   (a) Parasites benefit the animal or plant on which they live.
   (b) Parasites grow on a live animal or plant without affecting it.
   (c) Parasites take food, water, or shelter from the plant or animal on which they live, subtracting from the health of the other species.

5. A host animal or plant is one on which (saprophytes, parasites, algae) grow.

6. Which of the following are parasites?
   (a) a grub living in the hide of a cow
   (b) a fern growing out of a crack in the rock
   (c) a mushroom growing on the ground
   (d) a louse on a hen
   (e) a deer mouse living in a hollow log
   (f) a clothes moth larva in a woolen sweater
   (g) a live worm inside a dog
   (h) a bean beetle eating a bean leaf
   (i) a cow eating grass
   (j) a tick drinking blood from a blackberry picker
   (k) a termite in the wood of a building
   (l) an ant drinking juice from a plant stem
   (m) a worm inside an apple growing on a tree
   (n) a corn borer in a cornstalk

7. Which of the following are hosts?
   (a) a tree with a robin nest in its branches
   (b) a tomato hornworm with braconid wasp cocoons on it
   (c) a man with ringworm on his skin
   (d) a flower with a honeybee taking nectar and pollen from it
   (e) a dead animal with fly and beetle larvae living in it
   (f) a haystack with mice living in it
   (g) a dog with fleas
   (h) a bush with spider webs and spiders in it
   (i) a tree with engraver beetles under its bark
   (j) a partly hollow telephone pole with a family of woodpeckers in it
   (k) a cliff with a family of cougars in one of its dens
   (l) a fish with lice on it
   (m) a rock with lichens on it
   (n) soil with earthworms crawling through it

8. Many diseases of man are caused by (algae, parasites, symbiosis, saprophytes).

9. A host animal or plant provides for its own needs and those of (its young, other species living nearby, its parasites).

10. Which of the following is true?
    (a) A parasite is always an animal.
    (b) A parasite is always a plant.
    (c) Both animals and plants are sometimes parasites.

11. Mildews, wilts, blights, smuts, and rusts are (flowering plants, very tiny animals, thallophytes).

12. Smut, rust, and blight often (hinder, help) the host plant.

13. How did God use a fungi to punish the Hebrews when they were unfaithful to Him?

14. White pine blister rust and cedar-apple rust each have (one, two, three) hosts.

15. Nitrogen is taken from the air and changed to a form that plants can use by (algae, bacteria, lichens).

"Stand still, and consider the wondrous works of God." Job 37:14

2. Mammals

To the Mammals

Animals of sacrifice
    For the sins of guilty man,
Fliers through warm evening skies,
    Thundering herds on verdant plain,
Rangers brave through north's fierce cold,
    Scamperers on forest tree,
Climbers high on mountains old,
    Dwellers huge in earth's wide sea,
Burrowers beneath the ground
    Wrapped in hibernation's sleep
(Instinct strong in you is found;
    Each of you his place does keep),
Wanderers on desert sand,
    Friends obedient to man's call,
Mammal host on sea and land,
    God designed and gave you all.

"And out of the ground the Lord God formed every beast of the field." Genesis 2:19

7. Animals With Four Legs

God created mammals on the sixth day using the dust of the ground. Among the host of living creatures coming from His divine hand, this group has been most helpful to man. At the time of Moses when God directed the Hebrews in worship, He chose the mammals and the birds as sacrificial offerings.

Any living creature with a backbone is called a vertebrate ('vər-tə-brət, 'vər-tə-ˌbrāt). Mammals and birds are the only two warm-blooded, vertebrate classes of animals living on the earth. The other three vertebrate animal groups—amphibians (am-'fib-ē-əns), reptiles, and fishes— are cold-blooded. Birds have feathers while

Mammals
(warm-blooded)

Birds
(warm-blooded)

Amphibians
(cold-blooded)

Reptiles
(cold-blooded)

Fishes
(cold-blooded)

mammals have hair as man does. In their physical structure mammals have more in common with man than any other animals do.

The word *animal* is used to mean all living things (except man) that are not plants. Marine animals such as corals sometimes puzzle scientists who are trying to classify them as either plants or animals.

What is a mammal? Mammals are animals, but many animals are not mammals. Insects, reptiles, and birds are animals, but they are not mammals. Mammals are warm-blooded. Some mammals are able to remain active even during severe winter weather because they are warm-blooded.

All reptiles, amphibians, most insects, and other cold-blooded creatures must become dormant during freezing temperatures.

Another aid to winter activity is the coat of fur that God has given to many mammals. Fishes, amphibians, reptiles, and birds do not have hair.

Elephants and whales do not have very many hairs. But usually mammals are covered with a thick growth of hair. Each hair grows out of a pit in the skin. With its small muscle attached at the root, the hair can be raised. In fear or anger the mammal sometimes lifts its fur on end. It appears larger than before. Perhaps the enemy hesitates to attack.

Some hairs are sense organs. These are usually found growing around the mouth and eyes. Nerves carry a message to the brain when the hair is touched.

As a group, mammals are vertebrate, warm-blooded, hairy creatures. Another distinctive characteristic is the possession of skin glands. Most mammals have at least three kinds of skin glands.

The sweat glands ooze water that has been drawn from the blood stream. The skin is cooled as the sweat is taken up by the air. This causes the mammal to be more comfortable in hot weather.

Something to Do

Collect a human eyelash, a hair from an eyebrow, and an uncut hair from a human head.

Find one or more shafts of hair from a dog, cat, cow, horse, rat, mouse, squirrel, rabbit, and other species of mammals. Notice how each hair tapers at its end. Hair usually grows in one direction. The tapered hair tip helps the shaft to lie flat. Notice the stiffness, thickness, color, and length of the various hairs. Does an individual mammal have more than one kind of hair? What is the difference?

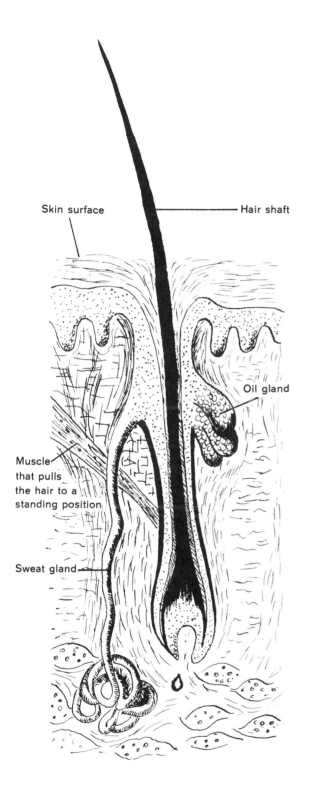

Skin surface

Hair shaft

Oil gland

Muscle that pulls the hair to a standing position

Sweat gland

The structure of a hair

Another important gland of a mammal's skin is the oil gland. Oil glands are usually located at the base of each hair. The oil keeps the hair glossy and soft. The fur of an animal sheds rain partly because of the oil that dresses each hair.

A third type of gland is the milk or mammary ('mam-ə-rē) gland that gives mammals their name. The young drink milk from the glands of the female at birth and afterward. Birds, fishes, amphibians, and reptiles do not have milk glands. When a young mammal begins to depend entirely upon food other than milk it is said to be weaned.

Mammals give birth to living young. Some reptiles, some fishes, some amphibians, and some insects give birth to living young also. But only two mammal species lay eggs. As a group, mammals bear living young.

A vertebrate, warm-blooded animal wearing fur, bearing young alive, having skin glands of various kinds, and nourishing its young with milk is a mammal. The only vertebrates that never bear young alive are birds.

Mammals are found everywhere on the earth's surface, underground, in the sea, and in the air. Their surface homes include those in the marsh, the desert, the plain, the mountain, the forest, and the Arctic.

The size of mammals varies greatly. Many species weigh less than an ounce. But the largest animals on earth belong to the mammal class. Some of those that live in the ocean are much bigger than the land forms. A blue whale may be 100 feet long and weigh 150 tons. The Lord has created a wide range of difference in size.

The beak of a bird usually indicates what type of food the bird eats. By noticing the feet of a bird one can guess whether it spends most of its time on the ground, on the water, or in the air.

In the same way God has made the teeth and jaws of mammals able to handle the food He has planned that they should eat. The teeth of those that eat meat and those that eat grass are shaped differently.

Likewise the Lord has provided a variety of limb and foot shapes, suitable for life in different habitats ('hab-ə-ˌtats). A habitat is the place where an animal or plant grows or lives naturally.

A water mammal may have webbed toes or flippers. A rudderlike tail may aid the creature in swimming.

A mammal living in trees will have paws that can grasp and sometimes a tail that can be wrapped around a branch to bear the weight of the body.

Burrowing mammals have long, strong claws used for digging.

Creatures that escape by running—such as deer, elk, and pronghorns—are supplied with hoofs and long legs.

God has given wings to mammals living in the air.

The sharp curved claws of the cat family catch and hold living prey.

How have mammals been helpful to man? Mammals are the chief sources of meat for man's diet and his only source of dairy products, such as cheese and milk. Beef, pork, mutton, veal, and lamb are meats that man obtains from domestic mammals. In this country there are many wild mammals that are used for food. Members of the deer

Man keeps herds of mammals for meat production.

Man milks herds of mammals.

Deer

Squirrel

Rabbit

Bear

Man hunts mammals and eats their flesh.

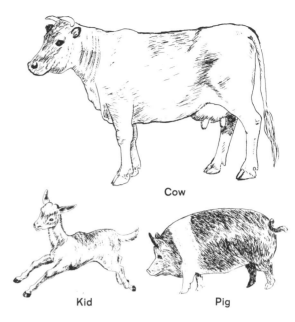

Cow

Kid

Pig

Leather is a product taken from mammals.

family, rabbit family, and squirrel family are appreciated as sources of meat as well as raccoons, opossums, bears, and armadillos.

Clothing products such as wool, leather, and fur come from mammals.

Before the machine age, mammals such as horses, donkeys, mules, camels, and dromedaries were used in working the soil, harvesting, marketing crops, pulling wagons and boats, traveling, turning mills, hauling fuel, mining coal,

Sheep

Angora rabbit

Llama

Man raises mammals for fibers from which clothing is made.

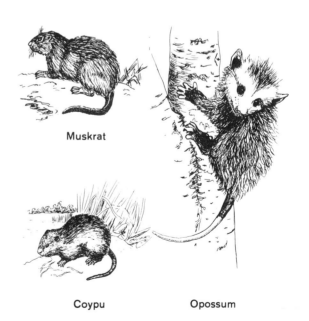

Muskrat

Coypu

Opossum

Wild mammals are trapped for their fur.

Camel

Malamute sled dog

Horse

Man uses mammals for power and transportation.

and many other essential tasks.

Mammals are more popular pets than other classes of animals. Probably everyone has become acquainted with at least one mammal, either in his own home or in the home of a neighbor. Dogs, cats, horses, rabbits, and other species are kept as companions for adults as well as for children.

Mammals are fascinating creatures. In the coming days we will learn to know various species and how God has made them to live together in our world.

Silver fox

Chinchilla

Mink

Man keeps mammals for fur production.

Dog

Hamster

Cat

Man enjoys mammals for pets.

Class Project

Prepare a list of wild mammals seen in your country by members of the class. How many families are represented? List the date seen and the location in which the creature was found. Describe the habitat. It may be marsh, swamp, grassland, lake, ocean, river, mountain, desert, forest, or cave. In which of these habitats is the highest number of species found?

Questions

1. God has created most species in the mammal class to (bear young alive, lay eggs, be warm-blooded, be cold-blooded, have backbones, have no backbones [choose three]).

2. Which statement is correct?
   (a) A mammal may be an insect, a bird, a reptile, or an amphibian.
   (b) An animal may be an insect, a bird, a reptile, or an amphibian.

3. Which of the following are habitats?
   (a) a marsh or swamp
   (b) a zoo
   (c) a forest or mountain
   (d) a lake, river, sea, or ocean
   (e) an aquarium

4. Some mammals live in very cold climates. They can do this because they (are cold-blooded, are warm-blooded, are very large, can run fast, can dig, have thick coats of fur, have no hair [choose two]).

5. (Five, Four, Three, Two, One) other animal (class, classes) (has, have) backbones besides mammals. Name (it, them).

6. (Five, Four, Three, Two, One) other animal (class, classes) (is, are) warm-blooded. Name (it, them).

7. (Five, Four, Three, Two, One, No) other backboned animal (class, classes) (has, have) fur besides mammals.

8. (All, No) (birds, fishes, amphibians, reptiles) bear their young alive.

9. (Some, No) birds, fishes, amphibians, and reptiles feed their young from milk glands.

10. Name six characteristics of most mammals.

11. Mammals are (more useful, less useful) to man than other classes of animals.

12. Which is true?

(a) All mammals have teeth shaped alike.
(b) Various mammals have differently shaped teeth.

13. Which is true?
(a) Various mammal families have differently shaped limbs and feet.
(b) All mammals have limbs and feet shaped alike.

14. Mammals live

(a) only in underground burrows
(b) only in the sea.
(c) only in trees.
(d) only in the air.
(e) only on the ground.
(f) in underground burrows, the sea, trees, the air, and on the ground.

15. Mammals are (usually very very small, usually very very large, found in sizes varying from very small to very large).

"Blessed be the Lord God, . . . who only doeth wondrous things." Psalm 72:18

8. Some Furry Chiselers

Just as beetles are by far the largest order in the insect class, so rodents ('rōd-ənts) are the largest order in the mammal class. Beetles are numbered in the hundreds of thousands of species, but less than two hundred rodent species appear in America north of Mexico.

Rodents do not inhabit oceans or large lakes. But they are found from the Arctic to the dry land of the Antarctic. Even most of the islands are home to one or another of these little sharp-toothed animals.

Rodents have two upper and two lower chisellike teeth called the incisors (in-'sī-zərs). These are in the front of the mouth with a space between them and the grinding teeth behind. These large teeth are very hard and sharp; they are used for gnawing. The incisors continue to grow as long as the animal lives. Nut cracking and wood cutting wear down rodent teeth so that they do not become too long.

Most rodents have four toes on each front foot, and five on each hind foot.

Rodents are a very important group of mammals. They destroy many weed seeds and many insects. They are often the main food of meat-eating animals that otherwise might prey on man's poultry or livestock. Beavers and musk-rats are valuable fur bearers.

While rodents destroy more of man's property than other mammals do, they are also more useful than most other wild mammals. Soil development and tree planting are tasks performed by rodents. Rodents build dams that preserve the water supply of forests.

Among the rodents that we know best are the rats. The black, ship, or roof rat came to the United States on ships with the earliest explorers. This creature grows to 7 inches with a 9-inch tail. It may be brown or black with a gray belly. The belly is never white. The black rat prefers areas apart from large numbers of people.

About 1775, two more Old World rodents reached American shores, both of them more serious pests than the black rat. They were the house mouse and the Norway rat, also called the house or brown rat. The brown rat has a

The black rat came from Europe with early explorers. Its back is either black or brown, its belly gray. Head and body length 7 to 8 inches, tail 8 to 10 inches.

The black rat lives in the extreme South and along the coasts of North America. It is most often found around buildings.

The brown rat and the house mouse are both found where man lives, in buildings in cities and on farms.

gray belly, a grayish brown coat, and a scaly tail shorter than the head and body which may be 10 inches long. The brown rat is by far the most common rat in North America.

Besides destroying the timbers in buildings and fouling tons of man's food, the brown rat carries various diseases, in the fleas and lice that are in its fur. Bubonic plague, trichinosis, rabies, tularemia, and typhus are all

spread by the brown rat.

The house mouse likes warmth and prefers heated buildings, where it multiplies all the year around. Valuable medical experiments are conducted with house mice and white mice.

Difference in size is the only basis for naming rats and mice. Smaller members of the group are called mice and the larger ones rats.

The brown rat is the most destructive mammal known to man. Gray bellied, brown backed, it has a head and body length of 7 to 10 inches and a scaly tail 5 to 8 inches long.

Second to the brown rat, the house mouse is a great mammal pest. This 3-inch creature often has a tail 4 inches long.

Something to Do

List damage done by Old World rats and mice in your community. What ways are used to reduce rat populations? What method works best?

The Lord has placed species from three groups of rats in North America— the rice rats, the cotton rats, and the wood rats. These rats rarely come into buildings with man, as the Old World rats and mice prefer to do. North of Mexico live the marsh rice rats, three species of cotton rats, and seven species of wood rats.

The marsh rice rat has a head and body measurement of 5 inches. Its scaly tail is lighter in color below than above, and is usually longer than the body. The short fur is grayish or reddish brown and the feet are whitish.

The marsh rice rat chooses moist, low ground near swamps, lakes, or rivers. This little creature is a good swimmer, cruising easily about underwater and coming out on moonlit or dark nights to nibble grasses, seeds, and sedges.

The rice rat begins to multiply when it is only 7 weeks old, and not even fully grown itself. It may have as many as seven litters a year. The nest is ball-shaped, either fastened above ground in vegetation or on some dry spot on the soil itself. Shredded dry leaves are carefully woven together, and the first young of the year are likely to be born in March or April. Litters may contain from one to seven young. They are weaned when only 12 days old.

The rice rat was so named because it was once very plentiful in the rice fields

The marsh rice rat lives in grasses and sedges near water in the southeastern United States.

The marsh rice rat has a soft short grayish-brown coat, whitish feet, and a scaly tail. Measuring up to 5 inches long, its tail may stretch to 7 inches.

of southeastern United States. But the rice rat likes to eat green grass stems more than it does rice and devours almost twice its weight in food each week.

The cotton rats are slightly larger with head and body measurements up to 8 inches long and a shorter tail. They were so named because they leave small balls of the white fluff along their tunnels, after their meals of cotton seeds. This active, plentiful rodent dines on a great variety of foods. Insects, carrion, eggs, and crabs are taken. Grasses, sedges, seeds, and juicy roots are favorites. Cultivated plants that they like are alfalfa, cotton, sweet potatoes, and sugar cane. Cotton rats are next to the Old World rats in their destruction of crops.

Before the coming of the white man to America, the animals that God had placed in this country lived together without great damage to each other or to the trees and vegetation growing here.

Then people moved in who killed

The hispid cotton rat lives in tall grass in the southern United States, Mexico, and Central America.

The cotton rat has long rough fur nearly hiding its ears. A mixed buff and black coat, whitish below, covers its 5- to 8-inch body tipped by a finely haired 3- to 6-inch tail.

large numbers of wolves, foxes, coyotes, bears, raccoons, cougars, bobcats, hawks, owls, snakes, weasels, and other meat eaters. The smaller animals, mostly rodents, that the predators had eaten were then limited in number only by their food supply. In many cases man grew or stored an abundant harvest at one location. Rodents gathered in granaries and fields, ate much food, and developed huge populations.

One species of cotton rats is named hispid, because its coarse hair is rough and rather stiff. The hispid cotton rat makes a small nest in an underground burrow or in a runway through the grass. Usually five to seven fully haired young are born. In only 18 hours their eyes are open. When they are about 5 days old the mother begins to wean them, and at the age of 10 days they no longer need milk. Where conditions are favorable the hispid cotton rat breeds all year around and may have a new litter each month. Six generations

These cotton rat footprints in mud are natural size. The hind foot shows a heel mark.

might be born in a single year.

Like the rice rats the wood rats are active at night and are rarely seen in the daytime. Wood rats grow to be as large as house rats. Their bellies and feet are white, their ears are large, and their tails are hairy. Wood rats of one species or another are found in most of the United States.

In mountains they climb along rock cliffs and ledges, leaving small piles of sticks and rubbish where they have been working.

On level places they build houses 2 to 4 feet in diameter and almost as high. One species adds cactus over the outside of its nest, which keeps away most of its enemies. On the western coast of the United States, wood rats nest in trees.

In cold climates they may have two or three litters a year. In the South they bear young all the year around. The eyes of the new-born open after 20 days, and they need milk for 4 weeks.

Wood rats are also called pack rats or trade rats. They are continually carrying objects in their mouths to add to their nests. If they see a wrist watch, silver coins, a jackknife, spoons, or a set of false teeth, they may drop the stick or pine cone they are already carrying and take the more unusual item. Because of this habit they are called trade rats. Their nests, if discovered, bring many of these sometimes-valuable belongings to light again.

When the wood rat is alarmed it will thump on the ground with both hind feet. Another signal is beating its tail up and down very fast. If the rat is sitting on dry leaves its thumpings and tail vibrations will be clear warnings to other woodland creatures.

The bushy-tail wood rat has a long, bushy, squirrellike tail. Pale gray and reddish or nearly black above, it is about the same size as a house rat.

Wood rats are good climbers, jumpers, and swimmers. They eat mostly

Seven species of wood rats without bushy tails are found in the cliffs, plains, brush piles, live oaks, and cacti of these areas. They are not often seen in the daytime.

This attractive 7- to 9-inch bushy-tail wood rat may be faintly yellowish-gray or very dark furred. Its squirrellike tail is shorter than its body and head combined.

The bushy-tail wood rat lives around cliffs from California, New Mexico, and Arizona north to Alaska and east to the Dakotas.

vegetable food; but they may also eat insects, snails, or dead birds.

How can you tell whether a rat is an Old World rat or a native rat? None of the Old World rats or mice in this country have white feet or bellies. All three foreign species have scaly tails without hair on them. The tail is the same color above and below.

The rice rat has a scaly tail that is lighter on the underside. The feet are also whitish and the belly is quite light.

The hispid cotton rat is different from Old World rats, because it has a whitish belly and a two-colored, finely haired tail.

Wood rats have larger ears, hairy tails, and usually white feet and bellies.

Someday you may see the hispid cotton rat with its long, grizzled, black and buff coat disappearing into the weeds by the road or along a stream.

Some night you may be sleeping in a mountain cabin and hear a scratching noise. Then your flashlight may shine on a small, white-bellied, bushy-tailed creature with big ears and eyes looking for one more object to add to its collection.

Class Project

Livetrap a rat. Identify it. How many toes are on the front and hind feet? Is the tail scaly, hairy, or bushy? Does the tail have one color or two? Is the fur soft and short or thick, coarse, and long? How does the length of the tail compare with the head and body length? How many colors of fur are present? What color are the feet?

Examine the teeth of a dead specimen, especially the incisors.

1. By far the most common rat in the United States is (the black rat, the brown rat, the marsh rice rat, the hispid cotton rat, the bushy-tail wood rat).

2. This rat (is very destructive, rather troublesome, does no damage, is a foreign animal, is a native animal [choose two]).

3. The (black rat, brown rat, marsh rice rat, hispid cotton rat, bushy-tail wood rat) lives in the South, and along the Atlantic, Gulf, and Pacific coasts.

4. What species of mice lives all over the United States, in western Canada, and along the coasts of Alaska?

5. Has this mouse been of any benefit to man?

6. The hispid cotton rat lives (all over the United States and Canada; in most of the United States; in the southern United States, Mexico, and Central America; in the northern United States).

7. The marsh rice rat lives in the (northeast quarter, northwest quarter, southeast quarter, southwest quarter) of the United States.

8. Various kinds of wood rats live (all over the United States, in most of the United States and British Columbia, in the southern United States, in the northern United States).

9. Foreign rats and mice do not have (scaly tails, hairy tails, white bellies and feet, dark bellies and feet, tails of one color only, tails paler below than above [choose three]).

10. What native rat when found in large colonies destroys crops?

11. Before the white man came, what prevented these rats from forming colonies large enough to permanently damage wild vegetation?

12. The young of the (black rat, brown rat, house mouse, marsh rice rat, hispid cotton rat, bushy-tail wood rat) are precocious; that is, they are born with fur coats and their eyes open the first day after birth. Their weaning begins when they are five days old.

13. The (black rat, brown rat, house mouse, marsh rice rat, hispid cotton rat, bushy-tail wood rat) comes out only at night. Its tail is (scaly, hairy, bushy). It lives only near water and is a good swimmer.

14. The (black rat, brown rat, house mouse, the marsh rice rat, the hispid cotton rat, the bushy-tail wood rat) comes out only at night. Its tail is bushy. It is often carrying something in its mouth. Its nest may have many strange objects in it.

15. Which of the following are found in your community: black rat, brown rat, house mouse, marsh rice rat, hispid cotton rat, bushy-tail wood rat, other wood rats?

"O Lord, . . . I will shew forth all thy marvellous works." Psalm 9:1

9. Nighttime Is Mouse Time, Vole Time, Lemming Time

"Thou makest darkness, and it is night: wherein all the beasts of the forest do creep forth. The sun ariseth, they gather themselves together, and lay them down in their dens" (Psalm 104:20, 22).

Twilight is a beautiful time. The sun drops from sight, rosy colors paint the sky, the stars prick out.

All across the land as shadows descend, active animals ease out of hiding. The bright light of day shows them to hungry hawks, snakes, herons, crows, and other dangers, including humans. The quiet darkness covering the fields and woods invites the timid ones to gather an evening breakfast.

Especially do the little mammals wait for night although some run about by day as well. One nighttime mammal is the deer mouse, a pretty little bright-eyed creature also called the white-footed mouse. Like a deer it has big eyes, big ears, and a pale brown or gray back. It may be 4 inches long with a 5-inch tail that is white underneath. Fifteen species of white-footed or deer mice live in North America. Most rural areas are home to several deer mouse families.

A deer mouse eats mostly vegetable food; but it also takes snails, worms, centipedes, millipedes, and insects.

Even where it is coldest, white-footed mice do not hibernate. Instead

The snowy nose and forepaws of this little deer mouse may be stained with pink juice in berry season. Its long tail, sometimes longer than its 4-inch body, is dark above and white below. Its fine soft fur may be grayish, reddish, tan, or brown.

Active at night and all year around, the deer mouse lives from Mexico to Alaska.

they store seeds away, as many as a quart at a time.

The females of this group are very good mothers. They nest in a wide variety of places, sometimes a hollow tree or even a deserted squirrel's or bird's nest. Grass or leaves roofing the nest provide a dry, warm place for the young that are born in several litters each year. A closed entrance shuts out cold air, rain, or snow. When in danger the young are carried away by the mother, who holds each one by the back of the neck with her teeth.

The eyes of the young open when they are about 2 weeks old. They drink milk for 3 weeks. At the age of 8 weeks they begin families of their own.

A white-footed mouse continually combs and cleans its pure-white under-

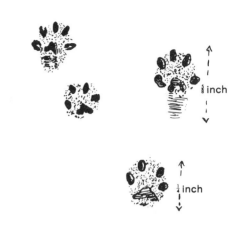

This deer mouse track was found in mud. Notice the heel mark on the hind foot. The front feet are smaller and have four toes.

parts and soft brown upper parts. When angry the deer mouse will stamp its little forepaws on the ground. The deer mouse occasionally sings, a birdlike trill so quiet that it cannot be heard more than a few feet away. At other times it sounds a buzzing hum.

Another mouse that does not hibernate in the winter, is the grasshopper mouse of the prairies and deserts. The northern grasshopper mouse measures 5 or 6 inches with a tail up to $2\frac{1}{2}$ inches long. Its soft fur coat is pinkish cinnamon or gray above and silky white underneath with a matching white tail tip.

Strange as it may seem, the grasshopper mouse eats very little vegetable food. It prefers to eat arachnids, insects, and other mice. It is very useful to the farmer.

Like a small furry hound the hungry little creature comes out from its burrow at twilight. It puts its nose to the ground and runs wildly about until it crosses a fresh track. Then indeed it

An old bird's nest is the foundation of this deer mouse home.

begins to squeak and follow the trail eagerly. As it draws nearer the prey, it becomes very excited. It shakes and jerks its short fat tail. At last it is able to spring upon the other animal and to kill it for breakfast.

It eats half its own weight every day when it can find sufficient food. With its keen sense of smell the grasshopper mouse detects grasshopper pupal cases and other hibernating insects below ground level. It is a good digger and easily unearths what it has found. Sometimes it hides along a trail and

Scorpions beware! The southern grasshopper or scorpion mouse dines regularly on your well-armed warriors. The gray or pinkish-cinnamon creature measures 4 to 5 inches, and the white-tipped tail 1 or 2 inches.

leaps out upon another animal as it passes.

Grasshopper mice have a sense of hearing so keen that they can even hear insects walking when they cannot see them. One man who was studying grasshopper mice allowed a pet mouse to roam his kitchen at night. Soon the many large cockroaches that lived there became few.

This little rodent hunts all the year around. As winter approaches, the

Like a hound picking up the trail, the grasshopper mouse cries aloud as it scents a food animal.

grasshopper mouse adds weight to its body and tail, which it uses when food is scarce. During blizzards or very cold weather it may stay at home, living on stored fat, and sleeping the time away.

The young are born naked with eyes and ears tightly closed. Three weeks later they have open eyes and ears and coats of downy fur. In time of danger

Western prairies and southwestern deserts are home to the grasshopper mouse and the scorpion mouse.

the young hold tightly to their mother's teats while she drags them to safety.

The southern grasshopper mouse, also known as the scorpion mouse, is a little smaller and lives in southern United States deserts.

The jumping mouse is another cunning little rodent. This animal may be seen during the day, and if it is jumping through grass it might easily be taken for a frog. Its sides are olive-yellow. A broad, dark band runs down the back, and the tail is tipped with black.

If you live in the northern United States, Canada, or Alaska, you have jumping mouse neighbors. Georgia and the Gulf states as well as some southwestern areas have no jumping mice.

The meadow jumping mouse has a 3-inch body and a tail twice as long. The tail acts as a balancer to prevent somersaults as the frisky ball of fur

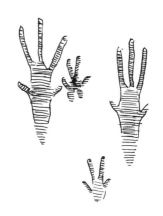

A jumping mouse landed here.

whizzes through the air.

The meadow jumping mouse may leap in a different direction at each hop, reminding one of a confused grasshopper. Like most of our native mice the meadow jumping mouse is white or yellowish underneath and darker above.

In wet marshy areas the jumping mouse hangs its nest in grass or bushes where the young can be dry. Four to nine young are usually born in June, hairless, whiskerless, with eyes closed and tails lacking adult length. Three litters are born in a season. In 3 weeks they see and hear, and in another 3 weeks legs and tails are developed for jumping.

The woodland jumping mouse prefers to live in the woods. It sleeps in the day and is abroad at night. When frightened it may flee, leaping 12 feet at a time.

This curious little creature has been seen on moonlit nights during the mating season behaving in a very entertaining fashion. Like a child with springs on his shoes, this mouse

Olive-yellow 3-inch body, big hind feet, a white belly, and a 4- to 6-inch tail set the meadow jumping mouse apart from other small furred ones.

bounces up and down turning in different directions and landing on all four feet. He breaks off to collect some nesting material in his forepaws. He disappears into the mouth of his burrow. In a short while he is back, leaping and hopping gaily around in the moonlight, neither tired nor dizzy. More nesting material is gathered, a second disappearance into the burrow and, like a ball on an elastic string, the little fellow is back, springing and dancing about again.

Grassy pastures, plains, and marshes hide the meadow jumping mouse.

By fall the woodland jumping mouse is plump and round. It often eats as much as its own weight in food every day. Below the frost line it burrows, and carries in large amounts of soft dry grass. Finally cold weather drives it deep into the ground. Dry grass is woven for a door, and the sleeping room is made as cozy as possible. Then, nose on belly, long feet behind ears, and extra-long tail wrapped round and round like the thread on a spool, the jumping mouse sleeps.

Its breathing slows, its body temperature drops, its heartbeat slackens.

Brownish-gray to dark brown, this very common little creature, the meadow vole, lives in country places. Long soft fur covers its 3- to 5-inch body and nearly conceals the ears. The two-colored tail is only 2 inches long.

It enters hibernation and may remain dormant 7 months. Warmth awakens it for another summer.

One of the most abundant of all rodents is the meadow vole. Although it is as short as a deer mouse, grasshopper mouse, or jumping mouse it may weigh twice as much, for it is round and chubby. Its brief tail stretches about 2 inches. Small, black, beady eyes and little, round ears are hidden in the plush, brownish-gray fur.

Tiny, inch-wide trails through the

This vole track in mud shows the marks of each toenail. The front foot has four toes, the hind foot five.

grass running in every direction advertise a vole town. Stubby pieces of grass stems dropped along the path are signs, too.

In the far North some voles hibernate. Others do not. One can see the wee exits they have made to the tops of the drifts. Where the snow-covered ground is not frozen hard, they continue digging, pulling loose soil to the surface and packing it into tunnels in the snow. After a complete thaw, the soil cores remain. These ridges may show in the same area as larger ones that are the work of the pocket gopher. Vole tunnels as long as 350 feet have been measured.

Tender stems, leaves, roots, tubers, seeds, fruits, berries, insects, snails, crayfish, and small rodents are eaten by voles. They hide food to use in winter, sometimes as much as 2 gallons at one place.

In Alaska voles climb willows and cut off willow tips, heaping them in piles around the base of a tree. As much as a bushel of the tender twigs may be collected. Under the snow of winter this

Voles climbing the willows in Alaska cut this pile of twigs for winter eating.

The meadow vole lives in wet, dry, warm, and even arctic regions.

food can be eaten, away from freezing winds and the constant prowl of foxes and owls. These rodents eat as much as their own weight in food each day.

Voles can swim well under water and on the surface. When upset a vole stamps its hind feet. These small mammals sit up like squirrels to eat, holding food in the forepaws.

Voles multiply very fast. As many as seventeen litters a year, of five to nine young are born. In 3 months the young themselves may have been parents two or three times. Many predators ranging in size from grizzly bears to weasels find voles very tasty.

Lemmings are much like voles. They live in the far North. They have long thick fur into which their ears disappear. Their tails are less than an inch long.

Every 3 to 5 years these little creatures migrate. Strangely enough, an abundance of food seems to trigger the migration. Under good conditions, four large litters may be raised in a single

The 5-inch brown lemming, gray on head and shoulders and reddish-brown on its back has a 1-inch tail. In spite of being a very good swimmer, this arctic rodent may drown. Do you know why?

The brown lemming lives in burrows on the mossy plains of the far North.

season. One female may bear twenty-five to forty young a year instead of the usual four or five in a single litter. Soon the burrows become crowded, food becomes scarce, and individuals go above ground to seek other areas. Then the few are joined by many others, until a flood of small brown mammals is moving like a river of molasses across the country, about 15 miles a day.

Snowy owls, Arctic foxes, wolves, Canada lynxes, otters, bears, minks, and many others eat their fill. Sooner or later the lemmings reach water too wide to cross. But they plunge in anyway. Back in the once-crowded burrows a few survivors carry on the species. In no time lemmings are again abundant.

How many of these little rodents live in your community? How many have you seen? God has filled the earth with creatures whose ways are well worth knowing.

Class Project

Visit an old pasture or an old orchard. Look for vole towns. See their burrows with grass cuttings scattered along the trails leading to them. Notice other signs, such as gnawed twigs and bark, tiny droppings, and nests.

Questions

1. Small mammals are most often active (at night, during the day, during storms).

2. Deer mice, also called white-footed mice, (store food for the winter; hibernate; live throughout North America; live only in the western mountains; eat many different kinds of food, including insects; eat

seeds only [choose three]).

3. A deer mouse has (one young one each year, one litter each year, several litters a year).

4. A deer mouse raises her young (in burrows only, in hollow trees only, on ocean beaches only, in many different places).

5. Young deer mice in danger are (pulled to safety by their tails, carried away one by one in the mother's mouth, hauled to safety on the mother's back).

6. The grasshopper mouse eats mostly (insects, arachnids, and mice; seeds; grass).

7. The grasshopper mouse (smells out and trails its prey, swims after and catches its prey, drops down on its prey from a tree, hides and jumps out as the other animal goes by, smells and digs out the other animal, chases its prey in 10-foot leaps [choose three]).

8. The grasshopper mouse (hibernates, stores food, hunts) most of the winter.

9. In time of danger the grasshopper mouse (leaves her young behind, kills her young, drags her young to safety while they hold to her teats).

10. The jumping mouse lives (in the United States, Canada, and Alaska; in the southern United States and Mexico; throughout North America).

11. The woodland jumping mouse sometimes bounces up and down (when frightened, when gathering nesting material, when hungry).

12. The jumping mouse (stores food, hibernates, hunts food all winter).

13. The meadow vole is (round and chubby, long and thin, long tailed, short tailed [choose two]).

14. Voles eat (plant food only, animal food only, food taken from the water, many different kinds of food).

15. Voles are eaten by (owls and hawks only, predators of the dog family only, predators of the cat family only, predators of the weasel family only, almost every predator).

16. Lemmings live in (the far North, the far South) and are most like the (deer mice, jumping mice, meadow voles, grasshopper mice).

17. When lemming colonies become too crowded, the lemmings (starve, stop having young, migrate).

"Blessed be the Lord God, . . . who only doeth wondrous things." Psalm 72:18

"The conies are but a feeble folk, yet make they their houses in the rocks" (Proverbs 30:26). The Bible writer Agur was speaking of a little rabbitlike animal that lives in Israel, Lebanon, and Sinai. This chubby mammal was noticed in Psalm 104:18 as finding a refuge in the rocks.

The coney of that country has a small round hoof; but in size, color, shape, and habits it is much like the American cony, also called pika ('pē-kə, 'pī-kə).

In the high mountains of western North America, this sturdy 7-inch creature lives among the boulders and fragments of the rockslides. It has round, white-rimmed ears, short legs, and a tail so brief that it is hidden by fur. Stiff white hairs growing out between small black toe pads give the pika traction as it scurries about on the rocks.

Pikas live near other pikas, about six to an acre. They are cheerful little fellows, whistling, calling, and bleating all day long. Each animal has several lookout points near his food pile where he sits like a ball of fur gazing out over the countryside far below with his bright shoe-button eyes.

At the edges of the rockslides grow alpine heather, grasses, sedges, clover, and perhaps two dozen other plants which pikas relish as food. They must leave the safety of their dens to gather these plants. Any predator will be announced with squeals of warning from the lookouts.

The first litter of three or four arrives in May or June. Until the beginning of September additional litters are born.

The pika does not hibernate. But it lives where winter is long and severe. Cold winds howl about the towering mountain peaks and snow lies deep on the summer food supply. How does the Lord care for this creature through the long winter months when plants are frozen?

As summer wears away, the pikas cut grasses, clover, and other favorites, spreading them out to dry. If rain

The pika, a perky high-mountain mammal, may store as much as 50 pounds of hay in the family provision pile. This grayish, buffy, or brownish mammal weighs less than ½ pound, but measures 6 to 8 inches.

Pikas enjoy life even in the high mountains of very cold areas.

threatens, the entire group rushes out, bundles the hay, and carries it below. These energetic $\frac{1}{2}$-pound mammals will work on after dark to save their provisions. Day after day plants are cut, cured, and stored. Connected with the burrow by a runway, a haystack is the center of each family's home range.

Freezing winter sets in. Frosts split the rocks. Bitter, icy winds rage across the boulders. Under the snows the pikas, warmly furred, gather about their hay pile.

Three species of pikas live in North America from the high mountains of Alaska and the Yukon to the upper altitudes of California and Arizona.

Cottontails are in the same mammal order as pikas. There are eight main species of cottontails in the United States. The smallest one, the pygmy rabbit, weighs only $\frac{1}{2}$ to 1 pound when fully grown. But the swamp rabbit in this same group, called cane-cutter, may reach 6 pounds and be 17 inches long.

The European rabbit digs burrows and lives in an underground community much as the prairie dog does in this country. Our domestic rabbits came first from Europe. Their young are born naked, blind, and helpless. The rabbit is a larger animal than any cottontail. Some students consider cottontails a group apart from rabbits.

Under a cactus or wild rose thicket the cottontail sits in its form, licking its fur clean and rubbing its nose with its paws. A form is an empty place in grass, light vegetation, or soft snow shaped by the animal itself. The creature's nose is continually wabbling. Its long ears turn one way and then another to hear every sound. At least one foot is pressed to the ground to pick up any warning message thumped out by a neighbor.

The cottontail brings forth its young, several litters in a year, in a shallow depression lined with grass and its own fur. The young are naked and

The eastern cottontail is a familiar, well-liked mammal. Brown or gray, it measures 14 to 17 inches in length. Its tail is short, white, and cottony. Weight, 2 to 4 pounds.

Cottontails of various kinds are found in much of the United States.

weasels that are small enough to go wherever the prey goes. When in danger, this timid animal sometimes covers 8 feet in a bound. Nearly always the cottony tail is held up against the back, showing its white lining.

Cottontails stand on their hind legs and scratch their chins on small trees, leaving scent. This habit tells the height of the visitor, how recently he was there, and the boundary of the territory he is trying to gain or wants to hold.

Cottontails often shelter in groundhog holes. But there is one species, named the pygmy rabbit, that digs its own home with two or more entrances. A sagebrush eater, it lives in the sagebrush country of southern Idaho and Washington, eastern Oregon, and northern California, Nevada, and Utah. Much smaller than cottontails, this pinkish-gray creature weighs $\frac{1}{2}$ to 1 pound when adult. Like the pika, it may squat at the mouth of its burrow and bark.

Grouped with pikas, cottontails, and rabbits are hares, which are largest of all. Hares have longer ears and longer hind legs than cottontails or rabbits. They are larger and have different digestive tracts. The European and American hares live in forms rather than digging burrows.

The young of the hares are born with thick fur and eyes already open. Eleven species of hares live in North America. The most commonly known hares are the jack rabbits, so named for their long ears which are like a donkey's ears. Jack

blind for a week or more. The mother covers them with a soft blanket of grass and fur and returns at night to give them milk. So well are they hidden that very few people have ever seen a cottontail nest. However, snakes, foxes, cats, dogs, skunks, owls, and others are very fond of these small tender morsels. Only about one-third of the young live to leave the nest. In 2 weeks they are furred, their eyes are open, and they are able to hop about.

Cottontails are peppered with various shades of brown and buff. They have no white or black markings on the ears.

Freezing, or remaining perfectly still, often enables the cottontail to escape the notice of enemies. Another defense is to be familiar with every part of the home range which may cover 2 acres. The trails, the brush piles, the briar patches, the cane thickets, the cactus clumps, and other shelters allow cottontails to keep out of the reach of predatory animals except for minks and

79

This nimble long-heeled creature is a familiar sight on the western prairie. A gray-brown and 20-inch body, black-tipped ears measuring 6 or 7 inches, and a black-topped tail identify the black-tail jack rabbit. It weighs 3 to 7 pounds.

rabbits may be 2 feet long and weigh up to 7 pounds.

Three species of jack rabbits live in the western United States.

When chased, jack rabbits tear along in great bounds, perhaps 12 feet or more at a time up to speeds of 35 miles per hour. Occasionally they leap as high as 5 feet in the air, looking back to see how closely they are being followed. Like cottontails, jack rabbits avoid danger by freezing.

Man has greatly increased cottontails and jack rabbits by killing off hawks, owls, wolves, coyotes, foxes, bobcats, snakes, weasels, minks, badgers, and other meat-eating animals. Man's hay crops are able to support large populations of these wiggle-nosed mammals. The best way to control large numbers of cottontails and jack rabbits along with overpopulations of mice and rats is to bring about the return of predatory animals.

Hares of the arctic tundra are still bigger than those in the United States. They weigh up to 12 pounds and may be 2 feet long. In summer they are various shades of gray or cinnamon brown. This fur is molted and a very heavy white coat grows in its place, covering even the soles of the feet.

These hares live in the treeless plains next to the arctic icecap. During winter they may come below the timberline. Extra-long incisors in the upper jaw enable them to scrape lichens from the rocks. Lichens, willow bark, and other plant materials are food for these great white hares. Only during a blizzard will they seek shelter in a thicket. At other times they sleep in their forms in the snow with the frigid subzero winds whistling around them and the northern lights flickering and climbing up the sky.

During the mating season there is a great deal of fighting among male hares. They leap high into the air biting, kicking, and scratching. Tattered fur and torn ears are the result. "Mad as a

The areas above are home to the black-tail jack rabbit.

These big handsome Arctic hares provide man with meat and fur. Two feet long and weighing from 6 to 12 pounds, these gray or brown creatures turn white in winter. In some areas they are always white.

Arctic, snowshoe, and tundra hares live in cold forests and swamps and on the Barren Ground of the far North.

March hare" is an old saying used because of the behavior of hares in the month of March.

The does have yearly one litter of three or four young. Like other hares the young are born fully furred in a nest on the surface of the ground lined with hair from the mother's body.

Most Arctic hares live solitary lives, but in far northern Canadian islands hares are seen in herds numbering up to one hundred animals. In Greenland the hares are also found in herds. When frightened, these animals rise on their hind legs and dance about until they discover the direction from which danger is threatening. Then away they all bounce leaving the field behind them empty.

Eskimos use the hares for meat, and the fur for lining mittens and making socks. They also use woven fur strips to make an unusually warm blanket.

Hares, rabbits, cottontails, and pikas were once considered rodents. They have long gnawing teeth as

Class Project

Bring a very tame pet rabbit to school. Feed it a blade of grass. Notice how the grass is drawn into the mouth without any help from the paws. Does the nose ever stop wabbling?

Do the hind feet and front feet have the same number of toes? How many?

Smooth dust or sand on the school ground or choose an area of unbroken snow. Allow the rabbit to hop across it. Do the hind feet show first or last in the prints?

rodents do. However, in the upper jaw behind the two incisors is another pair of teeth. An additional difference between them and rodents is in the use of the front paws. Squirrels, woodchucks, and various other rodents turn their forepaws in to handle food. Pikas, cottontails, rabbits, and hares cannot do this.

God has made the forest edges, meadows, and prairies a haven for these usually mild-mannered creatures. In the lush dewy grass and departing shadows of an early summer morning we may often notice a shy cottontail. How charming to see in the light of a fading sunset a small furry creature hop quietly along a hidden path or pause with wabbling nose to pull a grass sample.

Questions

Answer numbers 1 to 12 with the name or names of the mammals found in this lesson that possess these characteristics (pika, cottontail, European rabbit, jack rabbit, Arctic hare).

1. This mammal may weigh as much as 12 pounds.

2. This small creature weighs less than $\frac{1}{2}$ pound when grown.

3. These animals sit in forms in grass, light vegetation, or soft snow.

4. The young of these animals are born in a fur-lined depression in the ground and are covered with a blanket of fur.

5. This mammal lives in underground colonies as prairie dogs do.

6. They are born naked; their eyes do not open for a week or more.

7. They are born warmly furred with eyes open. They soon hop about.

8. This mammal lives in rockslides on high mountains.

9. When in danger they often sit perfectly still.

10. When in danger they thump their hind feet on the ground to warn others.

11. When danger threatens, it bleats or whistles loudly to warn others.

12. When danger threatens, this mammal sometimes rises to its hind feet and dances about to keep balanced until it sees what is coming.

13. Cottontails and jack rabbits are (very scarce, quite plentiful).

14. Man has (increased, decreased) cottontails and jack rabbits by (destroying predators, protecting predators) and (planting crops that are food for them, planting only those crops which cottontails and jack rabbits will not eat).

15. (Pikas, Cottontails, Jack rabbits, Arctic hares) store food for the winter.

16. Pikas, cottontails, jack rabbits, and Arctic hares have long incisors as the rodents do. However, they are no longer considered rodents because (they have a very small furry tail, they have an extra pair of teeth behind the upper incisors, they do not chew wood, their front paws cannot be turned inward to hold food [choose two]).

"Sing unto him . . . : talk ye of all his wondrous works." Psalm 105:2

11.   The Most Wonderful Ears

Have you ever been in a place where there was no light at all? God has created the sun, moon, and stars to shine upon the earth. On a moonless night the stars cast a dim glow. Rarely is there total darkness under the open sky. Owls, cats, flying squirrels, and other animals have pupils that open wide to take in every faint ray. But these creatures do not really see in the dark. Eyes are useless in complete gloom.

The Bible writer Moses tells in Exodus 10:21-23 about 3 days in Egypt when there was no light. Neither sun, moon, nor stars could be seen. The darkness was so thick that the people did not travel around. They simply stayed where they were until God mercifully removed the heavy pall that shut out even the brilliance of the sun.

How could you move about if you were in pitchy darkness? Some animals are guided in their burrows by the sense of touch.

Would you believe that God has made a mammal able to whiz at top speed between invisible walls without brushing against anything?

Hundreds of feet below the earth's surface are large natural caverns where total darkness reigns. Tiny mammals with wings of thin, crepey skin live in these inky regions. They come to the surface to find food, dashing along without touching walls or bumping into each other.

Since the seventeenth century men have studied bats and puzzled over their ability to travel without being able to see where they were going. At last, G. W. Pierce at Harvard developed a device that could pick up sounds that were higher in pitch than the human ear can hear. Bats were discovered to be raising loud, shrill cries, as often as thirty or more times a second. These sounds bouncing from everything near showed the location of each object. The bats' ears were able to pick up echoes and measure distances accordingly. This sense is known as echolocation.

Blindfolded bats released in rooms

The most nimble wings. Some birds fly faster than bats can. But not even a hummingbird is able at full speed to turn a right angle in little more than its own length as does this master of the air.

strung with wires 10 inches apart flew full speed between them without touching. A bat with its ears plugged hit the wires because it was unable to hear its own voice. Another with open ears and tied-shut, sealed jaws also blundered about, bumping into wires and walls. It could not squeak with its lips closed.

Bats with mouths and ears open sensed and dodged every wire even though seventy loudspeakers were blaring cries of the same pitch and two thousand times as powerful.

How does a bat pick out its own echo when flying with thousands of others that are all calling and receiving echoes from countless moving surfaces? Until the present time this mystery is one of God's ways "past finding out."

Bats use echolocation when catching insects. Echoes from a fluttering moth show exactly where it is. Some moths are able to hear. Scientists have surmised that they, too, notice the bats' high-pitched screeches and try to avoid being captured. These darting mammals gather beetles and mosquitoes every warm night. Bats in North America are insect eaters while those in the tropics are mostly fruit eaters. The fruit eaters are sometimes larger and may be called flying foxes.

The flying mammals of this country are divided into two groups, the cave bats and the tree bats. The cave bats hibernate through the winter and the tree bats usually migrate.

The bones at the tips of the front limbs are toe bones in most mammals. But in bats the Lord has created these

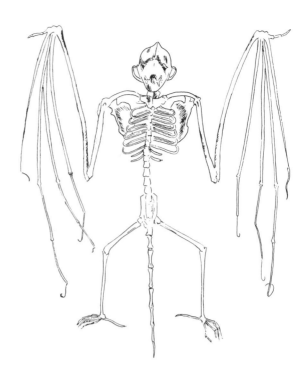

A bat's skeleton. Long, light bones support the membranes of a bat's wings.

bones very fine and light. They are even longer than most of their other bones. The wings extend between these long, fine bones and along the body to the hind legs. The soft skin stretches between the hind legs and is joined to the tail, as well. There is one claw on the outer bend of each wing. The hind feet have five claws each.

When a bat is ready to give birth she prepares no nest. Instead, she hangs by her wing hooks and feet like a flat, fuzzy sheet. Her tail membrane prevents the newborn from tumbling below. Soon the new infant has shuffled onto the fur on her breast and found a milk gland. Here it drinks contentedly for several days. Even when the mother bat leaves the roost and darts about catching insects,

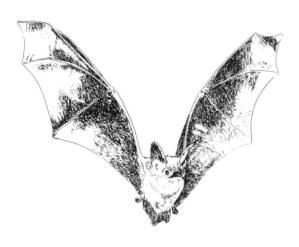

The little brown bat. Bats similar to the little brown bat are found throughout the world except in Antarctica, the Polar Regions, and a few islands of the sea.

the young bat feeds on. A human baby in similar circumstances would soon be discouraged.

Next to rodents, bats are the mammal order with the largest number of species. One hundred eighty species of bats live in North America.

The little brown bat lives from Alaska and Nova Scotia to California and Georgia. It hibernates in winter, many times in caves below the frost line.

The little brown bat is very common. It is about 4 inches long and has a wingspread of 10 inches. Its tail membrane has no hair. The little creature weighs $\frac{1}{3}$ ounce and has short, brown or black fur. It lives as far north as the tree line in Canada. If one listens to this bat closely one may hear squeaks, buzzes, clicking sounds, or soft calls. In winter the little brown bat hibernates.

Big brown bats are slightly larger with a wingspread of 12 inches. This bat often spends the winter in buildings,

The big brown bat lives over a wide area in North America. Most big brown bats hibernate in caves although a few may fly south for short distances.

barns, church steeples and similar places. If you find a little skin-and-fur creature all folded up, tucked away behind a shutter or in a chink of a wall it may be this species. It likes warm, dry spots.

When the big brown bat is thirsty it skims across the surface of some quiet lake or stream, gulping in tiny swallows of water as it goes.

The red bat is a trifle larger than the

big brown bat. The upper surface of its tail membrane is thickly covered with red hair. The remainder of the body is also red furred with white-tipped hairs that give a frosted appearance. Red bats live in central and southeastern Canada and in the United States and Mexico except for the higher, drier areas.

Unlike the little brown bat with only one young, the red bat may have three or four. Altogether they may weigh as

The red bat is common in most of the United States. This tree dweller flies south before cold weather, returning when insects are again plentiful.

A mother red bat with her baby. Red bats have as many as four young at one time.

much as the mother, but she carries them about with her while she hunts. When they are partly grown she hangs them up on the roost while she goes out to find food. She returns and feeds them until they are able to fly about and catch their own insects.

Autumn comes. Moths, beetles, and mosquitoes disappear. The red bat leaves the northern parts of its range and heads south. Migrating bats usually travel at night about 1,500 feet above

the ground or higher. The red bat may winter in Bermuda.

Six species of bats belonging to the free-tailed group live in the United States. Bats in this group have tail membranes that extend only partway along the tail. The naked tip of the tail is free for perhaps an inch. Southwestern United States has more free-tailed bats than any other kind.

The Carlsbad Caverns in southeastern New Mexico is the home of millions

The Mexican free-tailed bat lives by the millions in the Carlsbad Caverns of New Mexico.

The Mexican free-tailed bat lives in Mexico and southwestern United States.

of free-tailed bats. During the day a huge room $\frac{1}{4}$ mile long and over 100 feet high is hung full of myriads of these tiny creatures. At dusk they awaken. A low roaring sound arises from the swish of countless wings. One naturalist estimated that they emerge from the mouth of the cavern at the rate of three hundred per second. They are so close together that from a little distance they appear as thick clouds of smoke. Scattering over the landscape they hunt and pick up tons of insects that would probably injure crops. All night long they roam. Before the sun rises the millions of bats gather about the cave's mouth and fly underground again to sleep before the next night's food-gathering.

In caves where bats live their droppings form a very rich fertilizer known as guano ('gwä-ˌnō). The Carlsbad Caverns yielded 50 to 100 tons of guano per day, 6 months out of a year for 15 years. At last, the fertilizer companies had dug up and hauled away all the deposits. These tons of guano were the remains of billions upon billions of insects. The Carlsbad Caverns is only one roost in thousands used by bats. So we know that bats consume vast numbers of insects.

Wooden towers are sometimes built to attract bats. These squeaky, little creatures, besides ridding the countryside of various insects, may leave as much as 2 tons of valuable fertilizer in each tower every year.

Bats have few natural enemies. Storms and unexpected severe weather kill a few. A bat may live 10 years or even longer.

Swallows, swifts, flycatchers, gnatcatchers, and dragonflies reap the rich insect harvest of the air by day. And at night the bats, on wings of finest leather, swoop and dip and turn and cry.

Class Project

Search old deserted buildings or other likely places for sleeping or hibernating bats. Disturb the animals you find as little as possible. Notice the size, the color of the fur, and the structure of the ears. Examine the front and the hind claws. How often does the hibernating bat breathe per minute?

Questions

1. Bats are (birds, mammals, extra-large moths).

2. Bats (can, cannot) fly in total darkness.

3. Bats in complete darkness (feel their way along; travel by a very keen sense of smell; can hear their own tiny, high-pitched sounds echoing from objects and surfaces).

4. At the approach of winter a bat in the North may (hibernate; migrate to southern regions; stay active by finding shelter in heated places such as greenhouses, factory smokestacks, and poultry houses; freeze to death [choose two]).

5. Bats in the United States eat mostly (fruit, seeds, insects, leaves and grass).

6. Mother bats (build nests in hollow trees, burrow into the ground, build no nests at all).

7. Bats are (extremely light, of medium weight, solid and chunky).

8. When in total darkness bats use (wings and claws, noses and tongues, voices and ears, smell and hearing, eyes and ears) to find their way.

9. Name two ways that bats are beneficial to man.

"Dost thou know . . . the wondrous works of him which is perfect in knowledge?" Job 37:16

12. Hoofs, Horns, Antlers, and Special Stomachs

"As light of foot as a wild roe" runs the description of King David's nephew Asahel (2 Samuel 2:18). Eleven men of the tribe of Gad "were as swift as the roes upon the mountains" (1 Chronicles 12:8-13).

The roes of Israel were very fast and slender gazelles belonging to the antelopes. Probably they were the fleetest mammals of the country. When chased they are said to vanish rather than to run.

The swiftest mammal in the United States, considered the second-most speedy anywhere, is the pronghorn of the western plains. It is the only animal on earth in its family. It travels in 15-foot leaps at rates up to 60 miles per hour. Colored a warm cinnamon brown with touches of black on the ear tips and nose, it also has white lower sides and two white bands crossing the throat. A short, dark-brown mane stands up on the neck and a large, white patch of hair covers the rump.

The pronghorn's tan blends into the sand and dusty sage of its habitat. But when it is frightened the creature erects the white hairs of its rump patch and bounds away to safety. Like a mirror catching the light, the white flashing can be seen nearly four miles in the

The pronghorn is the only one of its family anywhere in the world. Body length of buck, 4 feet; height at shoulder, 3 feet; weight, 100 to 140 pounds. A flashing white rump patch is used to signal danger to other pronghorns.

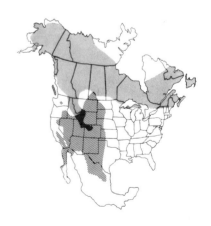

Pronghorns (lines) roam in grasslands and deserts. Moose (shaded) prefer the forests and shallow lakes with water plants.

clear desert air and bright sunshine.

Pronghorns in the 1700s were estimated to number 50 million animals. By the 1900s their homes had been taken for cattle pastures and farm fields. Careless hunting also reduced the herds until laws protecting them were passed. By 1953 they had increased again to 340,000.

The horns of the bucks and does grow over a core of bone. Each year the horn covering is shed and a new one extends from the tip of the permanent bone core until it reaches the top of the head. This speedy creature is named for the prongs on its horns. No other mammal has branched horns.

Very keen eyesight and ability to outrun other animals are its defense. A head poked over a hill a mile away will alert a pronghorn at once.

Late in May twin or triplet fawns are born that are soon running with the group. They have the special ruminant ('rü-mə-nənt) stomach to handle grass, weeds, and sagebrush.

Three species of wild cattle in this country also have the four-chambered

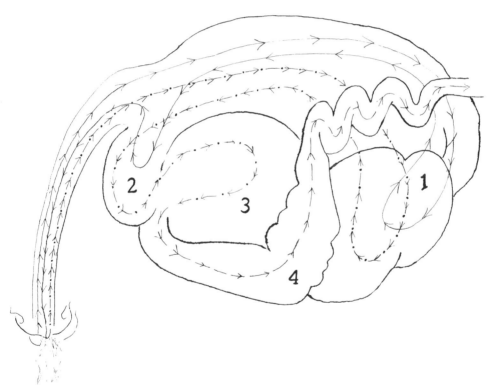

The four-chambered stomach of a ruminant. After a few chews the food is swallowed into number 1 where it is mashed, moistened, and broken down by bacteria. Passing into number 2, the food continues to be broken down for a total of about 8 hours. Here it is formed into cuds. A strong hiccup returns a cud to the mouth where it is chewed thoroughly for the first time. Reswallowed, it again enters number 1, then number 2, and on to number 3. Chamber number 4 receives the mixture, pours in digestive juice, and passes the food into the small intestine where nutrients are absorbed into the blood stream.

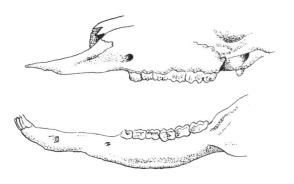

The mouth of a ruminant. The front lower teeth and the upper horny plate act in scissors fashion as the mammal nips off vegetation. The grinding teeth in the rear work on the cuds as they come into the mouth from the stomach.

ruminant stomach. They are the mountain goat, the bighorn sheep, and the bison.

High on cliffs and pika rockslides above the timber line lives the mountain goat, a white shaggy animal with small, backward-curving, black horns. The soles of its hoofs are spreading and cup-shaped, designed to grip the rocks. Even in the severest cold and blizzards the mountain goat stays in his wind-swept heights; for he is protected by a soft, wool undercoat that is 3 to 4 inches thick and a still-longer, coarse overcoat. Jaws and throat are swathed in a heavy beard. The wool is sometimes shed; where it is plentiful it is gathered, dyed, and made into blankets and robes. Single kids or occasionally twins are born to the does in May.

The brown or gray American bighorn sheep is also at home climbing the rocks of the high peaks. However its large horns which may be 16 inches around at the base and measure 49 inches around the outside curve make the sheep a target for trophy hunters. Two species live in North America, the Rocky Mountain sheep and the Dall's or white sheep. These mammals were in

The mountain goat lives above the timber line on high mountains. "The high hills are a refuge for the wild goats" (Psalm 104:18). Some individual mountain goats wear beards much longer and denser than this one. Body length of buck, 5 to 5¾ feet; height at shoulder, 3 to 3½ feet; weight, 125 to 300 pounds.

Mountain goats (lines) skip about the cliffs and graze the highland meadows above the timber line. Bison (shaded) live in little, protected colonies in this country. In Canada one wild herd roams free in northern Alberta.

The bighorn sheep lives in rugged western mountains. Body length of ram, 4½ to nearly 6 feet; height at shoulder, 3 to 3½ feet; weight, 125 to 250 pounds. Bighorn sheep have a creamy-white rump patch.

danger of extinction until laws were passed to preserve them.

In the fall rams and ewes move to the lower valleys away from the fiercest, winter storms. One lamb or twins are born in late May or June. Like pronghorns these creatures of the high peaks have a very keen eyesight and can see a gun barrel gleam several miles away. Like pronghorns the American bighorn sheep has a whitish rump patch. The coats of bighorn sheep vary in color from gray to black. Some individuals are all white with yellowish horns and dark hoofs.

Some desert bighorn sheep live in the dry lands of the Southwest. Here they quench their thirst by butting down water-storing cactuses and taking the damp juicy pulp.

Two hundred years ago the most useful native animal in this country was the bison. North into Canada and as far south as Mexico, from Oregon to Virginia the massive herds of huge, wild cattle wandered. Probably man has never before or since seen such vast multitudes of mammals, for it was estimated that they had numbered 60 million or even 100 million.

The Indians depended largely upon the bison for meat, fat, clothing, shelter, and fuel. Pounded together with wild berries a rich food called pemmican was prepared from the dried meat and fat. Leggings, moccasins, shirts, dresses, tents, shields, saddles, ropes, and even small boats were fashioned from the leather. The large, shaggy, dark-brown furs were used for bedcovers and robes. The sinews became thread and bowstrings. Boiled hoofs made glue. Bones were good for tools and sled runners. The dried dung was fuel for fires.

When the white men came they were unwilling to let the Indians continue to enjoy their way of life. Some European

The Dall's or white sheep (lines) lives in Alaska, the Yukon Territory, and British Columbia. Two hundred miles farther south, through the mountains and western deserts to northern Mexico and Baja California the Rocky Mountain sheep (shaded) are found.

The bison is the largest North American land animal. Body length of bull, 10 to 12 feet; height at shoulder, 5 to 6 feet; weight, 800 to 2,000 pounds; record weight, 3,000 pounds.

immigrants decided that all native peoples who would not give up their homes should be killed or driven away. They tried to starve the Indians by shooting the millions of bison. Hides and tongues were taken; the bodies were then left to rot upon the plains.

By 1820 all bison east of the Mississippi River were dead. In another 70 years the countless thundering herds were reduced to about eighty-nine free-ranging animals plus a few privately owned groups.

The stench of their carcasses hung over the whole West for years. It was said that a man might have walked on dead bison a whole day without touching the earth. Bones whitened the hills for miles in all directions. Then came bone pickers who collected the skeletons and shipped them east where they sold for $6 to $10 a ton. When the last bones had been ground for fertilizer, the last chips burned in campfires, the only traces of these magnificent animals were the old trails and the wallowing places now grown in with grass.

Scarcely in time, laws were passed to protect the remaining few bison from death. These have increased to about six thousand in the United States and twice that many in Canada. The only wild herd left is south of Slave River in northern Alberta.

Single bison calves are born in the spring while the cows and bulls are shedding their winter coats. Dense long fur clothes their shoulders, head, neck, and upper spine hanging down behind their front legs like a woolen scarf. Mud and dust wallows help rid these bearded, shaggy mammals of flies and mosquitoes. Sharp hearing and a keen sense of smell alert bison to the approach of enemies.

Few deer in the world are smaller than the very rare key deer, a subspecies of the white-tailed deer. Body length of buck, 38 inches; height at shoulder, 25 inches; weight, 33 pounds.

The deer family have ruminant stomachs as well as the pronghorns and the wild cattle. However, they wear antlers rather than horns. Antlers are solid bony structures that grow from the front part of the skull and are shed each year. Caribou does are the only female deer carrying antlers.

The key deer on the southernmost islands of Florida are the smallest ruminants in this country. All deer are strong swimmers and the little, reddish-brown creatures readily paddle from island to island of their home range. Only twenty five of this species were left in 1945. Since then a refuge has been set up. Many people hope that this sub-species of the white-tailed deer will continue to live and multiply.

The white-tailed deer occupies the greatest area of any native deer. Probably there are as many as $4\frac{1}{4}$

The white-tailed deer ranges across southern Canada and throughout the United States east of the Rocky Mountains. This widely distributed hoofed mammal also lives in Mexico and Central America.

million individuals. After the first year, the does give birth to twin fawns each season. In autumn the short, reddish coat of summer changes to the thick, protective, gray coat that shields from the cold of winter. This animal has chalky underparts and white inner surfaces on its upper hind legs and a short, wide, snowy tail that it holds up and wags as an alarm while it runs. Deer have long been used for venison, buckskin, thread, and bone tools.

The mule deer is of similar size. It, too, is reddish in summer and blue-gray in winter. Some individuals have a light rump patch. The tail is either black tipped or black on top. The does raise their one to three fawns at an elevation of 7,000 feet or higher. Like the bighorn sheep the mule deer descends to lower levels when the severe winter weather threatens.

Three species of caribous (called

The antlers of a white-tailed buck are a main beam with prongs. Body length of buck, $4\frac{1}{2}$ to $6\frac{1}{2}$ feet; height at shoulder, 3 to $3\frac{1}{2}$ feet; weight, 150 to 275 pounds. When it is alarmed its voice is a loud, whistling snort.

The antlers of a mule deer buck branch equally rather than being tines from a main beam. Body length of buck, 4½ to 6½ feet; height at shoulder, 3 to 3½ feet; weight, 125 to 300 pounds. Many mule deer have a whitish rump patch.

The mule deer lives from southern Alaska, throughout western Canada and United States and south to Baja ('bä-hä) California and Mexico. On the western plains, it lives in the same areas as the white-tailed deer.

reindeer in the Old World)—the woodland caribou, the Barren Ground caribou, and the Greenland caribou—live in North America. Like mule deer and pronghorns they are white on the rump. Caribous are no taller than white-tailed

deer and mule deer, but they may weigh 100 pounds more. A mane protects the neck from cold and even the nose is hairy. A record antler measured 74¼ inches long.

Lichens are the main food of the caribou; and the ruminant stomach of this mammal converts the leathery lichens, the dried grass, willow leaves,

The caribou, called reindeer in the Old World, is the only wild mammal still supporting large populations of human beings. Body length of Barren Ground caribou bull, 5¼ to 6½ feet; height at shoulder, 3½ feet; weight, 150 to 400 pounds.

Barren Ground caribou (shaded) and woodland caribou (lines) tramp the highland meadows and mountain slopes, grazing on lichens, mosses, and dried grasses. The woodland caribou ranges farther south than the Barren Ground species.

The thrilling voice of a bull elk begins low, rises sharply and clearly, and ends on a lower note. Body length of bull, 7½ to 9½ feet; height at shoulder, 4½ to 5 feet; weight, 700 to 900 pounds. Elks have a large, yellowish rump patch.

and twigs to body-building materials, heat, and energy. The Barren Ground caribou is known for its long migrations that take place in the fall and spring as the creatures seek winter and summer feeding grounds. Especially in the past, many people of Alaska and Yukon depended upon the traveling herds for food and clothing. A wounded caribou often swims to an island and remains there, out of the reach of wolves, until it is able to travel again.

In Europe the reindeer is a domesticated animal providing meat and milk. The hair is used for mattresses and the skins for parkas, mittens, and trousers. The sinews make thread and the antlers are turned into knife handles and other items. Reindeer pull the sleds of the Laplanders.

Elks once lived from the southern Appalachians to the Pacific coast and from northern Alberta to southern New Mexico. Today these large deer live in a much smaller area. Like bighorn sheep and mule deer the elks move down from high mountains to avoid the deep snows of winter. The reddish-brown coat is set off by a chestnut-brown mane, darker legs and underparts, and a pale-yellow rump patch.

Moose are the largest deer in the world. They live in deep forests near shallow lakes or other water, eating moss, lichens, buds, twigs, and juicy water plants. Their antlers are often 6 feet across and have large, flattened parts with many small prongs. A record pair was 78 inches wide, with 34 points. The pair weighed 85 pounds. The moose is the tallest ruminant on this continent. Dark brown like the bison it has an overhanging snout and, on its throat, a flap of skin and hair that may be a foot or more long. One to three calves are born each spring.

Next to the moose in size the elk is the second-largest American deer. This huge animal once lived over the northern two-thirds of the United States, also in Alberta and south to Mexico. Now it is found in national parks and in high mountains.

The moose is the largest antlered animal in the world and the tallest ruminant in North and South America. Body length of bull moose, 8 to 10 feet; height at shoulder, 5 to 6½ feet; weight, 900 to 1,400 or even 1,800 pounds. The voice of a bull moose sounds like a diesel horn and can be heard a long distance.

The mammals with special stomachs are among the most hardy on earth. The pronghorn and caribou have long hollow hairs that grow thickly on their bodies and protect against the fierce winter winds.

Ruminant young are "precocious" and in a short time are able to travel with their mothers. Adult females of this group are smaller than males of the same species. In almost every state the domestic dog is the most serious predator of deer.

During the mating season bucks, bulls, and rams fight with their rivals; the battle calls of both elk and moose ring through the woods. At other times of the year there is peace in the herds. Elks, caribous, and bison form bands, and their largest bucks or bulls guard the borders of their group.

The white man has slaughtered and wasted the millions of pronghorns and American bison that once roamed the plains. He has brought to a very low number the key deer and the American bighorn sheep. But we are glad that some of these animals yet remain for us to enjoy, and we hope that there will always be at least a few living in the national parks and the game refuges of this country.

Class Project

Study the structure of mammal horns and antlers. Look at the hoofs of various ruminants. Domestic sheep, cattle, and goats may be examined if available.

Questions

bighorn sheep
bison
caribou

elk
key deer
moose

mountain goat
mule deer
pronghorn
white-tailed deer

1. Which of the mammals above belong to the deer family? They have antlers of hard bone that they shed every year before growing a new pair.

2. Which of the mammals above belong to the cattle family? They have hollow horns that are un-branched and grow over a bony core. The horns are never shed.

3. Which of the mammals above is in a family by itself? It has hollow horns that are branched and grow over a bony core. The horns are shed every year. The new horns replace the old over the permanent bony core.

4. What adult mammals within the groups above have neither horns nor antlers?

5. Mammals with a ruminant stomach have (paws, flippers, hoofs, webbed toes, claws).

6. A ruminant stomach is (very simple, like most other stomachs, very complex).

7. A ruminant stomach is designed to digest (meat, vegetable matter, fish, plankton).

8. What five ruminants in this country have a rump patch?

9. What four ruminants have manes?

(a) The ——— has a short, dark mane standing up on the back of the neck.

(b) The ——— and the ——— have manes that protect the neck all the way around.

(c) The ——— has extra-long hair on neck, head, front legs, and the forepart of the back.

10. The ——— and the ——— have beards and the ——— has a flap of skin and hair hanging down from its throat.

11. What ruminant mammal in North America runs fastest?

12. What ruminant mammal on this continent is the tallest?

13. What ruminant mammal of America is the smallest?

14. What ruminant mammal of the United States and Canada is the largest?

15. Members of the deer family are excellent (swimmers, tree climbers, runners, fliers, diggers [choose two]).

16. Name fifteen products or services provided by the ruminant groups of mammals in this country and other countries.

17. Name two species of ruminant mammals with pure-white hair and colored hoofs and horns.

18. Females of the American ruminants are (smaller than, the same size as, larger than) the males.

99

19. Most ruminant mammals of this country have (long, strong, conspicuous tails; easily seen tails that are about one-third of the body length; rather small tails).

20. The ———— uses its tail as a signal when it is fleeing from danger.

"Stand still, and consider the wondrous works of God." Job 37:14

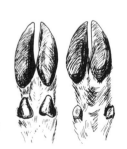

13.   Secret Claws and Ringtails

"Another mighty angel . . . cried with a loud voice, as when a lion roareth." In these words the apostle John described the deep awful sound of the angel's call. An elder at God's throne told the apostle that Jesus, the Lion of the tribe of Judah, had prevailed and was worthy above all men in heaven, in earth, and under the earth.

Agur, a Bible writer, says that the lion is "strongest among beasts, and turneth not away for any."

Lions once lived in Israel, although they have been extinct there for more than 700 years. Bible writers speak often of lions. Samson, David, Benaiah, and Daniel knew these great beasts very well. The first three fought hand to claw with them.

Another wild cat, still found in a few mountains of Israel, is the leopard. Jeremiah writes of the leopard's spots, and Habakkuk of its swiftness.

Mammals of the cat family are found in warm and cold climates except in Australia and in Antarctica. They are known as felines ('fē-ˌlīnz). Felines have very characteristic eyes. Most vertebrates have eye muscles that, in strong light, close the pupil to a small round hole. Cats have eye muscles that pull the two sides of the iris ('ī-rəs) together until only a slit shows. A feline's eyes are so sensitive that during the day a tiny crack is sufficient for seeing. At night the muscles relax and the pupil becomes large and round. Faint rays enter making it possible for the cat to see form and indistinct outlines.

Cats' claws differ from those of most other mammals, for they can be drawn into the paws or extended again at will. Sharp as an eagle's talons, these claws are useful in catching and holding live prey.

Cats have four toes on each hind

The bobcat is North America's most common native cat. Body length, 30 to 40 inches; height at shoulder, 20 to 23 inches; weight, 12 to 25 pounds, rarely 40 pounds; tail, 4 to 6½ inches.

foot, and five toes on each front foot. One toe on the front foot is so high on the inside of the paw that it does not show in the track.

The most common wild cat in the United States is the bobcat. Low regions, deserts, and mountain heights up to 12,000 feet are its home. Members of the cat family are rarely seen, even in the areas where they hunt. Usually they are most active at night. People who live near deep forests or rough mountains may hear an unearthly yell in the darkness and know that a wild cat is on the prowl.

The bobcat, like the white-tailed deer, lives close to man. As forests are cut, more areas are suitable for small rodents, the main food of bobcats. Mice, rabbits, squirrels, rats, beetles, grasshoppers, and sometimes birds are hunted by forest and mountain bobcats. In deserts snakes, lizards, and insects are killed. The bobcat creeps near its

Built-in snowshoes are God's gift to the lynx. Body length, 32 to 36 inches; weight, 15 to 30 pounds; tail, 4 inches.

prey quietly, then pounces suddenly before the animal can escape. Most frequently wild cats of this country take food killed only by themselves, but bobcats will eat carrion if it is still fresh.

The male bobcat gives no help with the kittens which come in litters of one to four in the early spring. The little velvet-furred, spotted creatures are born in a deep thicket, a cave, or a hollow tree, where their eyes open in about 3 days. An adult retains the dark spots that show on the legs and light underbody. The tail tip is black on top and there are short stripes on the upper side. The ears and a ruff underneath the neck are marked with black.

Except for a few details the lynx looks much like a bobcat. It has a two-color tail. The entire tip is solid black and there are no stripes. The lynx is a northern cat and its feet are large

Alaska and Canada are the home of the lynx (lines). The United States and Mexico are the range of the bobcat (shaded). In southern Canada and the northern United States the two live in the same areas.

and heavily furred for traveling over the snow. Long, pointed, black tufts adorn the ears. The spots of a lynx are few and its belly is not marked.

Both lynx and bobcat have various colors—yellow, tan, reddish-brown, dark-brown, or gray. Both animals eat any fresh meat that they can get, but the lynx eats more snowshoe hares than anything else. These cats have keen eyesight and hearing and a fairly good sense of smell.

The only unspotted wild cat in this country is the adult cougar, also called mountain lion, puma, and panther. Unlike the lynx and bobcat it has no ruff at the neck, nor does it have a mane. It is light in color on the insides of the legs and underneath. On the cheeks, the tips of the ears, and at the end of the tail are blackish markings. Clear yellow eyes, big heavy whiskers,

The cougar was found in recent times in the areas shown above. It seems to be extending its range to the northeastern and southeastern United States and around the Great Lakes.

and a long round tail characterize this quiet graceful creature.

Cougars seemed to disappear from most of the East as forests were cut and deer decreased. Now that the white-tailed deer are more plentiful, the cougar is being seen again, too. Deer are the cougar's most important food, although it kills even skunks and porcupines when other meat is scarce.

Two or three spotted kittens, weighing between $\frac{1}{2}$ pound and 1 pound, are born in a secret place and are protected and fed by the mother. The eyes open in about 2 weeks. At the age of 2 months the spots and the rings on the tail fade. The kittens go with their mother on hunting trips and learn to capture prey.

Like the leopard of Bible lands, the cougar likes to watch people. It has even been known to follow along behind travelers, keeping itself out of sight.

The jaguar is a little larger and heavier than the cougar and is covered from face to tip of tail with markings

The cougar is also called mountain lion, panther, and puma. Body length, 6 to 8½ feet; height at shoulder, 26 to 30 inches; weight, 100 to 175 pounds; tail, 26 to 36 inches.

The jaguar is the only American cat whose coat is marked with rosettes. Body length, 44 to 58 inches; weight, 150 to 225 pounds tail, 21 to 26 inches.

called rosettes. Rosettes are rings, sometimes with spots in the middle. The ground color of a jaguar's coat is yellowish or buff. The rosettes are dark-brown or black enclosing a slightly darker color and an occasional black center spot. The jaguar is most plentiful in Mexico, Central and South America. It lives in the coldest parts of southern South America.

Two to four cubs are born in a heavy thorn thicket or a cave. Their eyes are closed, and they are very woolly and spotted. In about 6 weeks the young are the size of house cats and ready to follow their parents on the hunt.

Jaguars eat a great variety of meat. Deer, jack rabbits, coyotes, armadillos, snakes, turtles, birds, squirrels, and many other small animals are taken. The jaguar even likes to play in shallow water on hot days, and while playing will hunt fish. The male jaguar brings

food to the female while she nurses the kittens.

One small pretty animal in the same family as the raccoon is the ringtail. This light, slim creature has shiny, golden-brown fur with pale-gray underparts, and a long, fluffy tail, crossed on the upper side with seven black bars and seven white bars.

Ringtails are frisky and playful, but are rarely seen because they come out only at night. Food eaten by these foxy-faced mammals is varied. Lizards, birds, toads, corn, bats, mice, oranges, figs, dates, nuts, wild berries, persimmons, insects, and acorns are all enjoyed by the ringtail.

Its claws are movable like a cat's but cannot be drawn entirely into its paws. There are five toes on both front and hind feet. It lives at altitudes up to

America's biggest cat, the jaguar (shaded), is found sparingly along the southern borders of Texas, New Mexico, and Arizona. It ranges throughout Mexico, Central America, and into the jungles of South America. The ringtail (line) likes Mexico, too, but also lives as far north as Oregon. Areas where both animals live appear dark.

6,000 feet and is an excellent climber. It can even leap spaces 10 feet across.

The ringtail is found in Mexico and Central America. The warm mountains and deserts of southwestern United States are its home, too.

It may bark, snarl, squeak, or scream when in trouble. Most of the time it is a quiet animal. Owls are its main predator.

All five toes of all four feet show in the footprints of the ringtail. The marks of the front feet are partly covered by the tracks of the hind feet.

This frisky little ringtail is abroad only at night. Body length, 14 to 16 inches; height at shoulder, 6 inches; weight, 2 to 2½ pounds; tail, 13 to 15 inches.

Usually three young are born blind, toothless, and deaf. The den may be in a tree near water or in holes among rocks. At between 4 and 5 weeks of age the kits' eyes open. In another month they are hunting with their parents. At 4 months they become independent.

Since ringtails roam at night they sleep during the day. They have been found dozing in tall trees lying along a branch with the black and white, barred tail hanging down. Early settlers, as well as present-day miners and ranchers, liked tame ringtails in their homes to catch mice and rats.

The raccoon is a nighttime animal, too; but it lives so near man and is so common along highways that many people know it.

The black mask covering the eyes and cheeks and the bushy tail with its four to seven dark bands give this creature a distinctive look.

The soles of a raccoon's feet are

A black-masked night prowler, the raccoon. Body length, 25 to 34 inches; height at shoulder, 9 to 12 inches; weight, 12 to 25 pounds; tail, 9½ to 10½ inches.

The raccoon is well known along the borders of southern Canada and throughout most of the United States and Mexico.

bare. Unlike many other mammals that walk only on their toes, the raccoon walks on its feet. Its claws cannot be pushed out or pulled in as can the claws of cats. There are five toes on both front and hind feet.

Like the ringtail, raccoons eat almost everything that is animal or vegetable. Nuts, berries, fruit, honey, corn, crayfishes, crabs, oysters, frogs, toads, turtle eggs, and many other foods are in its diet.

The raccoon swims well and is altogether at home in trees. Eagles, owls, and weasels take young raccoons. Adult raccoons are good fighters and can defend themselves. If they are attacked while they are caring for their young, they often put the young up a tree and remain on the ground to defeat the enemy.

Raccoons frequently wash food that they find near water, but away from water they eat unwashed food.

In the North during severe weather, the raccoon sleeps in a cave, a hollow

tree, or other sheltered place. In mild weather or in the South it comes out and hunts food.

Raccoon fur and flesh are both used by man. The background color of the fur varies. It may be grayish, brownish, blackish, reddish, or even pale gold or albino.

Usually four young are in each litter. A hollow tree is the den. The newborn young are very light, weighing only $2\frac{1}{2}$ ounces apiece. In 49 days they may weigh $1\frac{1}{2}$ pounds and be eating food other than their mother's milk.

You are more likely to see a raccoon than any of the cat family or the ringtail. Desert country, forest land, or ocean beaches are home to the raccoon.

This chubby masked mammal has many different cries—screechings,

The long heels of the hind feet and the five toes on all four feet are characteristic of the raccoon footprints. The right hind foot is placed beside the left forefoot as the mammal travels along.

106

snarlings, growlings, barkings, snortings, hootings, and hissings. If you hear a shrill whistling voice in the night it may be a raccoon.

The cougar and the bobcat are extending their range. Perhaps sometime you may even see one of these graceful, clawed creatures or hear its hair-raising scream in the night.

Class Project

Study a pet cat. Notice the elliptical pupils. Why does a cat have these elliptical pupils? Examine the sensory hairs on the cat's face. At what three locations are these hairs found? Count the toes on the front and the hind feet. Does every pad have a claw beside it? Gently squeeze the toes to move the claws in and out. Can the claws be seen when the foot is relaxed? Compare the width of the paw when the claws are hidden and when they are extended.

Questions

1. God has placed members of the cat family in (North America, South America, Europe, Asia, Africa, Australia, Antarctica [Choose five].

2. How are a cat's claws different from the claws of most other mammals?

3. What two wild cats were most common in Bible times in Israel?

4. Cats usually hunt during (the day, the night, both night and day).

5. Cats eat mostly vegetable food, fresh meat killed by themselves, carrion).

6. In this country most wild cats are (striped, spotted, plain in color).

7. The main food of the bobcat is (fish, birds, rodents, insects, fruit).

8. The main food of the lynx is (willow buds, seals, caribous, snowshoe hares, birds).

9. The cougar prefers (cactus pulp, deer, acorns, insects, earthworms) as food.

10. The jaguar is a (meat-eating, fruit-eating, leaf-eating) mammal.

11. The ringtail and the raccoon are both fond of (vegetable food only, animal food only, fishes and clams only, a great many different foods).

12. Members of the cat family are (often seen, not often seen).

13. The ringtail is useful as a (weed seed eater, rodent killer, frog catcher).

14. Ringtails are active (by day, by

night, both day and night).

15. Raccoons are (chubby, tall, thin) mammals.

16. Raccoons are used for (meat, milk, leather, fur, transportation [choose two]).

"O Lord, . . . I will shew forth all thy marvellous works." Psalm 9:1

14.   Trailers and Climbers

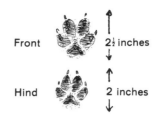

Front   2½ inches

Hind   2 inches

Dogs are very important workers. They may have begun as a single species, but through many generations men have developed various breeds that are quite unlike each other.

Pointers, spaniels, retrievers, and setters follow hunters afield. Terriers being small chase foxes, badgers, and rats and other rodents.

Hounds sniff the trail of game and pursue to trees or burrows. Greyhounds, deerhounds, and wolfhounds chase by sight, galloping swiftly after the prey and holding or crippling it until the hunters arrive. Bloodhounds are trained to find lost children or escaped criminals by tracking them.

Among the snow avalanches of the high Alps mountain ranges, the Saint Bernard dogs locate buried travelers and aid monks in rescue work. Over the centuries these big shaggy animals are said to have preserved 2,500 people. Another lifesaver is the Newfoundland breed that has rescued shipwreck victims.

Collies or sheep dogs move or herd livestock. German shepherds guide blind people, guard homes and stores, and assist policemen.

Strong dogs with big muscular bodies and extra-heavy coats pull sleds in the Arctic and Antarctic regions of extreme cold where other animals cannot go and machines are useless.

Various species of mammals belonging to the dog family, called canines ('kā-ˌnīnz), range the continents of the world except Antarctica. Unlike wild cats that usually eat only fresh meat killed by themselves, the canines eat carrion very willingly. Dead poultry, stillborn calves, small dead pigs, or other animals discarded in the fields by farmers will probably be found and carried to the den by foxes, coyotes, and wolves. The livestock owner losing an animal in a remote pasture by disease may come upon it partly eaten and surmise that coyotes have killed it. Ice storms and heavy snow may starve or freeze quails and game birds that are later feasted upon by a hungry canine. After hunting season, wounded rabbits and pheasants may have their lives quickly ended by a wolf, coyote, or fox that takes them for its food. Fires, floods, and landslides destroy animals that may later be cleaned up by a keen-nosed fox or coyote.

The remains of animals found at den locations do not show that the den owner has killed the animal. Many times the bones are of carrion found along the highway.

Several species of wild dogs live in this country, four fox and three wolf species. Like cats, dogs have four toes on the hind foot and five on the front foot with the inside toe too high to show in the track. However, the footprints of the two animals are slightly different. Dogs' claws are more blunt, cannot be drawn in, and often leave marks, especially in a muddy track. The leading edge of the heel pad is rounded. Cats claws rarely leave a trace. Two lobes share the foreward margin of the feline's heel.

Jaguars often enter the warm tropical waters of their southern homes, but most cats that live in the North avoid swimming if possible. On the other hand many dogs enjoy swimming even in cold water and their thick coats are good protection against dampness and

The kit and swift foxes (shaded) live in the deserts and plains of the west from Canada to Mexico. Limited parts of Missouri, Arkansas, Louisiana, and Texas have been the latest home of the now nearly extinct red wolf (lines).

low temperatures.

Foxes and wolves have a scent gland on top of the tail at its base. This scent is used to mark dens and trails.

The smallest mammal in the canine group is the kit fox. It hunts only at night and is seldom seen. The swift fox, fastest runner among the foxes, is slightly larger and darker, with smaller ears. When chased both species zig zag with lightning speed. However, they soon tire and must enter one of their many burrows. Eagles, coyotes, and wolves prey upon the swift and kit foxes. Four to seven young are born in the spring and live underground coming out only at night. Small rodents and insects are their main food, especially grasshoppers. Rabbits, birds' eggs, lizards, and some vegetable matter are also eaten. Swift and kit foxes are becoming scarce, for they are not clever enough to avoid traps and poison set out for coyotes.

Matching the desert sands in color, a buffy-yellow coat and fluffy tail adorn this beautiful mammal, the kit fox. Body length, 15 to 20 inches; height at shoulder, 12 inches; tail, 9 to 12 inches; weight, 4 to 6 pounds. The swift fox is slightly larger and darker with smaller ears.

Like the white-tailed deer and the bobcat, the red fox easily survives in areas close to man. It hunts by day as well as by night and gobbles mice, rabbits, shrews, birds, turtles, turtle eggs, muskrats, weasels, and even fruit.

The young are born four to nine in number and cared for by the parents. Mother fox gives milk to the young, and father fox brings back live juicy morsels that are released at the den to give the pups practice in catching food. The pups roll and play and frisk about, tossing up bones and seizing them again.

When the den becomes dirty or is flea infested the fox family moves to

Each of the variations of the red fox has black legs and feet and a white-tipped tail that floats gracefully out behind. The black phase of the red fox is called the silver fox. It is raised on farms for its beautiful fur. Some red foxes have black hairs over the shoulders and along the spine. These are called cross foxes because the dark markings form a cross. Body length, 22 to 25 inches; tail, 14 to 15 inches; weight, 10 to 15 pounds.

The red fox (shaded) ranges far throughout Alaska and Canada and in much of the United States. The gray fox (lines) is found in the United States, Mexico, and into Central America. Areas where both animals live appear dark.

another den dug by themselves or some other animal. By early fall the young are independent. In Israel the vineyard grapes were often spoiled by young foxes.

Foxes sometimes hide their food for a future use. Piles of dead mice or rabbits may occasionally be found.

The gray fox is slightly smaller than the red fox. Gray foxes form permanent pairs. They are also called tree foxes because they easily climb trees and often hide away among the branches. Like the red fox, the gray fox does not seek the most remote areas, but lives with man, skillfully avoiding traps and poison. Often it is never seen, for it hunts by night.

The coyote is a small wolf that is extending its range. As long as there are plenty of ground squirrels, woodchucks, jack rabbits, cottontails, mice, voles, moles, reptiles, acorns, prickly pears,

birds killed by traffic on the highway. Coyote parents teach and protect their pups until they are almost a year old. Coyotes are fast runners and travel at speeds up to 40 miles per hour.

Both coyotes and foxes are skillful at escaping from hunting dogs. One animal will lead the chase until it is tired. Then the other will show itself and take on the dogs, backtracking, cross tracking, and wading in water. In the end

The gray fox is mostly gray with a black stripe down the top of the tail. The feet and underparts are rusty, and the throat and sides of the nose are white. Like the kit fox it has a black tail tip. Body length, 21 to 29 inches; tail, 11 to 16 inches; weight, 7 to 13 pounds.

The smallest wolf in the United States looks like a small German shepherd dog with rusty legs, feet, and ears. The coyote may be reddish or plain gray with whitish underparts. Body length, 32 to 37 inches; tail, 11 to 16 inches; weight, 20 to 50 pounds. Unlike either foxes or other wolves, the coyote's tail is carried low.

kangaroo rats, gophers, and other small animals, the coyote will be able to find food. It rarely attacks domestic animals; but it does, like the fox, eat carrion of all kinds including dead stock discarded by farmers, and animals or

As in other members of the dog family this gray fox track shows the front foot slightly larger. Notice the hooklike projections on the rear heel mark. These footprints are only 1½ inches long.

the wild canines will escape while the dogs run in circles, trying to pick up the scent.

The red wolf has a body 42 to 49 inches long with a tail up to 17 inches. It weighs 30 to 80 pounds. It is larger than a coyote, but smaller than a gray wolf. One phase of the red wolf is sometimes blackish or all black. It lives in a few southern states directly west of the Mississippi and is nearly extinct.

The gray wolf, unlike the coyote, cannot endure living near man. Wolves, before the coming of the white man, lived throughout most of North America except in the very hot dry regions. In the east white-tailed deer were its main food. In the West it fed on bison, and in the North it followed caribou. After the coming of the white man most bison and white-tailed deer were destroyed. Wolves, deprived of their natural food,

The coyote (shaded) is widely distributed in Alaska, Canada, and most of the United States, and throughout Mexico and much of Central America. The gray wolf (lines) inhabits the far North, most of Canada, and is found in extreme northern United States near the Great Lakes. Areas where both canines live appear dark.

turned to domestic animals. Man poisoned, trapped, and shot wolves until in North America they are common only in Alaska and Canada.

During past centuries in Europe individual wolves sometimes attacked and killed people. Many stories are told of wolves killing people in this country, but evidence for such stories is lacking. Wolves avoid man as much as possible.

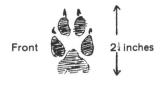

Front   2½ inches

Hind   2½ inches

This coyote track in mud shows larger toes on the outside of the paw and heel marks unlike foxes, dogs, or wolves. The larger print is of the front foot.

Wolves, as well as coyotes, send up mournful howls. Individual wolves that hear howling join in with their own cry until a chorus, reminding one of fire sirens, echoes through the empty wastes.

The gray wolf looks like a German shepherd dog with a broader head, and longer legs and ears. Body length, 43 to 48 inches; tail, 12 to 19 inches; weight, 70 to 170 pounds. Colors vary from all shades of gray and brown to reddish and yellowish specimens. When running, wolves carry their tails on a line with their backs.

113

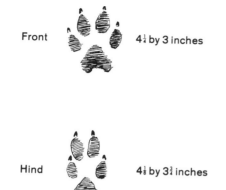

Front   4¼ by 3 inches

Hind   4¼ by 3¾ inches

This wolf track shows feet more than 4 inches long. Notice that the heel mark of the hind foot has three lobes on the rear margin. The front foot is larger and has no middle lobe on the heel. The middle toes are larger than the outside ones. Many dogs have this same characteristic difference between the front and hind feet. Some domestic dogs have five toes on the back feet as well as on the front feet.

In Israel the wolves hunted by night, and as darkness fell they crept out to satisfy their hunger. Jeremiah, Habakkuk, and Zephaniah speak of wolves in the evening.

Wolves hunt in packs. Together they bring down old and weakened moose, elk, deer, and caribou. Large numbers of rodents, ground squirrels, hares, and small mammals of all kinds are devoured.

Foxes and wolves have such a keen sense of smell that they hunt mostly by scenting the trail or burrow of their prey.

Two mammals that do not trail their prey but spend some of their lives in trees are the opossum and the porcupine. Neither of these is a canine. Each is the only mammal of its family in this country.

White hair covers the face of the opossum and is thickly mixed throughout with a rather long-haired, gray or black coat. A pink nose, round bright eyes, and ears of petal-thin, black skin adorn its head. Two special aids to climbing are the opossum's hind feet and its tail. The hind feet can grip a branch as human hands can. The extra-large toe that closes against the other four has no nail. The long wrap-around tail can bear the weight of the creature as well as a paw can.

Three million opossums a year are taken in the United States for their fur. Tens of thousands are eaten annually for their porklike flavor.

The baby opossums are born when they are scarcely any larger than flies. They crawl into a fur-lined pouch on the

This unusual mammal has a long, scaly tail that is pink and naked except for an inch or two of black at the base. No other mammal in North America can use its tail as the opossum does. Body length, 15 to 20 inches; tail, 9 to 20 inches; weight, 9 to 13 pounds.

The opossum inhabits the eastern United States, part of the Pacific coast, and most of Mexico.

mother's abdomen where they take hold of milk glands and remain for 9 weeks or more. The milk glands swell, filling their mouths and preventing them from being lost. Even at the age of 2 months eight of them can lie level with the rim of a measuring teaspoon.

After the young are safely inside the pouch, the mother contracts the muscles at the entrance. She pumps milk into their mouths when they are too weak to draw it out. At the age of 3 months the young are the size of mice and are climbing about over their mother's fur. At 4 months they are catching their own food, for the pouch is due to be refilled. Three litters a year are born in the South.

The opossum, although a tree dweller, does prowl on the ground, too. If overtaken by a hawk, owl, or bobcat that eats only food killed by itself, the opossum has one trick that is a sure escape. Either from shock or fright, it apparently loses consciousness. Heartbeats and breathing become too tri-

fling to be noticed. It seems to lose all feeling. Being swung by the tail or shaken by a dog produces no reaction. The limbs become helpless; the mouth falls wide open. Even wounds do not bleed. After the predator has discarded what appears to be a dead body and has departed, the opossum may recover and go on its way.

Opossums eat insects, snakes, carrion, and even rats and mice if they can catch them. Grain, wild berries, and especially persimmons are relished. Opossums during cold weather sleep whole days away.

The porcupine, America's second-largest rodent, is a tree dweller. It has thick black or brown underfur with

The porcupine, second to largest rodent in North America, is the only mammal in this country with long, sharp, easily detachable quills. Body length, 18 to 22 inches; tail, 7 to 9 inches; weight, 10 to 28 pounds.

The porcupine lives in the trees of Alaska, Canada, and northeastern and western United States.

yellowish or white, long guard hairs. It walks flat on the soles of its feet as bears and raccoons do.

In summer, fruits, buds, twigs, and other plant materials are eaten. In winter, the porcupine depends upon the inner bark of trees, especially poplar trees and aspen. It eats mostly at night and may stay in just a few trees if the food holds out.

The mother porcupine has a hollow log nest or goes into a crevice among rocks to bear her single young one. An hour after birth the quills of the newborn are hard and ready to prick. This infant is larger in relation to its mother than any other mammal. The mother may be 30 inches long, but the new arrival is often 11 inches long. This is larger than a day old black bear cub.

The porcupine is probably the best protected of all mammals. Among the heavy fur and the long, guard hairs are some thirty thousand quills from 1 to 4 or 5 inches long. The quills are very lightly fastened, and the tail is thickly set with them.

When a porcupine is attacked it finds a shelter for its nose under a log or a rock, sets all its spines on end, and begins to thrash its thorny tail.

Sometimes a quill flies loose to land where it will. Once fastened to the skin, the weapon swells. Barbs, all along the length, spread as moisture is absorbed from the flesh of the victim. Slowly it sinks deeper and deeper. If the mouth of the predator is struck, eating becomes too painful to be borne. If the quills are in the throat they prevent swallowing. Cougars and bears have sometimes died from them. If an animal lives through an encounter with a porcupine it usually avoids these creatures ever after.

Porcupines are protected by law in most areas. Porcupines in calm cir-

This porcupine track in dust shows the larger hind footprints ahead of the smaller ones of the front feet. The brush lines are left by the thick quills of the tail swinging from side to side as the plump mammal lumbers over the ground.

cumstances have a sad wail. They may wander through the woods, crying to themselves, or sit high in a tree, screeching away. Usually no more than one is found, for they do not stay together after the young one needs no further care.

Opossums are most active at night, but porcupines are abroad during the day, as well. Porcupines keep going all winter.

Unlike opossums, porcupines, and many other mammals, the wild dog group has a family unit that stays together for many months and mated pairs that run and den with each other year after year. They are among the most loyal of all the mammal families that the Lord has created.

Class Project

Find or mix some firm smooth mud in an out-of-the-way spot on the school playground. Have a pupil produce a clear hind foot print and front foot print by pressing the feet of his pet dog into the mud. Have another pupil do the same with the front and hind feet of his pet cat. This may be done after school hours if the prints are protected by an overturned shoe box, wooden box, large tin can, or the like. Compare the front and hind feet of each mammal until you can distinguish them from each other. Notice also the differences in the cat tracks and the dog tracks. How are they alike?

If a large muddy or snowy spot is available the animals may be induced to walk or run across it so that the patterns of movement may be observed also. Dust or sand will record footprints, too.

Questions

1. (Like, Unlike) the cat family, the dog family has been created with (four, five, six) toes on the forefeet and (four, five, six) toes on the hind feet.

2. Dog tracks in mud are different from cat tracks in mud because (dogs do not have the same number of toes showing, dogs' short toenails do not leave an impression and cats' long claws do, the heel mark is shaped differently).

3. Wild mammals of the dog family eat (carrion only; fresh meat killed by themselves only; fish, frogs, clams, and other water animals only; vegetable food only; some of all of these).

4. The skeletons, feathers, and other animal remains at a wolf, coyote, or

fox den (show, do not show) what the mammals living there have killed.

5. Name five sources of animal food other than what the fox or wolf has killed.

6. In what two ways do foxes and wolves benefit man?

7. Menno and Jacob live in northern Arkansas. they are visiting their uncle Elam in eastern Texas. One morning at daybreak as they are checking their uncle's beef cattle, they see a good-sized doglike mammal crossing an open space in the field below. Its legs and nose are reddish, and its coat is gray and black. A black-tipped, bushy tail is held out in a straight line with the back. Menno and Jacob are looking at a ———. Three other wild canines sometimes crossing their uncle's farm are the ———, the ———, and the ———.

8. Sam and Rebecca live in western Kansas. One evening they climb the hill to watch the sunset. A quite-small, buffy-yellow creature with big ears and a black-tipped tail is being chased by a dog. Zigzagging, the nimble mammal dodges the hungry jaws and then sails safely away to its burrow, leaving the dog behind. Sam and Rebecca have seen a ——— or ———. Another wild canine living in their area is the ———.

9. Anna and Paul live in Ontario, Canada. One evening as they are driving along a country road north of Lake Huron they see, running through the twilight, a large dark-gray doglike mammal with a darker tail. The tail is black tipped and held straight on a line with the back. "There's a ———," calls the children's father. Two other canines living in this area are the ——— and the ———.

10. James and Mary live in western Florida. One spring evening they are passing through the woods on their way home. Suddenly a gray-backed, white-throated mammal about 2 feet long bounds into a low-branched tree. The creature has rusty legs and feet. Its long, bushy tail is black on top and red underneath, with a long, gray side stripe running down toward a black tip. As they watch, the mammal climbs rapidly to the top of the tree. James and Mary have seen a ———.

11. Sarah and Joseph live in Indiana. One rainy, dark autumn day as they are riding home from school they see a gray doglike mammal about 3 feet long with whitish underparts. It is climbing the nearby hill. Its tail is held down close to its rusty feet and legs. Sarah and Joseph are looking at their first ———. Other wild canines in their area are the ——— and the ———.

12. Simon and Rachel live with their parents in south-central Ohio. Their cousins have come to spend

the afternoon. Simon, Abner, Mark, Rachel, and Elizabeth are perched on the old rail fence. Bounding lightly over the grass at the far side of the pasture is a reddish-yellow mammal with black legs and feet. It has a white throat and belly and a white tip on the tail. It is a ———. Another wild canine living in their area is the ———.

13. The opossum is a (good, poor) climber because it has (long sharp claws, extra-long legs, a wrap-around tail, a thick neck, hind feet each with one toe that opposes the others [choose two]).

14. When the opossum is caught by an enemy it (tries to run, fights, apparently faints, climbs a tree, swims to safety).

15. Opossum babies are (large, small, undeveloped, mature, active) at birth (choose two).

16. Opossums provide man with two things. What are they?

17. A porcupine is (very well protected, rather helpless to defend itself).

18. The porcupine avoids enemies by its (speed in running, swimming ability, coat of quills, quick climbing, strength in fighting).

19. Porcupines eat (almost entirely vegetable food, many insects and fruits, almost entirely animal food).

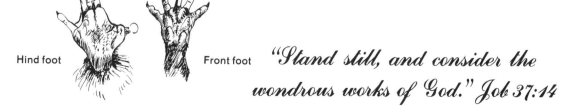

Hind foot   Front foot   *"Stand still, and consider the wondrous works of God." Job 37:14*

15. Soft Rich Fur and Bags of Musk

Many people refuse to accept God as the Creator. Some even are ignorant of His divine wisdom in putting the plants trees, reptiles, fishes, insects, birds, and mammals together into various habitats where each depends on the other for food and shelter.

Somehow such people imagine that they themselves could arrange animal and plant groups in a more rewarding way than God has. Often people feel that only man, who can produce crops to feed himself, has any right to kill an animal for food. They speak of predatory animals as greedy and bloodthirsty. They wish that predators were absent and that only human hunters were present to kill wild game. What would happen if this wish could come true?

In 1906 the Grand Canyon National Game Preserve in Arizona sheltered four thousand deer. State game officials estimated that many more deer could live in this area if predators were removed. Future deer hunters would be very happy.

So they forbade the taking of deer for a time. Then money was paid for each large predator killed. Records show that up until 1924, 4,889 coyotes, 781 cougars, 30 wolves, and 554 bobcats were destroyed.

By 1916, 30,000 deer were living in the forest. The plan to increase deer by removing predators had worked so far. Two years later, 40,000 deer were roaming the game preserve and in 1924 there were 100,000.

Young saplings and new shoots were devoured and larger trees died as the hungry deer chewed bark from the trunks and dug up the roots in a frantic effort to stay alive. Erosion of the bare slopes began. The whole country looked as though a swarm of locusts had passed through it. Forty thousand deer died of starvation and disease during the next two winters. More tens of thousands perished until the herd numbered a mere ten thousand deer, many of them quite weak.

Even with only ten thousand deer the food remained scarce for years. Other animal populations suffered, too. The cougars, wolves, coyotes, and bobcats had not only prospered the deer; but they had also protected the vegetation and trees, the animals dependent upon them, and even the land itself.

Let us accept God's wisdom in creating predators and not doubt their usefulness and beneficial influence on all other forms of life. Predators are meat eaters, also called carnivores ('kär-nə-ˌvōrz).

The smallest carnivore that we have

This longtail weasel has a velvety, brown coat with pale-cream underparts and a black tail tip. Body length of male, 9 to 10½ inches; tail, 4 to 6 inches; weight, 6 to 9 ounces.

studied so far is the kit fox that weighs only 4 to 6 pounds. Weasels are much lighter. The least weasel, the tiniest of all, weighs less than an ounce. A long slender body, little round ears, and short legs characterize this restless creature.

Weasels are known for the beauty and softness of their brown fur and for the little bags of musk carried in glands under the tail. Weasels living in the North turn white almost overnight when the first snow falls. Brown hair is shed and white grows in. This snowy plush is known as ermine. In Europe weasels are called stoats. Their pelts trim very showy clothing.

Weasels move quickly and continually. Heartbeat, breathing, and digestion are fast and much food is needed. Dogs and cats may maul or play with their prey, but weasels are hungry all the time. They kill their food at once. Weasels may store piles of dead mice in a burrow or under leaf litter. Shrews, insects, small snakes, earthworms, moles, and nestling birds are also taken. White-footed mice and

meadow voles are 50 to 90 percent of the weasel's diet.

In March or April seven or eight blind young ones are born in an underground den that may be the former burrow of a mole or pocket gopher. In 3 weeks the eyes open. At the age of 5 weeks they are weaned. Both parents take the young on hunting trips and teach them to catch live food. Normally a weasel family will hunt over 200 to 300 acres.

Weasels have many natural enemies. Dogs, cats, foxes, birds of prey, and larger relatives in the weasel family, such as badgers, like to eat them.

A number of other meat-eating, musk-bearing mammals belong to the weasel family even though many of them are very unlike the tiny creatures that bear the weasel name.

Probably the most common and

The longtail weasel ranges throughout the United States, along the Canadian border, all over Mexico, and south to Central America. The least weasel and the shorttail weasel are found in Alaska and the far-northern reaches of Canada where they are ermines a great part of the year.

This handsome furbearer, the striped skunk, has been trapped for its silky black and white coat which is sold under such names as Alaska sable, black marten, or tipped skunk. Body length of male, 13 to 18 inches; tail, 7 to 10 inches; height at shoulder, 7 to 8 inches; weight, 4 to 10 pounds.

well-known predator in this country is the skunk, six species of which live in the United States, Mexico, and Canada. The six species are the eastern and western spotted skunks, the hognosed and the eastern hognosed skunks, the hooded skunk, and the striped skunk. The furs of these creatures, both natural and dyed, are a significant item on the market.

Skunks eat hordes of crickets, grasshoppers, and beetles. These slow animals den under sheds and barns, finishing off their mouse populations. In New York state the skunk is protected for the sake of the hop crop that is eaten by a grub that the skunk likes to feed on. Skunks are said to destroy more insects than all other kinds of mammals combined. The young of ground squirrels and rabbits, frogs, shallow water fishes, and even carrion are welcome to this important little predator.

One farmer could not understand why ducks and fish were becoming so scarce in his pond. He had provided cover and food for them and they had been abundant. A wildlife expert solved the problem when he discovered that the farmer had killed the skunks that were formerly active around his farm. Skunks relish turtle eggs and dig them out of the banks of the waterways. Without skunks to check the snapping turtle population, young ducks and fishes were eaten in increasing numbers by the multiplying turtles.

All skunks carry the bags of musk common to weasels. However, they have spraying muscles that other weasels do not have. Skunks are quite peaceful and use their weapon only when alarmed by an enemy. As a warning the skunk raises its black plume of a tail. Then it paws the ground. If the enemy is still advancing, the skunk spreads a fine mist of its

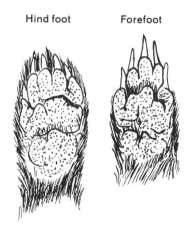

Hind foot   Forefoot

Second to the badger, the master digger of the weasel family is the skunk. See the long claws on the forefoot used for uncovering insects, earthworms, cutworms, grubs of all kinds, eggs of snapping turtles, and burrows of mice and voles.

The striped skunk is found from the Northwest Territories, throughout much of the rest of Canada and most of the United States, south into Mexico. The spotted skunk roams this country except for the Northeast, along the Canadian border, and most of the Atlantic states. With the hooded and hognosed skunks, the spotted skunk lives in Mexico and Central America.

powerful musk through the air. It can throw this yellowish liquid 8 to 10 feet. If it strikes the eyes they will burn and water. The nose and mouth are painfully affected by the attack.

Young skunks are usually born, six to eight in the litter, in an underground burrow sometimes dug by the mother or left vacant by a woodchuck. After a month the young have their eyes open and are able to follow their mother as she teaches them to hunt.

Birds of prey that do not have a sense of smell are the main predators of the skunk. The great horned owl captures more skunks for its food than other meat eaters dare risk taking although cougars and wolves may eat a few.

Another, much larger carnivore of the weasel family is the badger. This low, wide, powerful, clawed creature is the best digger among the United States mammals. It is simple for the badger to capture any creature that it smells in the earth. It merely burrows faster than the other animal can. Rabbits, ground squirrels, gophers, lizards, snakes, even rattlesnakes, insects, grubs, voles, and mice are its food. Like skunks, badgers also eat carrion.

Badgers dig complicated burrows, with sleeping and eating rooms where carrion is often stored. Several generations may live in the same maze of tunnels as long as food is plentiful. The badger mother, like the skunk and wolverine mothers, has all the care and training of the young. The males of these species do not stay with their families.

Both skunks and badgers become

This young badger, already equipped as a champion digger, looks out from his burrow. Body length of male, 18 to 22 inches; tail, 4 to 6 inches; weight, 13 to 25 pounds.

very fat by autumn. They do not hibernate, but will sleep for long periods of time during the winter.

Badger fur is still coarser than skunk fur, which is coarser than weasel fur. Shaving brush bristles have been made of badger hair in the past. The long, shaggy fur does have some value now for collars and coats.

Badgers are more scarce than they once were, probably because their main food, the prairie dog, has decreased. Badgers, like other members of the weasel group, have five toes on all four feet.

Badgers are fierce and aggressive and seldom meet any animal that they need to fear. Eagles or coyotes may manage to take off a few young badgers. Large predators, such as cougars or wolves, may sometimes succeed in killing full-grown badgers.

The wolverine is the largest of the weasel family living in this country. In

The badger lives mainly in treeless country from Alberta and Saskatchewan, through the western United States to Baja California, and into Mexico. It is found as far east as Ohio.

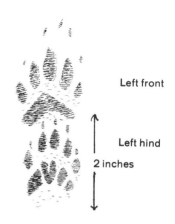

Left front

Left hind

2 inches

Notice the long claw marks in this badger track. One badger digging after a gopher was timed. It followed the gopher about 3 feet per minute.

disposition it is more like the small weasels than the skunks or the badger. Wolverines live in the far North and they may roam over 100 miles searching for prey. They look like a small chunky bear, and their musk bags carry scent as powerful as that of the skunk. Sometimes they are called by the nickname of skunk bear.

Some men on Mount McKinley in Alaska found where a wolverine had killed a Dall's sheep weighing about 150 pounds. The much-smaller animal had carried the sheep a mile and a half—down the mountain, across the river, and up a steep bank—before beginning to eat it.

Not only is the wolverine unusually strong; it is also very fast and can run down moose, deer, or hares. When chased by wolves it can leave them behind. The skunk bear is a strong swimmer and crosses lakes and rivers, searching for food. It can climb to the tops of trees.

Pound for pound, the wolverine is one of the strongest animals in the world. Body length, 29 to 32 inches; tail, 7 to 9 inches; height at shoulder, 12 to 14 inches; weight, 25 to 40 or more pounds.

Through the snowy frigid North, the wolverine travels in the worst blizzards, strong and dauntless. It does not hibernate, retreat to a sheltered den, or store food. Mice, lemmings, grouse, and hares are its most common food.

Trappers sometimes abandon a trapline because the hungry wolverine follows, emptying each set of bait or catch. Sometimes wolverines retreat before bears or packs of wolves. At other times they fight fearlessly and have been known to chase off cougars, bears, wolves, or coyotes from food that they both wanted to eat.

These hardy, tireless creatures live in places hard to find, and few have been studied very much. This giant weasel lacks keen eyesight and when trying to see ahead it will often shade its eyes with a forepaw.

The two to four young drink milk for about 2 months and then begin a diet of fresh meat. They hunt with their mother several months before going their own way.

Wolverines, like others in the weasel family, have valuable fur. Moisture will not freeze on wolverine fur, and it is usually cut into large strips and used to line the opening of parka hoods. Arctic travelers and dwellers have always preferred wolverine fur for this reason. Skiing and winter sports create a larger demand for wolverine-trimmed hoods.

Important predators and valuable furbearers are found in this strong, beautiful mammal family.

Class Project

Try to observe skunks or badgers if any are living in your community. What kind of den are they using? What food do they eat? Measure tracks if you can find any. Sketch tracks and bring the sketch to class.

Questions

Write the name of each mammal with the letters of the characteristics that describe it.

1. Weasel—

2. Skunk—

3. Badger—

4. Wolverine—
   (a) large, active, powerful
   (b) peaceful, slow, house-cat size
   (c) active, small, weighs from less than 1 ounce to $\frac{1}{2}$ pound
   (d) carries bags of musk
   (e) can spray and throw musk
   (f) is always active; dashes around hunting all winter
   (g) gets fat at the end of the summer
   (h) shades eyes with a forepaw when peering ahead
   (i) sleeps during cold severe weather
   (j) fur becomes white in winter except for the tail tip or a few hairs on the end of the tail
   (k) fur is used for collars and coats
   (l) hair has been used for shaving brushes
   (m) the fur of this species is used to trim showy clothing
   (n) fur is used next to the opening in a parka hood
   (o) eats mostly mice and voles
   (p) is an important predator of insects, grubs, and turtle eggs
   (q) is a strong fighter; protects itself and its young from attack
   (r) fearlessly drives away animals much stronger and larger than itself
   (s) is often eaten by other predators
   (t) is rarely eaten by other predators
   (u) lives in the far North and is seldom seen by man
   (v) is the most common predator
   (w) both parents teach the young to hunt
   (x) the male does not care for the young
   (y) is a champion digger; can dig faster than most other mammals
   (z) is nicknamed skunk bear

5. Predators directly or indirectly protect (game animals, trees, shrubs, grass, rodents, soil, birds, rabbits, wildflowers [choose more than one]).

"O Lord, . . . I will shew forth all thy marvellous works." Psalm 9:1

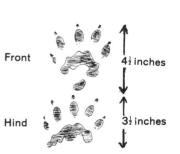

Front $4\frac{1}{2}$ inches

Hind $3\frac{1}{2}$ inches

16. Monarchs of the Forests
and the Ice Floes

Except for opossum babies, which are pocket carried and pocket fed, no mammal infants are so tiny in comparison to their mother as the bear young ones. Born during the mother's winter sleep, they may weigh $\frac{1}{200}$ to $\frac{1}{350}$ as much as she does. In the dark, cold den the rat-sized cubs are nearly lost in the long fur of their slumbering parent. Hairless and blind they snuggle contentedly into the warmly heated shaggy folds of their mother's thighs and abdomen. Milk glands hidden here and there yield sweet, rich liquid to comfort the restless stomachs. Drinking and dozing and wriggling through the long days and nights, the cubs grow strong until they are able to romp about the den and follow their mother out into the sunshine when warm days come.

God has created bears to be forest or mountain dwellers, except those in the Polar Regions. Large quantities of berries, twigs, roots, shoots, and new leaves are eaten. In the spring bears graze like cattle on the new tender grass. Later in the season they use their strong shoulders and long claws, ripping open the rotten wood of fallen logs to lick up ants, beetle grubs, termites, and many other insects. Tearing into ground

The black bear. This smallest and shortest clawed of American bears has two identifying marks. The face is brown and there is usually a small white patch on the chest. In the West the coat is often cinnamon colored. In British Columbia it is nearly white. The black bear in Alaska wears grayish-blue fur and is called the glacier bear. Length of body, 5 to 6 feet; height at shoulder, 2 to 3 feet; weight 200 to 400 pounds.

127

The grizzly bear has a silver-tipped coat and the longest claws (4 inches) among the American bears. Like the black bear its coat varies from nearly black to light brown and almost white in the Yukon. Length of body, 6 to 7 feet; height at shoulder, 3 to 3½ feet; weight 325 to 850 pounds.

burrows they find chipmunks, marmots, moles, voles, mice, ground squirrels, and lemmings. Crickets, grasshoppers, birds and their eggs, snakes, frogs, toads, nuts, acorns, fruits, and wild honey keep these big mammals well nourished.

The black bear is the smallest and most common of American bears, and like other bears it usually travels alone except when the mother is caring for young cubs. The same trails through forests and thickets and on riverbanks may be used as long as 50 years. Along these paths the bears stand on their hind legs and rub their backs against the bark of trees. They bite it until shreds come loose in places. Pitch oozes out and bear hair sticks to it. Sometimes bears rub out old itchy hair in this way. The next bear on the trail also scratches, rubs, and bites, leaving its scent behind for the next passer-by to read.

Next in size to the widespread black

bear is the grizzly bear. Originally this species lived in the western part of the continent from Alaska south to central Mexico and east to Minnesota. Now there are very few south of the Canadian border except in parks.

From 80 to 90 percent of the food eaten by a grizzly bear on the Barren Ground is vegetable. In Idaho the grizzlies come down to meet salmon as they run up the river from the sea. They watch the riffles and as a salmon is struggling up the waterfalls they dash in and with a blow of the paw knock it out onto the bank.

When injured or molested the grizzly will fearlessly attack. It can run as

The big brown bear, also known as the Alaskan brown bear or the Kodiak bear, is the largest carnivore in the world. Its color may be dark brown or yellow and the shades between. Like the grizzly, it may have white-tipped hairs in its coat. Both bears have a hump on the shoulders. Length of body, 8 feet; height at shoulder, 4 to 4½ feet; weight, 1,500 pounds or more.

fast as a horse, and a blow of its mighty paw will crush and break the bones of even the huge bison.

The big brown bear is the largest of all. Like the black bear it has its own trails along the rivers of British Columbia and southern Alaska.

When salmon come up the river by the thousands, the big brown bears have a feast. After spawning, the fishes die and float downstream, sooner or later coming to rest against a bank or a sandbar. Providentially, the great bears enjoy eating carrion; so the smelly heaps are removed and the riversides become clean and pleasant again.

The polar bear is the monarch of the arctic ice pack. On its snow-covered floes the great bears drift for hundreds of miles in the Arctic Ocean, the North Atlantic, or through the Bering Strait into the Bering Sea. They may swim 15 to 20 miles out to an iceberg in search of their most important food, seals. When seals become scarce the bears live on carrion. A sudden freeze may strand a white whale or a narwhal inside a little bay that later becomes so small that the creature finds it hard to breathe. A polar bear may kill even a whale that is 15 feet long. The powerful carnivore is able to drag an 800-pound animal out upon the ice. A large dead whale will provide food for bears, arctic foxes, gulls, and ravens all winter.

The bear's shaggy white coat, many inches thick, shuts out the frigid blasts, the freezing water that encloses the animal when it swims, and the low temperatures of the ice slabs where it sleeps. It also conceals the meat eater from other animals in the snowy white world.

A polar bear sees a seal sun-bathing or sleeping. While hundreds of yards separate the two the bear lies down on the ice, pushing with its hind legs while its front legs are folded against its chest. Sometimes the great creature pulls itself along with all four feet. As the seal raises its head and looks around occasionally, the bear will become still. When the seal lays its head down again the hunter creeps forward among the rough chunks of ice.

Observers have noticed that a polar bear will cover its black nose with a paw or else keep a piece of ice pushed along between itself and the seal. The bear creeps unseen to within 15 feet of the seal before showing itself and leaping upon the smaller mammal. One blow kills the seal, and the bear settles down to a warm dinner. Perhaps 10 to 40 pounds are eaten at one sitting.

Bears also capture their food at breathing holes in the ice. Seals breathe

With her back to the arctic wind a polar bear mother protects her cub from the icy blasts. Length of body, 6½ to 7½ feet; height at shoulder, 3 to 4 feet; weight, 600 to 1,100 pounds or more.

The big brown bear (horizontal lines) lives in the salty air of the northern coast of British Columbia, the southern coast of Alaska, and half a dozen of the Aleutian Islands. The grizzly bear (shaded) lives inland on high western mountains and halfway across northwest Canada. The polar bear (vertical lines) prowls the coasts of the Arctic Ocean for seals and fish. The black bear lives all over North America in many wooded areas, including the Mexican Plateau.

through these holes when the ice becomes too thick to break easily. If the ice is 4 or more inches thick the seal will keep a certain spot broken open. The bear enlarges this hole until it can put its paw down into the water. It waits there until the seal pops up to breathe. Then the bear pounces and drags it out on the ice.

In July the bears leave the ice pack and land on islands. Now they eat sedges, mosses, mushrooms, crowberries, cranberries, and blueberries. Lemmings, voles, ground squirrels, shrews, and puffins are dug out. Nestlings and eggs are gathered at the bases of the bird cliffs. Shellfishes are broken into and gobbled. The abundant food of the arctic summer nourishes and strengthens small cub and great shaggy oldster alike.

All pregnant bears in temperate or arctic regions retire into winter dens for weeks or months to give birth to their tiny cubs. Big brown bears, grizzly, and black bears also seek dens. Even where the weather is mild and the food plentiful they begin to sleep in early January and stay there for 8 to 9 weeks. While the bear sleeps, its temperature drops a degree or so and the heartbeat slows somewhat, but the change is not as great as in smaller animals that hibernate.

In smaller animals, like ground squirrels, hibernation is a deathlike sleep in which their temperature sinks to a few degrees above freezing. From 1 to 10 or more minutes may pass between breaths. Circulation is so slow that a cut-off toe bleeds very little. At the close of this dormant state the temperature of the animal may rise 60 degrees.

Bears, raccoons, and skunks are less perfect hibernators. They are much more easily aroused than are some other animals. When bears first emerge from their winter dens, they often eat a little tender grass or a few green twigs. It may be a week until they are eating their usual food.

The polar bear is the only bear that does not go in for the winter. Males, barren females without young cubs, and half-grown young bears continue to hunt through the long arctic night under the glittering stars, the many-colored northern lights, and the bright moonbeams.

Bears like to clown and play. Polar bears rock themselves on drifting ice floes or slide down slanting slippery glaciers. A bear student saw a young grizzly walking along a narrow wall of ice with an almost vertical glacier below. To his surprise the bear jumped onto the slick surface and without trying to slow itself whizzed along until it reached the very edge of the glacier. There was a sheer drop of 50 feet to the lake. The bear sailed through the air to plunge into the water. Soon it came to the surface, swam toward the shore, and climbed up to repeat its exciting ride. Sometimes a bear will start itself sliding by sitting down and jiggling back and forth just as a human being does.

traveled with four or five tame grizzlies that he had raised from cubs. They hunted game for him. One named Ben Franklin fought with a much-larger wild grizzly when it attacked his master.

In national parks today people approach bears closely to photograph or illegally feed them. Many times bears maul or even kill those intruding on them. Bears with cubs are especially touchy. The fierceness of a bear whose cubs have been taken away is mentioned by three Bible writers.

Two she bears once mauled forty-two children who were ridiculing Elisha, God's prophet. As Elisha climbed up the hill to Bethel he met a large group of young people who spoke

Class Project

Reproduce a big brown bear trail. Smooth some open soil with a rake or a broom. Draw the outlines of the feet life-size, placing the hind foot ahead of the front foot in each pair. The space between the pairs should be three-fourths as long as the hind foot print. The big toe on a bear's foot is the outside one. Tamp down the soil inside the outlines and for each of the toes. Claw marks may be made by a pencil point dug in well ahead of the toe marks. Tracks may also be laid out in chalk on a concrete walk or drawn on the blackboard.

Old-time hunters of the early 1800s agreed that grizzly bears did not attack people unless they were provoked, suffering from an old wound, or otherwise annoyed.

In the 1850s John Capen Adams

disrespectfully to him. When he called on the Lord to punish them, two she bears came out of the woods and tore them.

David, while still a lad, killed a bear that had taken a lamb from his flock.

The Bible writers Isaiah and Solomon speak of the bear's roaring. The yellowish-brown Syrian bear still lives in limited numbers in the highlands of Lebanon and northward.

For centuries Eskimos have depended upon polar bears for meat and clothing without causing the population to decline. But since the 1920s the great white giants are becoming few. Rich men hire airplanes to fly far over the ice fields until the bears are found. Then the plane lands nearby. The bear is killed with a high-powered rifle, skinned, and left behind. The head and hide are taken into the plane for a hunting trophy. In summer when the water is open, motorboats cruise around for days while men with telescopes and long-range guns wait to spot grizzly, polar, and great brown bears on their summer feeding grounds. Often only the head is taken. So many bears have been killed in this way that they may become extinct.

Since polar bears roam for hundreds of miles over the northern parts of various continents, several territories will need to cooperate if they are to be saved.

Watching wild bears is a rare privilege to be enjoyed with caution.

Questions

1. John's father is logging in western British Columbia. He sees a large light-brown bear. What species is it?
   (a) If it has a hump on the shoulders it may be a ——— or a ———.
   (b) If it has white-tipped hairs it may be a ——— or a ———.
   (c) If it stands 3 feet high at the shoulder it may be a ——— or a ———.
   (d) If it stands $4\frac{1}{2}$ feet high at the shoulder it may be a ———.

2. A nearly white bear with a brown face is a ———.

3. A pure-white bear 7 feet long is a ———.

4. A nearly black bear with white-tipped hairs and 4-inch claws is a ———.

5. Bears eat (grass, leaves, sprouts, roots; rodents of all kinds; carrion; fishes; all of these).

6. Bear cubs are born (at the beginning of warm weather, in the middle of the summer, in the middle of the winter, at the end of summer).

7. Bears in winter dens (have a very slow heartbeat and breathing rate, sleep lightly and can be awakened even in the cold).

8. Bears hunt food (in packs, in mother and cubs groups, in adult pairs, alone [choose two]).

9. At some time during the winter,

most (polar bears, grizzly bears, big brown bears, black bears) go in for a sleep (choose three).

10. The largest meat-eating mammal in the world is the ———.

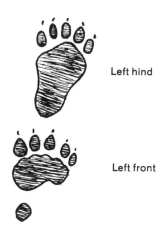

Left hind

Left front

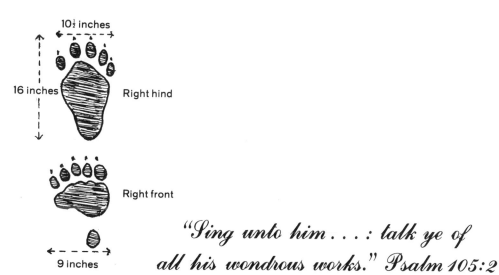

10½ inches

16 inches

Right hind

Right front

9 inches

"Sing unto him . . . : talk ye of all his wondrous works." Psalm 105:2

17.   Champion Divers, Pleated Throats,  and Mouths Full of Strainers

"Even the sea monsters draw out the breast, they give suck to their young ones" (Lamentations 4:3).

Jeremiah, a prophet of old Israel, knew about the order of mammals that spends its whole life in water. He called it the sea monsters and noticed the tender feeding of the young on milk.

The order Cetacea (sē-'tā-shē-ə) contains ninety species of whales, dolphins, and porpoises. Since cetaceans (sē-'tā-shənz) live only in water and have long streamlined bodies some people mistake them for fish. How do we know that they are mammals?

Mammals are warm-blooded vertebrates that have hair, usually bring forth their young alive, and nourish them with milk.

Cetaceans are warm-blooded vertebrate animals. Many adults have whiskers and some young have soft hairs early in life or before birth. All cetaceans bear their single young alive and nourish it with milk. Whales, porpoises, and dolphins have powerful flukes that spread horizontally, unlike the vertical tails of fishes. As other mammals do, they breathe with lungs. Most mammals have two pairs of limbs, but cetaceans have only one pair. The manatee is another mammal without a rear pair of limbs.

The cetaceans' most important sense is hearing, with sight coming second. Just as bats in complete darkness find their way by echolocation, so do cetaceans. God has so delicately constructed these almost-unbelievable hearing organs that the dolphin can sort out all the echoes of his own cries from dozens of signals raised by other citizens of the sea. By these sounds the size, shape, speed, distance away, and the direction of the movements of other creatures are understood as well as the outlines of sea bottoms, and other physical features.

During World War II listening devices in the ocean picked up the voices of cetaceans, fishes, shrimps, and other water creatures. The cry of the fin whale is a deep vibrant sound. The underwater call of a blue whale was measured off the coast of South America by scientists who were astonished at its length and power. They believe that it must certainly be heard for hundreds of miles. Sound travels about four times as fast in water as it does in air. By continually calling to each other, these far-ranging mammals

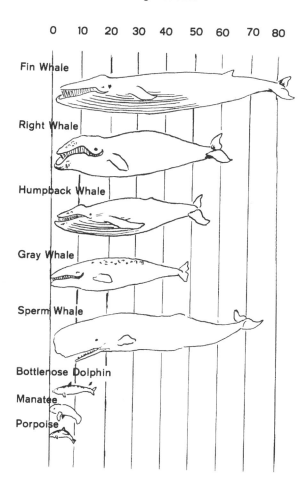

Length in Feet

God created water mammals in a wide range of sizes. The first four species are whalebone whales. The sperm whale, bottlenose dolphin, and porpoise are toothed cetaceans.

are able to feed and travel in family herds called pods.

Cetaceans are divided into two main groups. The toothed whales have a single blowhole and have flippers with four rows of bones. The toothless whales breathe through a double blowhole and have flippers with five rows of bones.

Toothless whales have hundreds of thin flexible bones called baleen (bə-'lēn) in their mouths. Fine mesh hangs from the inner surfaces of each one. The baleen whales do not swim below 325 feet. Their food is young shrimps, snails, sea jellies, lobsters, sponges, crabs, fishes, sea stars, and various one-celled creatures. These are called plankton or krill. The cold waters at the North and South poles hold more oxygen than warm tropical waters. During the polar summers when the sun shines for several months without setting, the waters are laden with food. Most of the whales migrate north or south in summer and stay for months, laying on blubber that may measure as much as 20 to 25 inches thick. Blubber is a layer of fat just under the skin. It protects the whale's body from the cold of Arctic and Antarctic seas.

The fin whale is the second largest of the baleen whales and grows up to 60 to 75 feet long. Three-fourths as large as the blue whale, this huge cetacean's throat and chest are creased by one hundred pleats that can expand to enclose large amounts of water and food. It finds its prey by echolocation. Circling clockwise around a school of herring, the fin whale turns on its side, flashing its white belly to drive the fish closer together. Then with wide-open mouth and a speed that fills the pleats with water, the whale rushes straight into the school. Closing its mouth and folding its pleats, it squirts tons of water out between the baleen strainers. When only herring remain they are gulped into the stomach. The fin whale has baleen as fine as wool so that very tiny

The fin or finback whale, 60 to 70 feet long and weighing 50 tons, resembles the larger blue whale and the smaller sei whale. This smooth silky gray and white mammal has a flat head, one hundred throat and chest pleats, and a fin on its back not far from the tail. The strainers in the mouth are purple and white. The fin whale's spout rises 20 feet with a loud whistling noise. This huge cetacean is a fast swimmer roaming most of the oceans of the world.

creatures can be strained out of the water. One fin whale was found carrying in its stomach 5 million shrimp weighing 2 tons. A large whale's intestine may reach the amazing length of 1,200 feet.

In former times baleen was used in making umbrella ribs, fishing rods, and buggy whips. In 1897 this whalebone sold for $5,000 a ton. Metal and plastics serve these purposes now.

Before the discovery of petroleum in 1859 whale oil was an important source of heat and light. Kerosene made from petroleum came next. In time, electricity replaced kerosene for light.

Before steam-powered ships were

The right whale grows to a length of 55 feet and to a weight of 40 tons in the Atlantic and up to 70 feet long in the Pacific. The spouts from its blowholes separate to form a V about 15 feet high. This black whale carries matching black baleen in its mouth. It has no throat and chest pleats or back fin. Light patches on the head show where parasites are growing.

The humpback whale is black with a white throat and chest creased with 10 to 25 furrows. From 40 to 50 feet long and weighing about 29 tons, this unusual-looking cetacean has rows of knobs on its huge head in addition to lumpy growths on its flippers and flukes. Extra-long white flippers, a large back fin, and a 20-foot spout identify this huge Pacific and Atlantic mammal.

The gray whale travels the 4,000 miles between Siberia and Mexico twice a year along the eastern shore of the Pacific Ocean. The grayish-black skin of this 35-to 45-foot cetacean is crusted with various parasites that give its 25- to 40-ton body a patched, gray look. Its yellowish-white baleen is a little longer than 14 inches. Its spout rises in brief spurts about 10 feet high. There are only 2 to 4 folds on the throat, but there is a fin-shaped hump on the back.

invented, the right whale was killed in the greatest numbers. It is slow, likes to travel near the coast, yields a rich supply of whalebone and whale oil, and floats when dead.

Another baleen whale easily killed was the humpback. It, too, is not a fast swimmer and keeps close to the coast. The humpback sings loud beautiful songs as it bounds along in the pod.

If one species became too scarce to be profitably chased, the whalers turned to another species. When the Atlantic gray whales were all dead the Pacific gray whales were pursued. One whaler discovered the breeding grounds of the Pacific gray whales and secretly visited it for years. In 1937 this species was found to be nearly extinct; so it was protected from all hunters. Now over 40 years later, it has slowly increased to good-sized herds that travel along the western coast of North America.

The sperm whale is by far the largest of the toothed whales. It lives in most of the ice-free waters of the world. It is named for the very fine oil, spermaceti (ˌspər-mə-ˈsēt-ē, ˌspər-mə-ˈset-ē), carried in a large well in its enormous head. This clear water-white oil is used to lubricate watches and other of the finest instruments. Another valuable product of the sperm whale, selling for $20 an ounce, is ambergris

The sperm whale is bluish gray above, and paler below. It grows to a length of 60 feet and to a weight of 50 tons. About one-third of this weight is in the huge square head. There are no furrows in the throat. A fin-shaped hump and a series of small bumps stand along the spine. The squids of ice-free oceans are its main food. The spout slants forward.

('am-bər-ˌgris, 'am-bər-ˌgrēs). Chunks of this odd material are often in the sperm whale's intestine. One extra-large block weighed nearly 1,000 pounds and was worth a fortune. Ambergris is used in expensive perfumes to prolong their scent.

A sperm whale was once found tangled in an ocean cable at a depth of 3,240 feet. Each square inch of its body was resisting 1,400 pounds of pressure. Yet the same cetacean breathes regularly at the surface where there is no pressure. God has given it an amazing body that operates perfectly, as His works do. This champion diver may hold its breath for as long as 1½ hours.

The whale's blowholes have powerful valves. As it comes to the surface the holes pop open. A volume of compressed air rises perhaps 20 feet, taking along any water that happens to be over the blowhole. A deep breath

rushes down into the lungs and in 2 to 3 minutes is absorbed by the blood. The whale blows again and refills its lungs. Finally after a number of blows, the whale is fully recovered and ready for another long breath-holding dive. Oxygen enters even the muscles. The lungs are folded flat. The whale jackknifes. Then as it goes down it raises its flukes from the water in a backward kick that sends it to the bottom. The heartbeat slows to about one-third its usual rate. In the cold, blood leaves the skin, flippers, and flukes to enter the heart and brain. The body temperature drops. The squid hunter prowls the dark ocean floor, sounding its search signal.

Many whales have heating systems that keep them warm in icy seas. This system overheats when the mammal is stranded on the beach. Without the support of ocean currents, the heavy blubber on a whale's body will prevent its lungs from filling. A large cetacean

The dolphin is a small toothed whale with a beak. The bottlenose dolphin is gray and grows to a length of 12 feet. The lower jaw is longer than the upper, and the beak measures only a few inches.

smothers under its own weight when it is not in water.

The smaller toothed whales, called dolphins, have been kept in captivity very successfully. They enjoy eating fish which they swallow whole. After they have been around people for a while they begin to imitate the sounds of human conversation as parrots and myna birds do. They can be taught many tricks and seem to enjoy performing them and cooperating with people after the manner of pet dogs.

One pilot whale named Morgan was trained in the U.S. Navy research center at Hawaii to dive 1,654 feet to the sea bottom and fasten lifting tools to items that the Navy wanted to raise to the surface. He followed the boat 7 miles out from shore and after attaching the tools would reappear in 15 minutes, ready for his reward of fish.

Common dolphins live far from land. They like warm seas and often frisk about ships, swimming alongside and leaping out of the water.

Any cetacean in trouble is lifted to the surface by its fellows so that while it is recovering it will not drown. A number of people owe their lives to this habit, for they reported that wild dolphins pushed them ashore when they were unable to swim out. One dolphin on a beach in New Zealand delighted visitors by making friends with bathers and coming every day to play with the children who petted it and frolicked with it.

Porpoises live on the northern Atlantic coast and on the Pacific coast

The harbor porpoise lives on both the Atlantic and the Pacific coasts, sometimes going up large rivers. It grows to 5 or 6 feet with a black back, white belly, and pinkish sides. This is our smallest cetacean. It has many teeth.

south to California. They feed mainly on fish which they gobble without much chewing. They remain underwater only a few minutes at a time. Dolphin and porpoise spouts are not visible.

Every 2 or 3 years mature cow whales bear a single calf. At calving time they are attended by one or two other females that gently receive the newborn and lift it to the surface for its first breath. Until it is able to manage its own breathing it is constantly tended so that it will not drown.

A great whale's milk glands can squirt milk a distance of 6 feet. Located in two folds of skin, they deliver a rich milk that is more than one-third fat. The cow usually turns on her side so that the calf can drink with its blowhole out of water. The calf adds about 230 pounds a day. Every 9 days it has gained another ton of weight. Rate of growth slows as the young one matures. Calves nurse for about 9 months. They may be 8 years old before they themselves can become parents.

This slow reproduction rate makes it impossible for the whales to multiply as fast as they are being killed. Speedy catcher ships equipped with bomb-carrying harpoons shot from cannons and with underwater detecting devices fan out from modern factory vessels that completely process a whale's body in less than an hour. Along with widely cruising spotter planes, these outfits regularly visit the whales' feeding grounds in the Antarctic and the Arctic. Since 1925, two million whales have been slaughtered and changed into oil, meat, and fertilizer. At present fifty thousand whales die every year.

A small manatee will weigh 400 pounds and measure 7 feet, but larger ones may grow to 13 feet long. Its slow swimming, water-plant diet, and very round tail fluke easily distinguish it from the cetaceans. It is found only in warm water.

No product made of the body of a whale can be legally brought into the United States. The Marine Mammal Protection Act passed in 1972 made it illegal for any U.S. citizen to disturb or kill marine mammals. Fifty-six other countries have agreed to protect completely the blue, humpback, right, gray, and bowhead whales. Only native peoples are not covered by this law.

Mr. Jacques-Yves Cousteau, a present-day Frenchman, has followed whales for years in every sea in the world. He says that he is continually astonished at the whale's size, strength, gentleness, and appetite.

In earlier days the dying struggles of wounded whales were sometimes fatal to the men who had injured them. Whales were reported to be ferocious. Now these same species are photographed by men who overtake them in small boats and jump into the water beside them, wearing diving suits and carrying waterproof cameras. They are unafraid of these big docile creatures.

The manatee, also called sea cow, is a tropical vegetation-eating water mammal. Like whales, it has no hind limbs and swims by up and down motions of its horizontal very round flukes. A fully grown manatee may eat as much as 100 pounds of water plants daily, scooping them into a big-lipped mouth with its flippers. Manatees feed with their heads and shoulders out of the water. They drift slowly about the warm bays and lagoons of southern Florida.

Manatee flesh tastes good, and the

quiet peaceful creatures were killed and eaten until they became very scarce. The Marine Mammal Protection Act and the sanctuary of the Everglades National Park will likely allow the species to continue.

The milk glands of the manatee are on its chest, and the mother floats upright in the water, clasping her single young one with her flippers while it nurses. As the mother manatee grazes on water plants the father holds the calf in his flippers. The manatee infant is cradled in the flippers of either parent for some weeks after birth. Nearly 2 years pass before the young is left to make its own way.

Perhaps enough government protection will be given that the great whales still remaining alive may continue to roam the oceans of the world as they have since God created them.

Class Project

Choose one or more species of whales. Measure its length on the school ground and outline the body with pebbles, twigs, trails of sand or other material. Heavy twine held in place by small sticks driven into the ground may also be used. Trace the outline of lips, flipper, and eye. Throat furrows and back fins may be added to the appropriate species. If the creature is pictured with its mouth open, show the baleen or teeth. Represent the spout with strips of white cloth or sprinklings of lime or flour. Species name, weight in tons, and length in feet may be indicated also.

Questions

1. The three main groups of cetaceans are (fishes, eels, and sharks; crabs, shrimps, and lobsters; whales, dolphins, and porpoises; clams, oysters, and snails).

2. How are the skeletons of the cetaceans and the manatees different from those of all other mammal groups?

3. What way of life do cetaceans and manatees have that is different from that of any other mammal group?

4. Cetaceans depend mainly upon (feeling, smelling, hearing, seeing, tasting).

5. What other mammal group exercises the same sense (answer to number 4) in the same way? What is that way?

6. Name five characteristics of mammals. Do cetaceans have all of

these?

7. Most whales (cannot bear icy water, cannot live in warm tropical water, have a body heating system that makes them comfortable at various temperatures).

8. Which is correct?
   (a) The giant toothless whales swallow 10- and 20-foot fish, digesting them in strong stomach juices as a snake does.
   (b) The giant toothless whales eat food animals as small as a gnat, straining them by the ton out of the waters through which they swim.
   (c) The giant toothless whales hold medium-sized fish in their mouths and crush them against rocks or the sea bottom before swallowing them.

9. The toothed whales (chew their food before swallowing it, swallow food whole, eat carrion that comes to pieces in their mouths).

10. The manatees (eat large amounts of water vegetation; feed on small fishes, turtles, and crabs; strain plankton and krill out of the water).

11. Whales of all the oceans numbered in the (millions, thousands, hundreds) before modern hunting methods began in 1923.

12. Today most large species of whales are (still plentiful, either altogether extinct or in danger of extinction, rapidly increasing).

13. Whales and manatees have (two front limbs and no hind limbs, two front limbs and two hind limbs, no limbs at all).

14. Whales and manatees (come out on land to give birth to young, come out on land to eat special foods, never come out on land).

15. Whales and manatees (use fins for swimming, use horizontal tail flukes in an up and down motion, use their vertical tails in a side to side motion).

16. Which of the following have mouths full of strainers (choose four)?
    fin whales, manatees, humpback whales, gray whales, porpoises, sperm whales, right whales, dolphins

17. Which of the following are toothed whales or smaller toothed cetaceans (choose three)?
    fin whales, manatees, humpback whales, gray whales, porpoises, sperm whales, right whales, dolphins

18. (The fin whale, The right whale, The sperm whale, The manatee) has a slender silky appearance with a white belly and a back fin. It is one of the fast whales.

19. (The fin whale, The right whale, The sperm whale, The manatee) eats vegetation in warm tropical waters. It spends its infancy being held in the flippers of either parent.

20. (The porpoises, The dolphins, The sperm whales, The gray whales) are champion divers that roam far from land. Their huge heads carry a well of fine white oil or wax. Valuable ambergris is sometimes found in their intestines.

21. (The humpback whale, The dolphin, The right whale, The gray whale) does well in captivity and learns many tricks easily.

"Dost thou know . . . the wondrous works of him which is perfect in knowledge?" Job 37:16

18. Finfoots and Kelp Dwellers

Whales and manatees are not the only mammals that prefer water to land. The seals are altogether at home there; and wherever cool currents flow and small food animals abound the finfoots gracefully dive, leap, and play.

Even though the seal's feet may have toes and nails their wide webs resemble fins. The order of the seals is named Pinnipedia (ˌpin-ə-ˈpē-dē-ə), meaning "fin-footed."

These mammals sometimes spend months of every year entirely in the water, but they also pull out on land and shuffle about. Some seals migrate; others feed along the same shores in every season.

God has designed the large brown eyes of a finfoot to see equally well in air or in water. In air the pupil is slit-shaped horizontally. In water it expands to a round shape to take in more light. Seals have no little duct on the inside of the head to drain away tears as most mammals have. For this reason when they are out on shore and their fur is dry they often appear to be crying.

About eighteen species belong to the hair seal family. The hair seal's coat does not keep out the cold water, but when dry it does protect against chilling winds. Another aid to warmth is the 3-inch layer of blubber that most seals have.

God has planned the flippers so that they do not need to be as warm as the other parts of the body. Little heat is lost through the flippers. In the same way the skin can be near freezing without chilling the animal or causing discomfort. A seal's food digests much

How do the hair seals and the walruses swim? The hind flippers provide power by what is called a sculling motion. The body swings to the right; the right flipper opens and scoops water back toward the left as far as a midway point while the left flipper is closed. Then the body swings to the left; the left flipper opens and pushes water with a sidewise motion. Seals can swim up to 12 or 15 miles per hour in short spurts by this method.

faster than a land mammal's food does, and the warmth from it keeps the finny one cozy.

Fur covers the flippers of mammals in the hair seal family. The bones of the front limbs resemble the leg and toe bones of other mammals. The long ones are inside the body, and the five rows of small bones support a wide spreading flipper complete with five toenails. When the hair seal swims, these front limbs are tucked into hollows somewhat like armpits unless the creature wants to turn or steer.

One student in the Arctic saw a seal dashing top speed toward an ice floe. Just before striking the ice it leaped up, landing neatly upon the floe.

Once on shore a hair seal's front flippers take over the main work of locomotion. The hind flippers cannot be turned forward. The finny fingers are curved, stiffened, and dug into the sand as the wet slippery creature wriggles along to a spot near or on its fellows.

Most mammals drop hair and flakes of skin all year around. This dead skin and hair would be uncomfortable when soaked with water. Each year most seals molt and emerge with an entirely new set of skin and hair. Seals often stay near land while the days or the weeks of the molt last.

Hair seals have ears that are only an opening in the side of the head. When the seal dives these ears are closed partly by water pressure and partly by the seal's own muscles. The nostrils close, too. Since sound travels so much better in water than in air the seals can still hear, just as whales can, while their ears are closed.

Squids, fishes, shrimps, crabs, clams, and mussels are food for seals. Short, sharp teeth are characteristic of these meat-eating mammals.

Whales have no vocal cords, and students have not yet discovered how God has made them able to call in audible voices. Seals, however, have vocal cords and they yelp, whimper, yap, bark, and roar. Sounds that are not vocal are often heard from seal pods. As the noisy chubby mammals lie dozing and basking, packed close together, one may hear loud sighs, grunts, coughs, snores, yawns, and sneezes plus the sound of scratching many itchy parasites on the skin.

The common or harbor seals also beep high squeaks beyond what the human ear can hear. Perhaps echolocation aids them in finding the fishes, shellfishes, and crabs on which they feed. Blind seals that were just as healthy as those with eyesight have been found.

The harbor seal is one of the hair

The harbor seal wears various shades of gray and brown with darker spots. It does not migrate but is found on sand flats, mud banks, bays, and inlets of both the Atlantic and the Pacific coasts of North America. Body length, 5 feet; weight, up to 255 pounds.

This elephant seal, giant of the seals, may be 20 feet long and weigh up to 4 tons. Females are much smaller being only 11 feet long and weighing 1 ton. After molting, the yellowish-brown coat is replaced by a fresh dark-gray one. The trunk of this male is blown up while he roars. The northern elephant seal lives on islands off the coasts of California and Baja California. The southern elephant seal is found on the Antarctic islands and mainland.

seal family living from the Arctic Ocean to Baja California, along the Pacific coast. Along the Atlantic the harbor seal is found south to North Carolina. It also occurs in other parts of the world.

This finfoot hunts by itself, but when it comes out on land it joins a group. An old male seal climbs to the highest point and keeps a lookout for danger. Most hair seals come out on land to sleep at night.

In late spring the harbor seal seeks shallow water and gives birth to its one light-gray woolly pup. The young seal drinks very rich milk from its mother's twin milk glands before its independence at the early age of 1 month.

The elephant seal, largest finfoot of all, is a hair seal that can dive to great depth and may go down as deep as 2,000 feet below the surface. The male has a trunklike nose that develops after the creature is 2 years old. It sometimes becomes long enough to overhang the mouth as much as 1 foot when it is relaxed. The roar of a big elephant seal may be heard for several miles. Since the food is eaten without being chewed, the intestine is very long. One elephant seal had an intestine 662 feet long.

Each year in late spring cow and bull seals choose a stretch of beach and repel other cows and bulls trying to come ashore at that point. Seals do not appear to be sensitive to pain, and even conflicts in which wounds run blood and eyes are lost do not keep them from fighting. The contests may dye the water red for yards around, but one animal rarely kills another. Bulls do not leave the spot even to hunt for food. For 1 to 2 months both cows and bulls bellow and battle.

Pups are born a week or more after the cows arrive on the beach, and a large number of them perish by being crushed in the fighting. At birth the pup has black woolly fur, weighs 80 pounds, and is 4 feet long. During the 3 weeks of being nursed the pup may gain 300 pounds, for the milk is four-fifths fat. The pups immediately lay on blubber that nourishes them as much as a month after their mothers leave them. However, many starve before learning to feed themselves; and only 50 percent survive the first year. The young form their own groups, chasing each other playfully and riding the breakers.

Another finfoot family has only one species, the walrus. This bulky, almost hairless creature is second in size to the elephant seal. Its hide may be 2 inches thick, wrinkled and lumpy, and the blubber 6 inches deep. A heavy mustache of about four hundred stiff white bristles droops from the huge nose, and from the upper jaw project two great tusks that may weigh 12 pounds each and reach a length of $3\frac{1}{2}$ feet in the male and 2 feet in the female. No flaps protect the holes that are its ears.

This big finfoot feeds in shallow water, digging up mussels and clams from the bottom and sorting out empty pieces with the bristles of the mustache. The shellfishes are taken into the mouth and ground apart with the short, sharp teeth. The delicious soft bodies are swallowed and the shells are spit out to sink gently through the water.

The scientific name of the walrus means "he who walks with his teeth." The walrus does pull itself up onto the edges of ice floes with its tusks. It can turn its flippers forward to travel more easily on land than the hair seals. These sociable creatures like to be close to each other. Latecomers to the ice cake have no choice but to begin another layer. Sometimes the floe is overloaded at one side. It tips, and the whole herd

This baby walrus is too young to wear tusks, but its whiskers are beginning to show. Walruses live beyond the Arctic Circle in both the Atlantic and the Pacific oceans. The nearly bare hide is dark gray or brown. Body length of bull, up to 12 feet; cow, up to 9 feet; weight of bull, 2,700 pounds; weight of cow, 1,800 pounds.

is dumped into the frigid water. Collecting themselves they hook up onto the ice to bask again.

Unlike the hair seals that usually rest on land the walrus often sleeps in the water in an upright position. Alongside the neck are pouches that the walrus can inflate at will. These hold as much as a cubic foot of air. Possibly they hold the head out of the water while the mammal slumbers.

A third finfoot family is known as the eared seals. They number twelve species. Like the walrus they have massive forequarters. Swimming is by a paddling of the front flippers. The flippers are naked, usually of black skin with arm and leg bones projecting from the body in addition to the hand and foot bones. The rear flippers can be turned forward to support the weight of the body. The eared seals have a shuffling walk and even a clumsy gallop about as fast as a man can run.

Worldwide there are five species of sea lions. Sea lions have the small pointed earflaps, the huge neck and shoulders, and the naked flippers of the eared seals.

California sea lions are often kept in zoos and can be tamed and taught many tricks. Like the harbor seals, they beep high-pitched sounds and may use echolocation to find their food. This sea lion is naturally playful and chases its fellows or its own air bubbles through the water. It does not need to come out on land to sleep as the hair seals usually do, but turns onto its back, and floats, dozing.

Eight species of fur seals live off the

This California sea lion has the heavy neck and shoulders, the naked flippers, and the ear flaps of the eared seals. Its coat is brown or blackish. This species is tamed and trained to perform tricks. Body length of bull, 8 feet; cow, 6 feet; weight of bull, 600 pounds; weight of cow, 200 pounds.

The rich beautiful pelt of the northern or Alaska fur seal with its dark-brown, slate-gray, and reddish tones is a source of great wealth. Body length of bull, 6 feet; cow, 4½ feet; weight of bull, 600 pounds; weight of cow, 135 pounds.

coasts of all the continents of the world except Europe. The northern or Alaska fur seal lives along the eastern and western coasts of the North Pacific.

These seals have very thick fine fur that traps air and insulates them against the cold. Fur seals molt by shedding hairs singly. Not all the hair is shed. Through the years the coat becomes thicker. Fur seals sleep on their backs in water.

Each September the females and young move down the Pacific coast, swimming perhaps 50 miles offshore. Some go as far south as California, returning home by June.

Fur seals find it easy to become too warm out on land in the summer. They lose heat by panting and by sweating through the many sweat glands of the flippers. Sometimes they wave their black naked fins like fans.

The sea otter, belonging to the weasel family, spends more time in the water than seals do. This creature, of the Carnivora order, eats all kinds of shellfishes and other sea animals. It has the most beautiful and valuable fur in the world, one skin bringing $10,000 in the early 1900s. Perhaps 650,000 shiny hairs are found in each square inch of pelt.

Sea otters nearly always swim on their backs, heads up. When sunshine glares they shade their eyes with their paws. Shellfish when brought up are held and cracked open on a rock resting on the stomach. The young otter is held on the stomach, too, and fed from the milk glands.

The sea otter was once a tame friendly animal coming ashore to sun itself. Now it lives out from the Pacific coast in the kelp beds within a mile of shore. Here in the kelp forest the young are born and the adults sleep with strands wrapped around themselves to prevent their drifting out into the open

The sea otter, a large gentle member of the weasel family, has the most magnificent fur in the world. The glossy brownish-black coat has a frosted effect from white-tipped hairs. Head and body length, 30 to 36 inches; tail, 11 to 13 inches, weight, 30 to 85 pounds.

water. These water mammals have experienced somewhat the same treatment from man that the whales have.

The walrus had always been used by Eskimos without reducing the population. Hides, tools, rope, fuel oil, and ivory were products gained from the walrus. When whales became scarce the whalers began killing walruses for oil until they could no longer be found in numbers large enough to be profitable. Since 1960, walrus cows and calves have been protected.

The elephant seal, being large, yielded much oil. California sea lions were also taken in great numbers for oil. The northern fur seal and the sea otter were nearly wiped out for their valuable fur. The international treaty of 1911 brought the killing to a halt. By this time an expedition cost more than could be gained by the selling of the now very-rare skins.

Twenty-two years after the northern elephant seal was no longer hunted, a single herd of less than one hundred was found. It is now illegal to kill a northern elephant seal.

After the treaty of 1911 no sea otters were seen and they were considered extinct. Then 27 years later, in 1938, a few were discovered in a very craggy spot where hunters, decades before, had failed to find the last specimens. Today they are completely protected.

In the treaty of 1911 nations agreed to kill the fur seal only on land, where three-fourths of the catch, normally sinking, would not be lost in the water and where cows could be distinguished from bulls. This beautiful fur is now harvested annually, some sixty thousand skins from bulls only. The Alaskan herd numbers 2 million.

The wide, far ocean with its rolling waves is home to the dozens of mammals that God has created to flourish in its waters. Often unseen they travel its swift currents in every season.

Class Project

Using commercial modeling clay, papier-mâché, or other preferred medium, model the five seal species of the lesson. Allow a given number of ounces for each 100 pounds of the animal's weight. The various species would have the following multiples of the basic weight: harbor seal, $2\frac{1}{2}$, California sea lion and northern fur seal, 6; walrus, 27; elephant seal, 80. If $\frac{1}{2}$ inch is allowed to represent 1 foot of length the various models would measure as follows: harbor seal, $2\frac{1}{2}$ inches; fur seal, 3 inches; California sea lion, 4 inches; walrus, 6 inches; elephant seal, 10 inches. Be sure to adjust the weight of the material used to the scale chosen for the length so that the resulting model animal has the correct proportions.

Questions

1. Seals (like whales, live only in the water; live only on the land; live both in water and on land).

2. Finfoots are found (in the Arctic, Antarctic, and cold currents of the temperate zones; in warm tropical waters only; in the Arctic and Antarctic only).

3. How do seals keep warm (state three ways)?

4. Seals eat (water vegetation; shellfish, fishes, squids, and crabs; plankton and krill).

5. Seals are (graceful, both on land and in water; clumsy, both on land and in water; graceful swimmers and clumsy as they travel on the beach; clumsy swimmers and graceful as they travel on the beach).

6. Seals (like to lie on the beach close together; like to be alone on the beach; prefer the company of only one or two other seals when they are out on the beach).

7. Seals when out on shore at calving time are (very quiet, very noisy, very peaceful, very timid).

8. Which statement is correct?

(a) Elephant seal pups are given excellent care by their mothers and nearly all live to grow up.

(b) Elephant seal pups are often crushed to death in the battles at calving time. Others die before learning to feed themselves, so that only about half live to grow up.

(c) After elephant seal young leave their mothers, predators take off a very few. The majority survive to be adults.

9. (Elephant seals and harbor seals, Sea lions and walruses, Fur seals and sea otters) have beautiful, valuable fur.

10. Seals are divided into (one, two, three, four) families. Name them.

11. Some seals have (skin pouches on the neck or head that are some- times filled with air, strong tails that help them get about on land, mouth strainers that remove sea food from the water, large ivory tusks [choose two]).

12. Match the animal to the product or products taken from its body.
elephant seal
California sea lion
Alaska fur seal
walrus
sea otter
(a) oil
(b) fur
(c) ivory

13. Man also captures the California sea lions for two other uses. What are they?

14. A sea mammal living in the kelp beds of the east Pacific Ocean is the _____.

15. Lists One, Two, and Three tell how God has made the three families of the finfoots. Name the seal family that each list describes.

	List One	List Two	List Three
Flippers	Covered with fur; rear flippers never point forward	Naked, rear flippers can be turned forward to bear the body weight	Naked, rear flippers can be turned forward to bear the body weight
Swimming method	Rear flippers move in a sculling motion	Rear flippers move in a sculling motion	Front flippers move in a paddling motion
Teeth	Short and sharp;	Short and sharp; also has two long tusks growing down from the upper jaw	Short and sharp

(Lists continued on next page.)

Coat	Hair that protects from cold only when dry	Little or no hair except mustache	Some species have hair that protects from cold only when dry. Others have thick fur that traps air and keeps the species warm underwater
Ears	No ear flaps	No ear flaps	Small pointed ear flaps

"Blessed be the Lord God, . . . who only doeth wondrous things." Psalm 72:18

19. In Cozy Burrows

The burning sun of summer, the howling blizzards of winter, sandstorms, tornadoes, driving rains, deep snow, and heavy ice are uncomfortable and dangerous to the many furred and feathered creatures of God's world. When such weather grips the land, the small mammals like nothing better than to retreat to some safe burrow beneath the sod where even a tornado or a blizzard cannot reach.

The shrew, smallest mammal of all, digs its own home at the rate of 1 inch per minute. Each tiny foot moves alternately in rapid motion until a vertical shaft is sunk. Another passage is dug from the shaft horizontally. The soil is smoothed out on the surface with nose and forepaws.

Here in a soft nest of grass that is 6 to 8 inches across the pink naked young are born. These tiny creatures about the size of honeybees have both eyes and ears closed. The mother tends and feeds them until they are able to see and hear and collect their own food. Two or three litters are born each year.

The adult shrew has a pointed nose, beadlike eyes, and ears mostly concealed in short fur. Shrews have five toes on all four feet rather than only four on the front feet as most mice have.

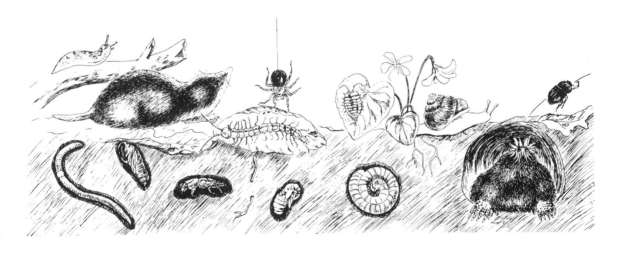

The short-tailed shrew darts about over or under the leaf litter of the woods, looking for small animals to eat. Body length, 3 to 4 inches; tail, 1 inch; weight, ½ ounce. The star-nosed mole hunts just below the surface. Body length, 4½ to 5 inches; tail, 3 to 3½ inches; weight, 2 ounces. Juicy tidbits picked up by these furry insect eaters are garden slugs, earthworms, sphinx moth pupae, mole crickets and other crickets, soil centipedes, spiders, young cicadas, sow bugs and pill bugs, millipedes, land snails, and various beetles.

The short-tailed shrew (shaded) gobbles insects from Saskatchewan to Florida and from Nova Scotia to Texas. The gray shrew (lines), also known as the desert shrew, darts about in all the North American deserts except the Great Basin desert.

Shrews rarely sleep more than a few minutes at a time. They patter frantically about, devouring their own weight in food every few hours. They even attack animals twice their size and eat them. Poison glands in the mouth of the short-tailed shrew charge the saliva, and small food animals are weakened as the poison enters wounds left by its bite. Shrews uncover prey in the upper levels of soil.

Because shrews and moles eat mostly insects they are in the mammal order named Insectivora (ˌin-ˌsek-ˈtiv-ə-rə). Moles rarely come above ground. Their eyes are pinhead size or even so small that they do not show through the skin. Their ears are just a hole under soft plushy fur. The senses of hearing and smelling are very keen in this small creature. It is also quite sensitive to the vibrations of the ground that are picked up through its nose, tail, and even hairs on its feet.

A mole's front paws and shoulders are quite large, for moles are perhaps the hardest workers among all mammals. Pink bare palms with big claws shovel soil away, sometimes at the rate of a foot per minute. The upper few inches of earth hold the many insect forms that are its main diet. Farther down are the rooms where this furry miner is sheltered from summer's heat and winter's cold.

The mole comes above ground to gather dried grasses. They are carried below and form the nest where the young are born. Pink and hairless at first, they are well furred at 3 weeks.

The star-nosed mole has twenty-two soft fleshy tentacles bordering the disk of its nose. Twenty of these wiggle about and locate food as their owner burrows

The star-nosed mole (diagonal lines) tunnels and swims in the southeastern part of Canada and in northeastern areas of the United States. The California mole (vertical lines) burrows mostly in California; the Pacific mole (shaded) is found shoveling soil in California, Oregon, Washington, and British Columbia. Moles are absent from the Great Basin and from the Rocky Mountains.

along. Some mole passageways end in water. Liking to swim, the star-nosed mole cruises around catching tiny crayfish, insects, and minnows to eat.

Another burrower is the pocket gopher. Like other rodents this mammal has two large gnawing teeth above and two equally large ones below separated from the smaller hind ones by narrow bare spaces on the jaw. Unlike other rodents whose mouths close over the incisors, the pocket gopher's lips close behind them. The big teeth are never covered. The outside cheek pouches are used for carrying food and nesting materials.

A gopher eats tubers, roots, and bulbs that are found as it digs. The main den is usually 3 to 4 feet down, but it may be as much as 6. The central tunnel measures to 500 feet long with many shorter side passages leading to the food piles, the room for waste, and

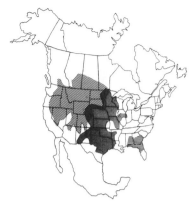

The northern pocket gopher (diagonal lines) digs from central Alberta and Saskatchewan south through the Great Basin desert. The plains pocket gopher (shaded) burrows and eats roots from west of Lake Superior south to Louisiana and Texas. The southeastern pocket gopher (horizontal lines), also called "salamander," tunnels around Florida and Alabama.

This pocket gopher has come above the ground, looking for seeds and grains to eat. He will carry the surplus in his outer cheek pouches to a hidden storeroom. These pockets can be turned inside out and are filled through slits on either side of the mouth. Notice the large digging claws. Body length, $5\frac{1}{2}$ to 9 inches; tail, 2 to $4\frac{1}{2}$ inches; weight, $\frac{1}{4}$ to $\frac{1}{2}$ pound.

the nest chamber.

Three to five young are born in March, April, or May. Naked and helpless, the young drink their mother's milk and in 6 weeks have fur and are able to eat other fare.

Even in severe climates the pocket gopher, like the vole, continues its usual activities during wintertime. This small living snowplow works unseen through the drifts, then fills the vacancies with dirt and gravel from its diggings. During a thaw this material sinks to form ropelike cores. These traces are like those left by voles, only somewhat larger.

Moles push up just under the surface, leaving little ridges interrupted by small round hills. The entrance to the burrow is usually closed, but the earth is nosed out in all directions and allowed to roll where it will.

In cold climates the chipmunk is a true hibernator. Woodchucks, marmots, jumping mice, ground squirrels, and many species of bats hibernate, too. Eastern chipmunk: body length, 5 to 6 inches; tail, 3 to 4 inches; weight, $\frac{1}{6}$ to $\frac{1}{3}$ pound.

A pocket gopher dumps all the soil to one side, making a fan-shaped mound. The last soil is left plugging the burrow itself.

The southeastern pocket gopher is known as a "salamander."

Rodent groups belonging to the squirrel family also burrow in the ground. These include marmots and woodchucks, prairie dogs and ground squirrels. All have inside cheek pouches. The smallest and handsomest are the chipmunks. Five dark stripes and four light stripes run from the shoulders to the base of the tail. The face is also striped. In North America around eight species of these frisky midgets chitter and chatter in every kind of habitat from high moist forested mountains to low deserts, rock piles, wood lots, and country gardens.

Chipmunks benefit the forests in which they live. Many evergreen tree seeds buried by them sprout and produce new growth. The very animals that destroy forests are relished by chipmunks. Beetles, caterpillars, pupae cases, and various injurious insects are eagerly gobbled by this little mammal. Hundreds of weed seeds are eaten or carried in the inner cheek pouches to pile in the storeroom below ground.

One or two litters a year are raised to maturity. The new babies weigh $\frac{1}{10}$ ounce apiece. They grow very fast and in 6 weeks are weaned and running about.

Another burrowing squirrel relative is the thirteen-lined ground squirrel.

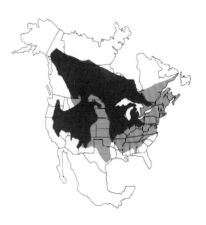

The eastern chipmunk (vertical lines) chatters from southeast Canada to Alabama and the northern parts of other Gulf states. The least chipmunk (shaded) is even more widely distributed from western Canada and the Great Lakes region into New Mexico. The thirteen-lined ground squirrel (horizontal lines) digs and whistles from Alberta, Saskatchewan, and the Great Lakes south to Texas. Areas where two or more species live appear dark.

A thirteen-lined ground squirrel. Chipmunks have stripes on both face and body. Ground squirrels are usually without stripes. This is the only striped ground squirrel in its range. These bright-eyed mammals are found from Alberta and Saskatchewan to Ohio, southern Texas, and west to Arizona. Body length, 4½ to 6½ inches; tail, 2½ to 5 inches; weight, ¼ to ½ pound.

About the same length as the chipmunk, but slightly heavier, this little creature has the usual inside cheek pouches of this mammal group. The thirteen stripes are light on a darker background. Some lines are rows of dots.

Unlike the moles and gophers, which distribute soil in a pattern about the mouth of a burrow, both chipmunks and thirteen-lined ground squirrels carry dirt away in their cheek pouches and sprinkle it around. Their young are born and raised in these well-hidden nurseries.

Both rodents gather food to eat after hibernation. Depending on the climate they may not hibernate at all. But where the weather is severe they retire to a cozy grass-lined bedroom, curl up, and become stiff and cold. Body temperature may be 37 degrees, the heartbeat slowing from 350 times per minute to only 5 times per minute. Breaths may be taken 4 times in 60 seconds rather than the usual 50 times.

Both chipmunks and ground squirrels whistle and churr, scold and chatter, often flicking their tails with each chirp.

The black-tailed prairie dog is named for its short sharp alarm call and its black-tipped tail. Many other ground-dwelling rodents live next to each other by chance, but these little diggers cluster together in towns. All through the squirrel city, furry watchmen sit up on their hind feet. At the first sight of an owl, hawk, coyote, fox, or other meat eater the guard squeals a warning and plunges below with a flip of the tail. The next lookout hears, likewise shrieks, and dives. The warning passes from throat to throat, and shortly all those within reach are safely underground. As the predator passes, heads pop out at a safe distance behind and the all-clear signal goes out. The hunter finds himself in an empty open space, while at a safe distance the little squirrels are sitting, watching and ready to drop into their tunnels if he comes near.

In early pioneer days prairie dog towns stretched for miles. In 1900, Vernon Baily found on the high plains of Texas a stretch of 100 by 250 miles that was home to perhaps 4 million prairie dogs. The mounds in a town are 25 to 75 feet apart and 1 to 2 feet high.

Now very few towns are left and the

These alert noisy little prairie dogs always live in colonies. Black-tailed prairie dog: body length, 11 to 13 inches; tail, 3 to 4 inches; weight, 2 to 3 pounds.

remaining ones are just a few acres in extent. Poisoning has wiped out most of the colonies.

The little creatures eat almost entirely roots, stems, leaves, blossoms, seeds, and other vegetable food. Eatables are carried in the cheek pouches and fed to the young ones below ground. Prairie dogs are dormant for a short time during the winter, but the fat stored on their chubby bodies lasts until spring comes.

Two or three times as large as the black-tailed prairie dog is the woodchuck. Like the prairie dog this burrower builds up a large mound at the entrance of its burrow. This mound is a dike against flooding, an observation deck, a basking platform, and a spot to lick and groom fur.

The yellow-bellied marmot in the West is known as the rock chuck. It does not store food as prairie dogs, ground squirrels, and chipmunks do, but it lays on fat. When so heavy that waddling is the only way to travel, it goes into

hibernation.

The young of both woodchuck and marmot are cared for in the family burrow.

A very skillful miner is the armadillo, the only species of its order in the United States. With poor eyesight and hearing but a good sense of smell the armadillo is sensitive to vibrations of the ground and when frightened usually dashes swiftly for its burrow. These dens may be 10 to 15 feet long with an entrance 6 to 8 inches across.

The armadillo is covered with heavy

This yellow-bellied marmot is lighter brown than the woodchuck and darker than the hoary marmot. The marmots are the largest members of the squirrel family. Yellow-bellied marmot: body length, 14 to 19 inches; tail, 4½ to 9 inches; weight, 5 to 10 pounds.

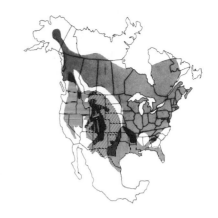

The scales of the armadillo may remind one of a reptile; but this unusual creature is warm-blooded, feeds its young with milk, and has a few fine hairs growing between its plates. Armadillos are mostly found in tropical countries. Nine-banded armadillo: body length, 15 to 17 inches; tail, 14 to 16 inches; weight, 9 to 15 pounds.

The black-tailed and the white-tailed prairie dogs (diagonal lines) live from the Canadian to the Mexican border in the Middle West. The woodchuck (shaded) is found from Alaska and the extreme northeast of Canada to the northern part of the Gulf states. The yellow-bellied marmot (horizontal lines) occupies the Great Basin and the Rocky Mountain areas. The armadillo (vertical lines) roots in the Chihuahuan (chə-ˈwä-ˌwän) Desert and east into the Gulf states and Georgia.

horny plates even on its tail and feet. The species living in the United States and Mexico has nine bands with joints between extending over the back. South American species have six bands or three bands.

The young are born underground in a nest of grass and leaves. Nearly always four young are born and they are either all males or all females. Their skins are soft and flexible, becoming harder as the animals mature.

The female nurses them and after they grow up, leads them on food hunting trips. In perhaps 3 months they go out and dig their own dens. Armadillos like to be together and feed in herds. This night-prowling mammal feeds almost entirely on insects and

Class Project

List the burrowing mammals that live in your community. Learn the size and characteristic forms of their various den entrances. Walk in the woods and in the fields and locate as many underground mammal homes as possible. Tracks in mud, dust, and snow will aid in identifying the owners.

other small animals found in the soil. Its snuffling, rooting habits suggest a feeding pig. It even grunts as it presses its nose into the earth, searching for food.

Animals that live in underground homes are sometimes dug out by badgers or bears. They can be followed by weasels and snakes. But many of the dangers that haunt other small mammals do not bother the dwellers in cozy burrows.

Questions

Match the characteristic with the mammal it describes.

1. Shrew—

2. Mole—

3. Gopher—

4. Chipmunk and thirteen-lined ground squirrel—

5. Black-tailed prairie dog—

6. Woodchuck and yellow-bellied marmot—

7. Armadillo—
   (a) builds up a large high mound that serves as a lookout post or uses a boulder for spying
   (b) carries dirt away and hides main entrance as much as possible
   (c) leaves soil at burrow, but smooths it evenly on all sides
   (d) pushes dirt out in one direction, making a fan-shaped mound
   (e) burrow entrance rarely found open
   (f) digs along or below the soil surface as it looks for food
   (g) uses its burrows for shelter and raising young
   (h) uses burrow for hibernation or long winter sleep
   (i) uses burrow for food storage
   (j) has inside cheek pouches characteristic of burrowing members of the squirrel family
   (k) burrows all winter, pushing soil into snow tunnels; soil shows in the spring like ropes lying on the surface of the earth

8. What mammal likes to live in a community of its own kind?

9. What mammal likes to go food hunting with others of its own species?

10. What burrowing mammal also swims and catches fresh-water animals for its food?

"Sing unto him . . . : talk ye of all his wondrous works." Psalm 105:2

20. In Leafy Treetops

"The trees of the Lord are full of sap; the cedars of Lebanon, which he hath planted; where the birds make their nests: as for the stork, the fir trees are her house" (Psalm 104:16, 17).

Birds are the animals most commonly seen in the woods, but mammals seek the shelter and food of the forests as often as do the feathered ones.

A ball of leaves and twigs high in some oak or hickory is a familiar sight. In wintertime when branches are bare and snow is lying all around, these little homes are revealed. Perhaps no one suspects that even while the white flakes sift softly, silently down, several furry mammals are snuggled together in the center of the leaf cluster. More often the nest is deserted and the warm-coated rodents are safely tucked away in a nearby hollow trunk.

In this country most woodland mammals are rodents although creatures of other orders likewise seek the safety and the freedom of the treetops.

In the spruce-fir forests along the California and Oregon coasts live the tree *Phenacomys* (fə-'nak-ə-ˌmis), also called the red tree mouse, a volelike creature with a blackish hair-covered tail. This bright reddish-brown blob of fur creeps about, eating pine or spruce needles and building half-bushel nests of soft material 15 to 100 feet above the ground. Here the miniature young, each weighing $\frac{1}{9}$ ounce, are born, nursed, and kept warm and dry until their eyes open and their fur grows out. In about 1 month they leave the parental nest and run about nibbling evergreen needles for themselves. The young males descend to the ground and burrow under the litter there, not climbing above until the next breeding season. The young females live on in the evergreens, occasionally cutting and storing twigs for future eating.

Farther east among the branches of the piñon ('pin-ˌyən) pines and junipers a small furry mouse scurries about picking up seeds and nuts. This little

The little tree Phenacomys, also called red tree mouse and red tree heather vole, likes the Douglas firs of the Pacific Coast rain forest and may live 100 feet above the ground, feeding on needles and tender twigs. Nests have been found that encircle the entire trunk with as many as five chambers connected by tunnels. Body length, 4 inches; tail, 3 inches; weight, 1 ounce.

This grayish-brown, large-eared piñon mouse lives among rocks or in the piñon pines where it nests and finds its food. Body length, 4 inches; tail, 3 to 4 inches; weight, 1 ounce.

grayish-brown creature with the dainty white underparts has large ears and a tail of two distinct colors, dark above and light below. It also nests among rocks. Probably it has more than one litter a year.

Honeysuckle, Spanish moss, and forest trees are home to the coppery cinnamon-colored golden mouse, with the snowy-white belly and feet. Its nest

of leaves and shredded bark is 6 to 8 inches across and from 5 to 10 feet above the ground. During spring and summer new litters are born and cared for briefly by this beautiful mammal. It is active throughout the winter and continues to eat seeds, acorns, and any dormant insects it may find.

Abroad only at night is the flying squirrel, which glides rather than flies. As it kicks off from some high point it stretches the loose skin between its legs into a wide furry sheet that easily slows its descent. The hairy tail is flattened and held rigid as well; and in a second or two the daring acrobat has swept the desired distance, landed, and whisked out of sight. Up to 125 feet have been covered in these exciting dives.

Beech and maple woods are the favorite haunts of this tree dweller. Seeds, nuts, insects, and birds' eggs are its diet. Some food is stored in the

The golden mouse is one of the white-footed or deer mouse family. Yellowish-cinnamon with a white belly, this little rodent collects a small round ball of soft plant materials where its young are sheltered. Body length, 3 to 4 inches; tail, 3½ inches; weight, less than an ounce.

Ranges of three tiny tree dwellers. The tree Phenacomys (horizontal lines) of the Pacific Coast is rarely seen. The piñon mouse (shaded) lives in the warm dry Southwest. The golden mouse (diagonal lines) is at home in mountains, forests, or plains of the southeast.

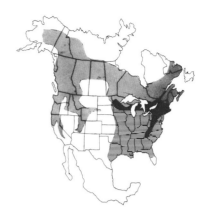

This tiniest of squirrels, the southern flying squirrel, will come out at dusk to glide about between the beech trees with playful boldness. Body length, 5½ to 6 inches; tail, 3½ to 4½ inches; weight, 1¾ to 4 ounces.

The northern flying squirrel (shaded) ranges into Alaska, Canada, and through the mountain areas of the United States. The southern flying squirrel (lines) lives in the eastern half of the country.

crotches of trees or in the nesting chamber that is built of leaves, twigs, and bark.

Attics of buildings afford cold-weather shelter. An old woodpecker hole may house twenty of these bright-eyed rodents through winter storms until spring comes with its warmth and delicious tree buds.

The red squirrel is another active little body slightly larger than its gliding cousin. Unlike the rarely seen flying squirrel, this little beast is very noisy. It frequently sits on a branch 10 feet or so above the ground, chattering away and making remarks to all within hearing.

The chickaree may have a favorite eating spot marked by a pile of nutshells and other remnants. It stores food for winter as does the flying squirrel.

Occasionally the red squirrel is out after dark, but usually it scampers around during the day. When winter comes its appearance changes slightly. Tufts of hair grow on the ears and the black lines of fur on the sides disappear.

Two litters of young are raised each summer. When cold weather arrives, this noisy rodent sleeps, but does not

Noisiest and liveliest of the American tree squirrels is the red squirrel. This spunky fellow sits in a white pine where feasts of seeds grow every 2 years. Beside him are mushrooms drying for later use. Body length, 7 to 8 inches; tail, 4 to 6 inches; weight, 5 to 11 ounces.

163

The red squirrel (shaded) lives in almost all of Canada and in Alaska. It is found as far south as South Carolina. The chickaree (lines) is a similar mammal living along the Pacific Coast.

hibernate, and often is abroad on bright sunny days. House cats and owls feed on red squirrels.

Twice as large and not nearly so agile is the gray squirrel, the beautiful silvery-furred resident of city parks and of oak and hickory woods. White

This beautiful friendly fellow has a silvery-gray coat that is slightly reddish in summer. Here a gray squirrel opens a hickory nut shell with its sharp incisors. Eastern gray squirrel: body length, 8 to 10 inches; tail, 8 to 10 inches; weight $\frac{3}{4}$ to $1\frac{1}{2}$ pounds.

bordered very bushy tail, and white behind the ears in winter characterize this familiar mammal. Like the red squirrel, each year it has two litters of blind naked young. These are born in a hollow trunk or bough or in a leaf nest lined with grass built among the branches of the home tree.

Buds, seeds, fruits, and mushrooms are relished by the gray squirrel in

The eastern gray squirrel (horizontal lines) is a common sight in the eastern half of the United States wherever food trees grow. In city parks and on lawn and street trees this furry rodent gracefully hops about feeding on seeds, nuts, and cones. The Arizona gray squirrel (diagonal lines) and the western gray squirrel (shaded) are slightly larger.

summer; but as fall comes on, the busy rodent begins to store provisions against the months of cold. Acorns, hickory nuts, and butternuts are stored separately in little holes dug by the forepaws. Later, even under a snow cover, these tidbits are found and eaten. Often the rich food of spring appears before the hoards are used. The nut

This young fox squirrel is pale yellow to orange below and rusty above. When grown, it will be the largest of American squirrels. Body length, 10 to 15 inches; tail, 9 to 14 inches; weight, 1½ to 3 pounds.

sprouts, a small seedling appears, and in a few years a new tree is growing toward maturity. In this way the forest is renewed by the very animals that profit most from the harvests of the nuts.

A small fox squirrel matches the gray squirrel for size, but a large fox squirrel will grow to twice the weight. In different parts of the United States this mammal has various colors in its coat. In the South the fur may be black and white. In Pennsylvania a steel-gray form lives and some fox squirrels have grizzled, reddish fur suggesting a fox.

Oak, hickory, and cypress are their favorites and they prefer forest borders rather than deep woods. The fox squirrel nursery is a hollow tree or a loose nest of bark, twigs, and leaves as other squirrels have. But when a fox

squirrel builds a winter home, the top and sides are tightly woven of plant materials that keep the rodents sleeping inside dry and comfortable.

Bobcats, foxes, and man enjoy eating this species that is probably fatter and slower than the smaller squirrels. At places it is becoming quite rare.

God has given every habitat in His creation predators that remove the sick, weak, and old individuals to prevent the crowding that often results in disease. Starvation comes when food plants or animals disappear into the mouths of an ever-increasing army. In the treetops hawks, owls, and weasels can easily chase the mice and squirrels that live and feed there.

One mammal weighing slightly more than the fox squirrel and carrying

A marten. This beautiful member of the weasel family has soft thick fur of yellowish brown that becomes darker on the tail and on the legs. A light spot adorns the breast. It dashes through the treetops and can overtake the fastest squirrel. Red squirrels are an important food of the marten. Body length of male, 16 to 17 inches; tail, 8 to 9 inches; weight, 2 to 4 pounds.

the little bags of musk used by the weasel family is the marten. Martens have been trapped for years that man might wear their fine rich yellowish-brown pelts in coat trimmings and scarfs. A lighter spot covers the chest and throat.

Mice, birds, frogs, fruits, berries, and other foods are eaten by the marten. Its litter of three or four young may be born in a hollow tree, a rotted-out log, or a rock pile.

Realizing that martens are valuable predators the lawmakers of several states have forbidden their killing. After 30 years of protection these flesh eaters are again found in New York and Maine. New Hampshire, Wisconsin, and Michigan have introduced martens into their wilderness areas, hoping that a group will become established. These creatures need large trees and heavy woods to be at home, and when forests are cut they suffer. Fires, road building, and city expansion destroy their homes.

Another predator that lives around swamps and other bodies of water is the fisher. This musk bearer was once plentiful, but has nearly disappeared. Its dark-brown fur is even more beautiful and valuable than the fur of the marten. White-tipped hairs give the coat a frosted appearance.

It is active day and night and can race through the treetops at high speeds. Like its big cousin, the wolverine, it travels much farther than the marten that is often satisfied to roam about over 1 square mile. The fisher normally ranges over 10 square miles,

The fisher prefers the flavor of porcupine and knows how to avoid the dangerous quills while gaining a delicious dinner. The white-tipped fur of this musk bearer is nearly black. Body length, 20 to 25 inches; tail, 13 to 15 inches; weight, 4½ to 10 pounds.

feasting on small mammals, birds, carrion, fruits, and fern tips. It is the one mammal that prefers to eat porcupine.

Wisconsin produced most of the timber in the United States around 1900. By this date most of the beavers, wolves, coyotes, and fishers had been trapped out. Over 50 years of timber cutting stripped the great trees from the forests. When the logging boom was past, lumber companies moved away. The large deposits of scrap wood left behind were excellent fuel. Fires raged throughout the state.

Then the government established national forests, planted trees, purified water, and protected wildlife. Many mammals and birds roamed and sang again in the new growth.

But predators were scarce and porcupines increased. Bobcats, cougars, and fishers can flip the porcupine over and escape the deadly quills while gaining a warm dinner. In the winter in some areas, porcupines ate so much bark from trees that all or part of the trees were killed.

Wildlife managers and foresters decided to bring some live-trapped fishers into the state from Minnesota. Sixty fishers were released between 1956 and 1963. Sixty more were carried in by the spring of 1967. These active furry animals feasted on squirrels, rabbits, porcupines, and other prey species. Traveling away from their first territories they spread through the northern quarter of the state and into a few southern counties also. The balance of nature is being restored in Wisconsin's growing forests.

Seeds from the cones of pines, serviceberries, the red fruit of the hawthorn, cedar berries, black walnuts, mulberries, hickory nuts, hazelnuts, butternuts, pecans, beechnuts, maple seeds, and acorns are known

The marten (lines) hunts in most of Canada, in Alaska, and in the high mountains of the West. The fisher (shaded) lives in a smaller area and is not usually found north of Canada. Areas where both furbearers live appear dark.

as mast. Then there are persimmons, wild cherries, wild plums, crab apples, papaws, and other delicious fruits of the forest. Squirrels, mice, wood rats, opossums, raccoons, ringtails, gray foxes, and porcupines find abundant food as well as shelter in the treetops.

Class Project

Locate food trees near the school, near private homes, or along roadsides. Watch to see what species of squirrels or other animals are eating the mast. Find den trees and mammal nests among the branches. Try to determine what creatures built the nests. Are any of the dens or nests in use as winter shelters?

Questions

1. What very small white and yellow mammal usually builds its nests in trees and bushes within 10 feet of the ground?

2. What quite-small tree dweller lives in the Southwest and is identified by unusually large ears?

3. What tree dweller lives high above

the ground and eats mostly evergreen needles?

4. Name the tree squirrels in the order of their size beginning with the smallest.

5. Squirrels enjoy various advantages by living in trees. Name three.

6. Squirrels find many foods growing on trees or dropped on the ground beneath them. Name ten.

7. What squirrel is seldom seen because it usually comes out only at night?

8. What squirrel living in trees chatters the most?

9. What predator often feeds on red squirrels?

10. What musk bearer hunts porcupines?

11. New York, Maine, New Hampshire, Wisconsin, and Michigan (have passed laws encouraging the killing of predators, are suffering severe damage to their forests from predatory animals, have brought in fur-bearing predators to protect their forests, have passed laws against harming certain predators [choose two]).

12. What squirrel have you seen most often?

"Dost thou know . . . the wondrous works of him which is perfect in knowledge?" Job 37:16

21. By Flowing Waters

"He lieth under the shady trees, in the covert of the reed, and fens. The shady trees cover him with their shadow; the willows of the brook compass him about" (Job 40:21, 22).

Here the Lord tells Job of a large animal that lives in the marshes (fens) and in the shelter (covert) of the reeds. Willow trees surround (compass) his watery home and cool shadows fall where he lies.

The Lord has created various mammals to live in the marshes and the streams. Just as He has given many of the ocean animals streamlined bodies, so He has provided the furry creatures of lakes and rivers with long tapering forms. To them He has given webbed or hairy toes, and thick waterproof coats to shut out the cold.

The water shrew, an insect eater, has stiff hairs on its feet that hold little bubbles of air. It can actually walk on the surface of still water. An expert swimmer and diver, it comes out mostly at night; but it has been seen during the day, cruising like a silvery fish encased

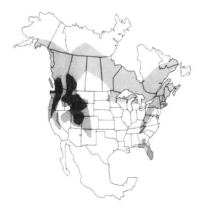

If you live in the areas shown above you may sometimes glimpse these small water mammals by brooks, springs, or marshes. The northern water shrew (shaded) hunts insects and other tiny animals from the Pacific to the Atlantic and south in the high mountains. The dark-brown Pacific water shrew (vertical lines) is active from British Columbia south to California. The Richardson's vole (horizontal lines), up to 6½ inches long, likes to swim in the streams of northwestern United States and southwestern Canada. The 8-inch Florida water rat (diagonal lines) is like a small muskrat, but without the muskrat's flattened tail.

Northern water shrew. This blackish-gray swimmer with the flattened tail is found along northern streams and in western mountain waters as far south as California and New Mexico. Body length, 3¼ inches; tail, 2½ to 3 inches; weight, ½ ounce.

Mink. This very dark brown fur bearer has a white chin patch and a slightly bushy tail. Body length of male, 13 to 17 inches; tail of male, 7 to 9 inches; weight, $1\frac{1}{4}$ to $2\frac{1}{4}$ pounds.

fishes, aquatic insects, and animal eggs of all kinds are its food.

The mink is a quick graceful creature with very dark brown fur. It is often raised in captivity for its beautiful pelt. Three hundred thousand wild mink are trapped and used annually.

Mink dens may be among tree roots at the water's edge or in an empty muskrat lodge. Burrows in the stream

The mink hunts (lines) from the shores of the Bering Sea and the Arctic Ocean east to the Atlantic Ocean and south to the Gulf of Mexico. Wetlands in every state except Arizona are its home. The river otter (shaded) fishes along with the mink except on the shores of the Arctic Ocean. It inhabits a larger area in the states bordering Mexico than its smaller relative, the mink. Areas where both furbearers live appear dark.

in a layer of air held by its coat. Its long bare tail is flattened at the sides like a muskrat's.

The water shrew nests in a small burrow on the bank. An underwater door and a ground-surface entrance lead to the tiny creature's home. Small

banks are homes as well, and the four to eight young are born in the spring and fed by both parents until they are able to care for themselves.

Like other weasels the mink is a predator and dines on fishes, marsh birds, crayfish, frogs, snakes, and rodents.

Another mammal that prefers the security of the wetlands with their

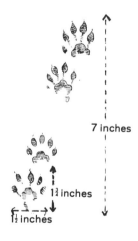

7 inches

$1\frac{1}{4}$ inches

$1\frac{1}{4}$ inches

A mink running through mud in Wyoming left this track.

This chocolate cottontail, the marsh rabbit, has coarse hair and small reddish-brown feet that are darker below. Its tiny tail is dingy white. Body length, 14 to 16 inches; weight, 2½ to 3½ pounds.

abundant plant cover is the marsh rabbit. This dark-brown cottontail with small reddish feet and a little dingy white tail hides in reeds or ventures onto floating vegetation. It swims readily and often walks rather than

The marsh rabbit (lines) lives in coastal wetlands from Virginia to Alabama and Florida. The swamp rabbit (shaded) lives in sloughs and along the rivers of Alabama west to Texas and north along the Ohio River to Illinois and Indiana.

hopping as most members of its order do. Its larger relative, the swamp rabbit, haunts sloughs and streams in the lower Mississippi River valley and north along the Ohio. These wetland rabbits feed entirely on plants.

The young, five or six in a litter, are born in a well-hidden grass nest above ground, lined with fur from the breast of the mother. Four or more litters each year replenish the rabbits taken by predators. Somewhere near water, un-

Most cottontails hop along, but the marsh rabbit often walks. Here is a marsh rabbit walking-track pattern.

der overhanging plants, one may find the forms where these two species disappear during the day.

One of the most widespread and important of the water mammals is about a foot long with an almost typical vole shape: chubby body, small ears and eyes, and no visible neck. The one exception is its long, naked tail, flattened on the sides. Perhaps for this reason it was named muskrat, although it is not a rat and its musk is mild

The muskrat. Fine soft fur topped with a thick layer of coarse red-brown guard hair warms this oversize volelike mammal. Its black tail is flattened on the sides. Body length, 10 to 14 inches; tail, 8 to 11 inches; weight, 2 to 4 pounds.

enough to be used in perfume.

It is a very tidy animal and like a cat keeps its fur shining and smooth, its teeth and claws washed, and its home clean.

In honor of its delicious flesh the legislature of Louisiana in 1944 officially changed the name muskrat to marsh hare.

The furs of the marsh hare are used in greater quantity than the pelts of any other creature in this country, about 5 million skins being harvested each year.

In warm weather one may see fragments of stems, roots, and leaves floating on the water or a pile of clam or mussel shells on the bank, showing that muskrats live nearby. Three to seven young are born in each litter and are fed first on warm milk and then on vegetable dainties until they are able to collect their own food.

Occasionally these mammals scoop

out dens under river banks. More often cone-shaped lodges may be found on ponds or lakes, their walls built of stems, reeds, grass, weeds, leaves, rushes, cattails, and other edible vegetation held together with mud. In freezing weather this material becomes very hard and is excellent protection against predators that walk out to the lodge on the ice. Meanwhile, inside, the plump creatures can eat the walls of their own homes in safety. As many as two dozen have been found in a single house.

Muskrats like to keep up a scent post to inform travelers or visitors of their presence. The post is a little mat of cut stems, leaves, and mud, topped with a few drops from the musk glands.

The muskrat (lines) lives from the shores of the Bering Sea and the borders of the Beaufort Sea east to the Atlantic Ocean. It is absent from most of California, Texas, Florida, and the areas next to Florida on the northeast. The beaver (shaded) mostly avoids the far-northern seacoasts, but like the mink, otter, and muskrat ranges throughout most of Canada and the United States. The beaver is found along the northern edges of eastern Mexico and in parts of the southwestern states as well. Areas where both muskrat and beaver live appear dark.

172

The coypu, a furbearer introduced from South America, is large and brownish with a long, round, finely haired tail. Body length, 22 to 25 inches; tail, 12 to 17 inches; weight 15 to 18 pounds.

Coypus ('kòi-püs) are big brown South American animals with round finely haired tails. They were brought into this country and released to provide a source of fur. Lately skins from 400,000 of these animals were sold per year.

The coypu hollows out a large den in the bank next to the water. As soon as they are born, the young are taken swimming by their mother, who carries them along on her back. The milk glands are high on the flanks of the female, and the young can be seen feeding as she paddles about. The male has a scent gland that gives off a very strong smell. Like the muskrat this mammal eats almost every kind of water vegetation. The soft underfur is known as nutria ('nü-trē-ə) and is sold under that name. Sometimes the live furbearer is called nutria.

The river otter, a member of the weasel family, is smaller than the sea otter and the wolverine. The badger is smaller than the river otter and is fourth in size of the North American weasels.

Medium-large members of this furry family are the fisher and the hognosed skunk.

Little species of this group in North America are the marten, the small skunks, the mink, and the weasels.

The river otter lives along freshwater streams and lakes and also in the salt water around islands and the mouths of rivers where the tide rises and flows. Its burrows are in soil next to the water. It is short legged with highly prized fur that appears on the market by twelve thousand skins annually.

Slower fishes are its main food. Toads, frogs, and crayfish are taken also.

River otters like to be together especially when they are playing. A single mink will coast along an icy trail and use slippery slides, but a whole family of otters will group and frisk

The river otter, related to the mink and other weasels, is a rich brown above, lighter below, with a heavy round tail. Body length, 26 to 30 inches; tail, 12 to 17 inches; weight, 10 to 20 pounds.

God has given the playful otter very skillful feet for swimming. Notice the web on the hind toes. This web shows when the otter walks in mud. The front foot is smaller.

about. In winter there is snow and ice to glide over. In summer wet clay or smooth grassy slopes will do. They tuck their front legs by their sides and whiz down the bank into the water, swimming out to climb to the top and dart down again. They play tag. They pretend to battle each other.

The largest rodent in North America is the beaver. Next in size is the orange-toothed porcupine. Coypu is third and either the woodchuck or marmot fourth.

Muskrat, prairie dog, and fox squirrel are medium-sized rodents. Voles, lemmings, mice, squirrels, gophers, and rats are groups of small species in this very numerous order.

Beavers in North America were estimated to number 60 million or more (probably 100 million) before the coming of the white man. Beavers live in Europe and central Asia and their furs were already the main source of felt for hats. The new continent was widely explored and the valuable pelts of these rodents were removed by the million. By 1845 they were too scarce to trap in numbers. Nutria skins began to be used more, and since then beavers have increased. They are now found in thirty states, and nearly 200,000 furs are taken every year.

Beavers live where their food trees—aspen, cottonwood, birch, and willow—grow near water. Their diet is entirely plant parts.

The Lord has created the beaver able to build three structures: the dam, the lodge, and the canal.

A dam may rise 4 to 5 feet or even up to 12 feet. Depending on the width of the river to be crossed it may be $\frac{1}{2}$ mile long.

The beaver's long yellow incisors can cut through a trunk 6 inches thick in 10 minutes. These teeth grow continually; otherwise they would soon be worn down to useless stubs.

The sharp-toothed mammal begins building by cutting down several

This mother beaver and her kits live inside the lodge, protected in summer by the deep surrounding water and in winter by the freezing of the thick mud in its walls.

trees. These, arranged lengthwise with the heavier base upstream and the branches pointing downstream, remain in place and are not carried away by the current. Mud and stones weighing up to 6 pounds are carried, with the forelegs against the breast, to fill in the spaces between. More of the same materials are piled up, layer after layer, along with sticks, logs, weeds, leaves, and grass until the dam is tight and the river rises and pours over the top.

Above the dam in the growing pond the beaver builds its lodge. There are several rooms, the most important ones being above the surface. All the entrances are below, usually near the bottom where winter ice does not form and hinder traffic. In the center of the dome mud is omitted. Warmth rising under the roof melts snow and ice above, allowing pure cold air to flow into the nest.

Near the lodge a food pile of young branches covered with bark is weighted to the bottom with stones and mud. Here the beavers feast during the winter, safe from predators. A beaver eats 3 pounds of bark in an average meal.

When trees are cut they must be dragged or floated to the building spot. Canals 2 to 3 feet wide and 18 inches deep are sometimes dug to float logs. Beaver ditches have been measured that were 1,000 feet long with one or more forks or branches. These busy workers even construct locks in their canals, low dams that cause water to rise and level off. Logs then are dragged over the dams.

Beaver ponds hold rainwater and help to prevent flooding. They are water-storage spots in times of scanty rainfall.

The beaver's tail is a paddle-shaped, scaly, heavy prop which is very useful when the mammal woodcutter stands on its hind legs to fell a tree. The tail is also used to give an alarm signal to others in the colony. A dive into the water along with a slap of the tail on its surface alerts all within hearing that danger is near. Each rodent as it dives slaps the water, and the warning

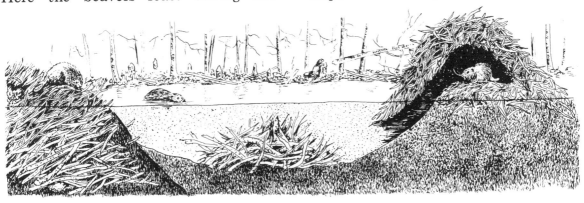

Beavers restrict the colony to three sets of young. Two-year-olds are expelled, if they have not gone already to begin colonies of their own. To the left is the dam and underwater is the food pile, gathered before ice covers the surface. On the right is the lodge. In the background, colony members fell trees to add to the food pile, the dam, or the lodge.

spreads until the banks are deserted and work is at a standstill.

Beavers mate for life. Two to six kits are born in the annual litter. Like muskrats, beavers maintain scent posts that may be as much as 1 foot high and 3 feet across.

Many rodents seem to live only as food for other animals or to make God's world a more interesting place. But muskrats, coypus, and beavers are rodents with valuable fur.

In addition God has given the beaver unusual ability to store water and to control its level. This strong worker has been called an animal engineer.

Class Project

Visit nearby wetlands, rivers, or lakes. Look for tracks, scent posts, lodges, burrows, and dams. Find where vegetation has been cut down for food or house building. Are there any animal trails? How many mammals of today's lesson do you think are present?

Questions

The mammals of today's lesson are: water shrew, mink, marsh rabbit and swamp rabbit, muskrat, coypu, river otter, and beaver. Answer the questions by writing the name(s) of the mammal(s) described.

1. We eat plants only.

2. We eat animals only.

3. We eat mostly plants; but we like clams and mussels, too.

4. We live in burrows on the bank.

5. I live in a burrow on the bank or I put together a lodge.

6. We build fur-lined nests on the bank among the reeds and grasses.

7. I sometimes live in a burrow. At other times I live in an empty lodge left by another species.

8. I almost always live in a lodge constructed by our family.

9. My tail is 1 foot long or longer, with fine hair on it.

10. Our tails are naked and flattened from side to side.

11. My tail reminds some people of a table tennis paddle. It is flat and scaly. I use it to make a slapping sound on the water.

12. Our tails are too small and furry to help us swim.

13. My tail is more than 1 foot long, covered with fur, round, and very thick.

14. My tail is covered with fine

beautiful fur. It may be 7 inches long.

15. I am an insect eater.

16. We are members of the weasel family.

17. We belong to the rodent order.

18. We are cottontails that swim.

19. I have been called the most playful mammal because we spend so much time frolicking together.

20. I have been described as an animal engineer because for our own safety we control the levels of the water in our own neighborhood.

"Stand still, and consider the wondrous works of God." Job 37:14

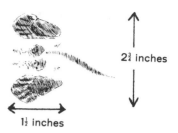

2¼ inches

1½ inches

22. In Sunny Deserts

"Be not afraid, ye beasts of the field: for the pastures of the wilderness do spring, for the tree beareth her fruit, the fig tree and the vine do yield their strength" (Joel 2:22).

What are the pastures of the American wilderness? What food supplies are found in the deserts and what beasts eat them?

Summer travelers across the American deserts rarely see animals in any numbers. They may imagine that dry places are rather empty of wildlife. They would be surprised to know that about five thousand species of insects, reptiles, mammals, and birds live in the arid lands of North America. Some of these we have already heard about: voles, shrews, deer mice, grasshopper mice, wood rats, cottontails, jack rabbits, bats, bobcats, weasels, skunks, badgers, deer, bighorn sheep, ringtails, and armadillos.

How is a desert different from other areas?

Dr. Koppen of Austria, measuring rainfall and temperatures around the world, found that about 14 percent of the earth's 56 million square miles of land area had less than 10 inches of rainfall annually and generally high temperatures. He identified these as deserts.

Other lands of about the same expanse had 10 to 20 inches of yearly rainfall. These steppes ('steps), or semiarid regions, added to the deserts totaled about 16 million square miles.

The largest desert is the Sahara Desert in Africa. The Australian is second biggest, and the Arabian third.

The North American desert is the fifth in size, 5 percent of its own continent's total area.

Naturally, along with scanty rainfall, dry places have very low humidity. There is no haze in the air to protect the earth from the sun's full strength. The

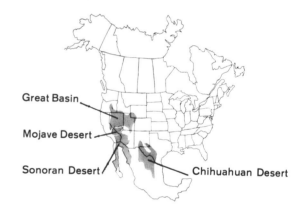

Great Basin

Mojave Desert

Sonoran Desert

Chihuahuan Desert

Four main deserts stretch over 500,000 square miles in the United States and Mexico. The Great Basin desert runs from Oregon to northern Arizona. Directly south of it on the west is the Mojave (mō-'hä-vē) Desert, lying in California and Nevada. Bordering the Mojave and extending into Baja California and Mexico is the Sonoran (sə'nō-rən) Desert. The easternmost desert spreads from New Mexico and Texas into Mexico. It is named the Chihuahuan (chə-'wä-ˌwän) Desert.

atmosphere has very little humidity to act as a blanket to retain the warmth received during the day. Desert soil heats far more than landscapes shaded by an overcast sky. But night temperatures may drop 50 degrees because there is no shielding cloud cover. Daytime desert air temperatures often reach 120 degrees and the surface can be as much as 30 to 50 degrees hotter.

In these arid places showers often evaporate in midair. Rain that falls is all absorbed by earth or atmosphere. Soil minerals from weathered rocks are not dissolved out and carried away. Some deserts are very fruitful. Plant products such as hay or grain, grown here, are richer in nourishment than the same species maturing where fertility has been lost in rainwater runoff.

A few wastes have such abundance of minerals that there is no vegetation. Mines may be profitable. Potash for fertilizer is taken from Utah's salt flats and borax and gypsum from the Mojave Desert.

Perennial plants and bushes space themselves away from each other and send out networks of shallow roots to drink up the surface soil moisture and a deep taproot to discover underground dampness. Cactuses hold water in thick pulpy trunks. Many plants that discard their tops after the growing season store liquid in bulbs and tubers.

Annual grasses, herbs, and weeds survive in seed form during periods of drought. Then a shower comes. Within weeks they have germinated, grown, matured, bloomed, and are again in seed state, well able to live through the next arid months or years.

A scientist, Lloyd Teveis, studied the supply of seeds on an acre of soil in a California desert and was able to estimate that 1.45 billion seeds were present even in an average dry year.

With the first good rains the desert is alive with many ants, wasps, beetles, crickets, grasshoppers, moths, and bugs. Besides these hosts of insects, many arachnids flourish. Spiders, ticks, scorpions, as well as millipedes, centipedes, sowbugs, and snails become active. These creatures along with the never-failing seeds of woolly plantain and comb-bur are the basic food supply of the small rodents.

The earth is a very good insulator. Burrows only 4 inches down were found to be 31 degrees cooler than the sun-drenched surface above. When the sands of the Mojave reach 150 degrees, the temperature is 61 degrees at a depth of 18 inches. Dens are far more humid than the air above; and many mammals, insects, and reptiles pass the heat of the day in holes with closed entrances.

We are already acquainted with the jumping mice of the moister areas of this country. The western jumping mouse is found in the northern part of the Great Basin desert. It has long hind feet, an extensive tail, and soft fur. When traveling at top speed, it leaps 6 to 12 feet. Damp places are its home, and, like most mice, it needs water to drink. It has no outside cheek pouches.

The pocket mouse, as well as the

The silky pocket mouse is one of the smallest mammals in North America. It has soft, pale-yellow fur sprinkled with dark hairs. The belly is white and the ears are set in a yellow patch of velvet. Head and body, 2½ inches; tail, 1½ to 2 inches; weight, ⅓ ounce.

jumping mouse, has long hind feet. Tail length varies among species. Far from being champion jumpers, the pocket mice hop quietly about, a few inches at a time.

God has provided the pocket mice with fur-lined cheek pouches, somewhat like those used by the pocket gopher. This mammal family lives almost entirely in deserts. The Lord has made these creatures able to take hydrogen from the food they eat and oxygen from the air to form water in their bodies. The flesh of these small seed eaters may be more than half water.

As is true in moister climates, the small rodents are the most plentiful of mammals; and in the desert it is the pocket mice and their relatives that feed the meat eaters.

The silky pocket mouse is a tiny fellow that lives on the soil of sandy prairies. Nineteen other species of pocket mice are found on arid lands of this country with colors varying from pale yellow to dark gray. None of them

have striking patterns on the face or body, and the tail is about the same length as the head and body, or slightly longer.

The spiny pocket mice, numbering five species, are found in California, southern Texas, Baja California, and Mexico. Litters of five young are born at any time of the year. At first the hair is silky and the spines on the rump are soft and flat. Two months later the young molt and the new coat has stiff sharp bristles on the lower part of the back. Four species have a crested tail. Snakes, foxes, cats, and weasels eat them, spines and all.

Spiny pocket mice enjoy nuts, seeds, and grass. They come out at dusk to pack their cheeks with ⅛ to ½ teaspoon of

The silky pocket mouse (horizontal lines) lives from South Dakota and Texas west to Arizona and south to Mexico. Kangaroo mice (vertical and diagonal lines) gather seeds in Oregon, California, Nevada and Utah. Ord kangaroo rats (shaded) hop about in the area bounded by Saskatchewan and Alberta on the north, Washington and Oregon on the west, Nebraska and Oklahoma on the east, and Texas and Mexico on the south. Areas appear dark where kangaroo mice and silky pocket mice are found along with ord's kangaroo rat.

A black-tipped tail, thicker in the middle than at either end, characterizes this dark kangaroo mouse. Its relative, the pale kangaroo mouse, has a similarly shaped tail, but without the dark end. It likes fine sand and some plant cover near its burrow. Head and body, 3 inches; tail, 2⅔ to 4 inches; weight, up to ⅔ ounce.

seeds. These foods are hidden in their burrows for days of cold and drought. Pocket mice live alone except when the mother is caring for the young. Their runways may be 7 feet long.

In lean times the pocket mouse saves its food supply by becoming dormant. Its temperature falls to about that of the burrow. In summer its sleep is not so deep or long as in the winter when the body temperature drops much lower. Dormancy during hot weather is called estivation (ˌes-tə-ˈvā-shən).

Two species of kangaroo mice, the pale and the dark, live in the Great Basin desert. Their short-haired tails are often a full inch longer than their 3-inch bodies. They have fur-lined outside cheek pouches as the pocket mice do. Their coats are without spines or outstanding patterns. Fine sandy soil in sagebrush and rabbit brush offers them shelter. Each warm night they hunt for seeds and insects, bouncing along in short hops.

Kangaroo rats are attractive fellows.

Most of them have white- and black-marked faces and a white band beginning at the nose, crossing the sides and thighs, and running onto the tail along its entire length. Sixteen species of these handsome mammals inhabit the American deserts.

Pocket mice and kangaroo mice weigh less than an ounce, but the largest kangaroo rat may weigh 6 ounces. Although kangaroo rats live alone except when a mother is nursing her young, a single mound may protect a collection of burrows. When feeding, the rodents drop down on all fours and hobble about gathering seeds into their cheek pouches so quickly that there is a steady clicking sound. The seeds are pushed out with paws or blown into the underground storeroom.

If a badger digs into the nest, the mother will gather the pink young into her forepaws and bound, 2 feet at a

½ inch

A kangaroo mouse in Black Rock Desert, Nevada, hopped along on its toes in sand. It left this track.

In low places where water seeps down from mountainsides and high snow fields, mammals, reptiles, and birds gather each evening. All are thirsty. But if a band of collared peccaries ('pek-ə-rēz) trots up to the spring, other visitors fall back. Peccaries are hoofed mammals without the ruminant stomach possessed by grass

The ord kangaroo rat may have either four of five toes on its hind feet. White adorns the feet, the belly, the thigh stripes and the sides of the plumed tail. Its coat is a pale, reddish-brown. Head and body, 4 inches; tail, 5 to 6 inches; weight, 2 ounces.

time, to safety. Kicking sand into the face of an enemy that draws too near is a favorite defense. Dens are often dug 20 or more inches below the surface.

By flicking its tail like a whip the kangaroo rat changes direction in midair.

The collared peccary ('pek-ə-rē), or javelina (ˌhä-və-'lē-nə), is mostly a Central or South American animal; but it does range north into the United States. Long coarse grizzled hair covers its piglike body, and there is a collar of light hair across the shoulders. Head and body, 34 to 36 inches; height, 20 to 24 inches; weight, 40 to 50 pounds.

The collared peccary ('pek-ə-rē), or javelina (ˌhä-və-'lē-nə), roots and roams in Arizona, New Mexico, and Texas and south through Mexico into Central and South America. It lives up to altitudes of 8,000 feet.

and lichen eaters.

Because of two very long sharp teeth like javelins ('jav-ə-lənz) in each jaw, these bristle-haired creatures are called javelinas (ˌhä-və-'lē-nəs). A javelin is a light spear used in hunting.

Javelinas travel in herds, digging with their noses for the roots, bulbs, and insects that are their food. Fruits, eggs, arachnids, and reptiles are in their diet as well. Javelinas do not hesitate to attack rattlesnakes and, if bitten, are not harmed by the venom. They have nothing to fear from coyotes, bobcats, or dogs, for the group fights unitedly to defend its members. These fast piglike mammals are agile, and readily leap 6 feet or more when startled.

Peace-loving and gentle, peccaries do not attack unless cornered or wounded. They shed scent from a musk gland on the back and probably use this method of keeping together because their eyesight is poor.

By day each one shelters from the sun in underground burrows or hollow logs. By night or in cool weather the band travels about looking for food.

Peccaries squeal, grunt, or bark. When angry they chatter their teeth together.

The usual litter is two or three reddish young, each having a dark stripe down the back.

If you want to know God's desert at its best, wander out after soaking rains have fallen. Sit still near a water hole at dusk and you will see the dryland creatures come to drink. Some small rodents that we know can be found hopping quietly about in the moonlight, picking up seeds.

Class Project

Whether or not you live on a desert there is probably a watering hole nearby where the wild mammals of the neighborhood come to drink. What signs do you find? Identify tracks if you can.

Better yet, wait motionless with a strong flashlight trained on the spot during the early part of the evening. When you hear movement turn on the light as quietly as possible.

Put out cereal grains, nut meats, or hamburger bits as bait. Keep a record of the mammals you see.

Questions

In questions 1 through 6 write the name of the animal being described, choosing from the following list: kangaroo mouse, pocket mouse, spiny pocket mouse, jumping mouse, kangaroo rat.

1. The —— lives in damp places, has soft fur, and hops 6 to 12 feet at a time.

2. The —— has no outside cheek pockets, no spines on the back, and no tuft on the tail.

3. The —— has outside cheek pockets, spines on the back, and usually a tuft on the tail. It hops a few inches at a time.

4. The —— has outside cheek pockets, soft fur, and a tail swollen in the middle. The tail is smaller at the base and tip than it is along its main length. Short hops of a few inches carry it about.

5. The —— has outside cheek pockets, soft handsomely patterned fur, and a tuft on the tail. It bounds 2 feet in a single hop.

6. The —— has outside cheek pockets and soft fur. It hops a few inches at a time.

7. The peccary, or javelina, is (deerlike, ratlike, skunklike, piglike, catlike, doglike, rabbitlike).

8. The peccary, or javelina, travels (alone, in family groups, in herds).

9. In summertime most desert mammals are above ground during (the day, the night).

10. In cool weather (more, fewer) mammals are above ground at midday than are abroad at the same time in summer.

11. In which of these ways do desert mammals avoid becoming too warm (choose three)?
    (a) remain in their burrows during the day
    (b) submerge themselves in deep cool pools of water
    (c) seek the shade of forests
    (d) seek shade in canyons, caves, and behind high rocks
    (e) become dormant in their burrows

1½ inches

1½ inches

"O Lord, . . . I will shew forth all thy marvellous works." Psalm 9:1

184

23. On the Barren Ground and in Polar Seas

Mysterious and isolated are the wide lands of the Arctic. Only those who live there know her secrets and understand her ways. The clean air is free of dust, smoke, noise, and germs. The bright sunshine and the abundant life of the ocean and the bird cliffs are very pleasant in the summer.

Winter nights flash their brilliant stars. Brighter still flicker the colored bands of northern lights.

What plants are found in the Arctic? Lichens, grasses, mosses, and other low plants prevail. Red mountain cranberries, blue bilberries, black crowberries and yellow cloudberries are food for people and animals. In some places the ground is covered with low scrubby plants and there are thickets of dwarf birches, dwarf pines, and dwarf willows.

What mammals live in the Arctic? The North American mammals have been divided by scientists into thirteen orders. God has created nine of these groups with one or more species that are naturally at home there.

The Steller's sea cow, in the same order as the manatee, lived in the Bering Sea until 1768. Men from Russia discovered the large gentle animals when they were on a voyage. There were no laws to protect wild mammals then, and in 27 years the last one was killed. No other species of this order is found in cold climates now.

Four other orders—represented in North America by the opossum, the armadillo, the horse, and the monkey (in southern Mexico)—do not have any members living in the far North. The remaining eight orders do very well in the Arctic. Meat eaters and rodents have the largest numbers of species, whales and seals next, the hoofed mammals fifth in number, down to the mammals with extra teeth (the hares),

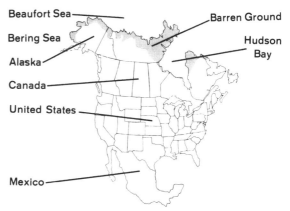

North of the timber or forest line, cold summers and permanently frozen ground prevent trees from growing large. This map shows the area bordering the Arctic on the south. Here snow blasts, and hard winds driving over frozen seas limit the vegetation to low stunted growth.

This buffy-gray mammal with the black-striped spine wears long fur that almost conceals its ears and tail. This species, the Greenland collared lemming, and the Hudson Bay collared lemming are the only rodents with fur that turns white in winter. Cold weather also brings double claws to the two middle toes of the front feet. Head and body, 4½ to 5 inches; tail, less than 1 inch; weight, 1 to 2 ounces.

the insect eaters (the shrews), and the flying mammals, the bats.

The hoary bat and the red bat gobble insects north and west of the Hudson Bay. Then before cold sets in they migrate. Various seals and whales swim south, avoiding ice-covered waters. Grizzly and black bears, and cub-bearing polar bears den up before February or earlier. River otters and muskrats seek the shelter of burrows and lodges. But other mammals keep going all winter. From the 3-pound snowshoe hare to the 900-pound musk ox God's creatures are well equipped with fat and fur to travel, hunt, and sleep at below-zero temperatures.

Snow is a poor conductor of heat. The smallest mammals weighing from $\frac{1}{10}$ ounce up to $\frac{1}{4}$ pound each—such as the shrews, weasels, lemmings, and voles—remain beneath its protecting crust all winter.

When soil freezes and snow appears the collared lemmings come up above ground to build their tiny round homes of sticks and straw. Inside the 8-inch nests are warm linings of musk ox wool, bird down, or caribou fur. The temperature of the nest may be as high as 50 degrees while above the 5- to 6-foot snow cover a subzero wind howls.

The brown lemming and four species of voles, including the common meadow vole, live in rodent cities of their own.

Small meat-eating mammals are below snow cover as well. The Arctic and masked shrews are hunting. The least weasel and the shorttail weasel in their coats of snowy plush are as hungry as ever. Minks, foxes, wolves, bears, and wolverines dig out lemmings and voles.

The spotted, bright-eyed Arctic ground squirrel cannot dig as deeply as its relatives in unfrozen ground. Whole colonies live together in several levels of tunnels down to 3 feet 8 inches below the surface. Burrows extend as far as 70 feet. Nests are lined with dry grass, their own fur, small bits of lichens,

This gray Arctic ground squirrel is touched with red on the top of its head. Its back is thickly flecked with light spots. The hoary marmot and the Arctic ground squirrel are the only mammals in the far North that hibernate. Head and body, 8 to 13 inches; tail, 3 to 6 inches; weight, 1 to 2½ pounds.

green leaves, and the fur of the caribou. An Arctic ground squirrel may carry in as much as 4 pounds of vegetable food from low plants and roots to eat when awaking from hibernation.

Born in June, the young have a very short time to prepare for their first hibernation that will last for 7 months. God has made them able to reach a nearly adult size in only 6 weeks. By 4 months they are as large as their parents and fat enough to hibernate until the next April.

Hoary marmots live on open grassy hillsides near loose rocky slopes in Alaska. Their shrill alarm whistles alert the ground squirrels to dive for cover. Hoary marmots themselves hibernate through the long winters.

The Arctic fox also lives on these open grassy hillsides, digging its den

A ringed seal. This dull yellowish to brownish seal has spots with dark streaks on its back. Pups, born on ice, are woolly white, but soon molt and grow a darker coat. Head and body, 4½ feet long; weight, up to 200 pounds.

The Arctic fox has short round ears and thick deep fur. In summer it is brownish or bluish with yellowish-white underparts. In winter its fur may become snowy white all over. Others of the same species may grow slate-blue coats, sometimes with touches of brown. Head and body, 20 inches; tail, 11 inches; weight, 7 to 15 pounds.

above the frozen layer of soil. This lovely creature with the soft puffy fur is the scavenger of polar lands. Whales, fishes, and seals that are washed up on the shores are eaten by the fox. In the summer it stays by the bird cliffs, eating eggs and nestlings that fall and catching adult birds as well. Excess birds are stored in piles among the rocks to be visited if food is scarce in winter. In the fall the fox enjoys the abundant berry harvest. Later it follows the polar bear on seal-catching expeditions, waiting until the bear has feasted, and relishing the pieces left by the king of the ice.

Lemmings are a main food of the fox, and its usual litters of five or six may increase to fourteen during years when lemmings are overrunning the country in large numbers.

Just as lemmings and voles provide food for many other mammals, so the ringed seal is the important item of diet for polar bears and man during the long winter. The ringed seal is a hair seal with hair-covered flippers. It eats shrimp and other marine animals. A ringed seal may keep a blowhole open all winter even though the ice becomes 10 feet thick. Then it must come up through a tunnel twice as long as its own body to scratch with toenails and bite with sharp teeth to keep the ice broken away from an inch-wide hole.

The ringed seals do not gather in herds as the walrus does. The female digs a cave under the snow on the ice. This shuts in her body heat and there out of sight of bears the single young is born in March.

The narwhal, a mottled gray creature with a white belly, may grow to a length of 12 feet. Males have one tooth on the left that comes out of the mouth and extends in a twisted tusk that may be 9 feet long. Early explorers brought back these ivory spirals, claiming that they had come from the forehead of the unicorn. They were sold for handsome prices.

This white-bellied, mottled, gray, toothed whale does not venture from the Arctic. The adult male has a long spirally twisted tusk on the left, and some individuals grow a shorter one on the right. Here a narwhale drifts through clear icy water. Length, up to 12 feet; length of tusk, up to 9 feet.

The white whales, or belugas, are close relatives of the narwhals. They have no back fins or grooves on the throat. Pure white, like various other arctic residents, this toothed whale ventures up the mouths of rivers, into Hudson Bay, and along the North Atlantic coast. Length, up to 14 feet.

The narwhal is used for meat and its sinews make thread or harness for Eskimo dogs. Narwhals scratch the bottom of the sea to bring up their favorite food, the halibut. The tip of the hollow tusk is always worn from working in the mud.

The white whale, a relative of the narwhal, also called beluga (bə-ˈlü-gə), lives only in cold waters. It has a blunt nose, no fin on the back, and no grooves on the throat. White whales travel in schools eating cod, catfish, halibut, and other fishes. Occasionally they are heard whistling. White whales have some unknown method of communication. If hunters molest one animal the entire herd will flee, even those around behind an island.

Part of the white whale population remains in the Arctic all year as do individual narwhals.

The bowhead, a white-chinned black whale is most closely related to the right whale. The head is very large and the 300 to 600 black baleen plates may be 14 feet long. The bowhead stays close to the edge of the ice. Length, up to 65 feet.

The bowhead is one of the whalebone whales related to the right whales. It has a very long head, about one-third of its length. As many as 360 black 12-foot baleen plates hang from each side of the upper jaw. Sometimes certain layers of the ocean seem to be all krill, a gelatinous mass that lies thick in the water. The bowhead whale opens its mouth and swims ahead. The sea water drains away through the baleen, leaving many pounds of krill to be swallowed. The bowhead whale is never far from the drifting ice of the polar seas. Like the right whale it has been hunted until it faces extinction.

The musk ox appears to be wrapped in shawls. It has a compact body, very short tail, stout legs, and thick broad neck. Its face is rounded and its ears are almost hidden in fur. Its underfur is silky soft, extremely thick and woolly. It grows strands up to 20 inches long of heavy outer hair. This long hair has been used for mosquito nets.

Musk oxen eat willow twigs, grasses, mosses, and sedges. Through the $4\frac{1}{2}$-month-long winter night they dig down through snow, if necessary, to graze. God has made them well able to endure the temperatures of 50 degrees below zero that last 10 weeks each winter. Sometimes the temperature drops to 70 degrees below zero. Snowstorms are frequent. But musk oxen do not seem to mind.

The musk glands of this creature are found on the face under the eyes. The musk is rubbed out by the front legs, spreading its odor on the air.

Musk oxen travel in herds of eight to one hundred animals. In blizzards they huddle together and keep each other warm. When wolves attack they find themselves facing a circle of horns. The larger animals surround the younger and face the enemy side by side.

These long-skirted mammals were

This unusual-looking arctic mammal with long, silky, brown hair is the musk ox. The musk ox is a creature that God has prepared to withstand frigid blasts in winter and hordes of mosquitoes in summer. All adults have horns. Height, 3 to 5 feet; weight, 500 to 900 pounds.

in danger of extinction until laws were passed to protect them. Several herds have been introduced into Alaska, the north of Norway, and Siberia, places where they were killed in years gone by. Lately some have been domesticated in the Green Mountains of Vermont. The unusually fine warm wool sells well. About 6 pounds can be harvested at one time.

In some arctic areas both caribou and musk oxen are found. Neither species pays attention to the other. The reindeer is a caribou introduced from Siberia.

Toothed whales eat fishes; baleen whales eat krill and plankton. Walruses flourish on clams, and seals gobble shrimp and other marine animals. Wolves depend on caribou, and foxes upon lemmings. Polar bears feast on ringed and other seals. The lynx follows the snowshoe hare. On the Barren Ground as well as everywhere else, God has designed mammals and plants to benefit each other.

Class Project

List the mammals of your state or province that also live in the Arctic. Use the map of the Arctic accompanying this lesson and the area maps in a field guide. A state or province mammal check list would be helpful.

If you live in a coastal state, include the whales, porpoises, dolphins, and otters swimming along your shores that summer in the Polar Regions or are found there all year around.

In what way might a mammal living in your community differ from another individual of the same species living in the far North?

Questions

1. Various species of mammals live and breed in the Arctic that do not spend the winter there. What species of mammals move out of the Arctic during the dark cold months (choose three)?
shrews, bats, hares, lemmings, some seals, some whales, foxes and wolves, musk oxen

2. A very few species of arctic mammals spend the winter in hibernation (choose two).

Arctic shrew, tundra hare, hoary marmot, lynx, least weasel, moose, Arctic ground squirrel, meadow vole

3. Some mammals go into dens and sleep for weeks or months at a time, living on their fat as hibernating animals do (choose three).
dusky shrew, snowshoe hare, black bear, Barren Ground caribou, muskrat, female polar bear expecting the birth of cubs, Greenland collared lemming, grizzly bear, bowhead whale

4. Write the name of the mammal with the letter of the food that it eats.

bowhead whale
Arctic fox
narwhal and white whale
collared lemming and Arctic ground
    squirrel
musk ox
ringed seal

(a) willow twigs, mosses, sedges
(b) shrimp and other marine animals
(c) plankton and krill
(d) birds, berries, lemmings, carrion
(e) fish
(f) low plants and roots

5. I am an arctic mammal. I keep my brown fur all year around. It would take five to ten of us to weigh an ounce. Of course I never come up into the freezing arctic air during the winter. I stay far below under the deep snow, eating any animal food I can find. I belong to the ―――― family.

6. I am an arctic mammal. I am brown in summer and white in winter. I eat twigs, bark, and buds. In summer we eat tender leaves. Wolves, foxes, lynxes, and owls chase us. Sometimes we dig through the snow cover to reach our food. Some of us weigh only 2 pounds, but others of our relatives may reach 6 to 12 pounds. Sometimes we let the snow blow over us to protect us from blizzards. I am one of the ――――.

7. I am an arctic mammal. My fur is always faintly spotted brown. I am a meat eater and I hunt hares all winter. Lemmings are good eating and so are birds. I always travel alone. I usually weigh 20 or 25 pounds. I am the ――――.

8. I am an arctic mammal. I live on grassy hillsides near loose rocky slopes. I am in the same family as the woodchuck and the prairie dog, but weighing up to 20 pounds I am much larger than they are. I am sometimes called Whistler because when I see an enemy coming I sound a shrill whistle that causes every relative in sight, including the Arctic ground squirrel, to dive for shelter. I am the ――――.

9. I am an arctic mammal. My fur is brick red tipped with white. It would take two of us to weigh an ounce. We fly about taking in mosquitoes, gnats, and other delicious creatures. We like to roost in trees. When autumn comes we fly south. I am the ――――.

"Blessed be the Lord God, . . . who only doeth wondrous things." Psalm 72:18

3. Sponges, Mollusks, Sea Worms, and Sea Jellies

Sea Creatures

Pearl and silk and jelly fair,
Mollusk's shine and polyp's hair,
    Sponge's still slow straining way,
    In God's thought Creation day.

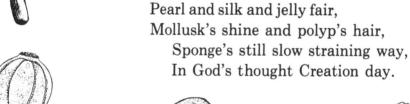

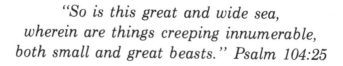

"So is this great and wide sea,
wherein are things creeping innumerable,
both small and great beasts." Psalm 104:25

24. Mollusks, the Soft-bodied Ones and Sponges, the Pore-bearers

God has created many water animals that do not swim. Some cling to rocks or sand. Others crawl slowly and additional species float.

Among the many animals of the sea are the shells. Most of these creatures belong to a group called the mollusks ('mäl-əsks). *Mollusk* means "soft bodied." Nearly 100,000 species are known. This group is second in number only to the insects. Some of them live in deserts; others prefer damp spots on land. Many are found in freshwater. But most mollusks inhabit salt water.

The shells that protect them may be divided. Each piece is called a valve. Animals like clams or oysters are called bivalves, because they have shells of two parts. A snail is a univalve ('yü-ni-ˌvalv). Its shell has only one part.

Mollusks are divided into five classes: the chitons ('kī-tənz), the bivalves, the tooth shells, the univalves (snails), and a fifth class that includes the octopuses and the squids. Octopuses and squids are not enclosed in a shell as the others are.

Mollusks, except squids and octopuses, have a mantle, a fold of skin that covers most of their body. Numerous small glands lie along the edge of the mantle, oozing a material that hardens into one or more valves.

From the eggs of many mollusks breaks a tiny bit of life called a larva. If the eggs hatch in seas, lakes, or rivers, the larvae are part of the plankton that drifts around in the waves. The mantle of the small one soon forms a tiny thin valve from minerals taken out of the water. If the larva is a bivalve it has two mantles, one on the right and one on the left. Each of the mantles forms a valve, and the two are joined by a hinge even when the animal is still very, very tiny. In addition to the mantle and the valve that comes from it, mollusks have a mass of soft inside organs. The heart, the reproductive and digestive organs, and the nerves are in this tender mass.

The third body part is a large fleshy foot. The mollusk glides along by stretching the forepart of its foot ahead, then pulling up the body. The gills (except in land snails) lie between the mantle and the other organs. As water is drawn through, the gills absorb oxygen and food is trapped. Land snails use lungs for breathing.

Many animals, as well as people, enjoy the good-tasting meat of these sea creatures. A sea star wraps its arms about an oyster and pulls hard for a long time. At last the oyster becomes tired, opens its hinge, and is eaten. Big crabs crack the shells in their strong pinchers. Out from shore sharks and other monstrous fishes swallow them whole in large numbers.

Sometimes a low tide strands a mollusk on the beach. A gull finding it carries it high into the air and drops it on a rock below. If the shell does not break the first time, the gull drops it until it does break. The delicious meat is quickly gobbled.

The chitons are sometimes called sea cradles because they can curl into a cradle-shaped form. Up to 3 inches long, they have eight overlapping platelike valves bordered by short spines along the sides and in front. Chitons crawl around at the water's edge, licking algae from the wet rocks and holding tightly with their big sucker feet. People of the West Indies call them "sea beef." They pry them up with knives and cook them.

In another mollusk class are found the tooth or tusk shells. These look like small elephant tusks. Little inch-long tooth shells are like thick curved needles. Big ones may be 5 inches long and rather heavy. They live in shallow or deep water usually on sandy bottoms. Both ends of the shell are open. The foot and mouth are on the larger end. The foot digs in mud or sand, searching for small food animals.

The most common tooth shell of the Atlantic coast is 2 inches long and is found from North Carolina to the Arctic Ocean. Along the Pacific coast north of California live shiny white tooth shells

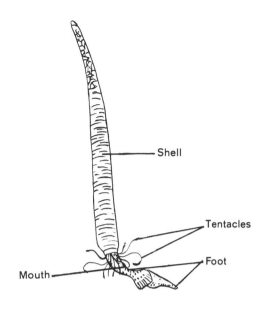

Tooth or tusk shells grow up to 5 inches long. This common tooth shell is 2 inches long and ivory white in color. It lives on the shores of the Arctic Ocean and in the northern Atlantic on both the American and the European sides. It digs for small food particles in sand and mud.

little more than an inch long. Indians in the past made necklaces of them and used them for money.

Octopuses and squids belong to another mollusk class. These creatures have sacklike bodies. Octopuses have no shells. Squids have a straight shell enclosed in their flesh. Both are fast swimmers. Their eyes are similar to human eyes and they have very good vision. A large brain lies between their eyes. A strong hooked beak juts from the center of the animal, around which the arms cluster and hold food to be eaten.

These creatures also carry an ink sac containing a thick dark-brown liquid. Only a few drops color a large amount of water. When squids and octopuses want to escape enemies they shoot out jets of ink that spread like smoke. After the cloud scatters, the mollusk is nowhere to be seen.

Octopuses and squids have spots of different hues on their skins. These areas can stretch or shrink. The animal may reduce all the cells around the brown places so that only the brown shows. In a change to purple all the

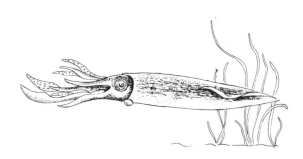

The common squids that live on our eastern shores may reach 8 inches. Both deep and shallow waters are their home. The squid has a total of ten arms, no two pairs exactly the same length. Eight of them have suckers in two rows. The two longest arms have four short rows of suckers on their club-shaped ends. This swift creature is steel gray with reddish spots.

The little octopuses that live in deep water off the Atlantic coast are about 3 inches long. Notice the suckers on the arms.

colors diminish but purple. When the mollusk is angry its skin flushes darkly. A frightened squid turns pale. Often many different tints show at once as the spots open and close quickly.

After the eggs are laid the female octopus watches over them until they hatch. Even though months pass, she

will not leave them to find food. Unless animals she can eat come within reach she may die guarding her eggs.

Squids and octopuses squirt jets of water from their bodies with such force that they shoot backward almost faster than the eye can follow. Arms and beaked mouth trail behind. Often they leave the sea and travel through the air,

This cuttlefish is an inhabitant of the Mediterranean Sea. Its central bone is fed to canaries. The common cuttlefish has a body length of 15 inches and tentacles that extend 20 inches more. The margins of the mantle form two long narrow fins. India ink is obtained from its ink sac.

196

even landing on the decks of ships.

Sepia, or cuttlefish, is a 3-foot squid living in the Mediterranean Sea. The ink sacs of this creature are used to make India ink. The central shell is fed to canaries and is called cuttlebone.

are quite different from mollusks. Countless tiny openings pierce their body walls. Three thousand species live in arctic and tropic seas, and in freshwater. Altogether some five thousand species are known to live in

Giant squids are the biggest of the mollusks. They sometimes have bodies 10 feet long and arms 50 feet long. Sperm whales like to eat giant squids. Naturally they fight to save their lives, sometimes leaving large scars on the whales with their wide suckers. Usually they are eaten. Butchered whales are often found to be carrying squid fragments in their stomachs.

Another very common marine animal group is the sponge tribe. Sponges

Earth's waters.

A sponge is either a single animal or a colony of animals. A young sponge may begin as a bud on the parent. The bud develops until it is able to live alone. Dropping to the ocean floor it holds fast and continues to feed and grow. Another way that sponges multiply is by means of reproductive cells

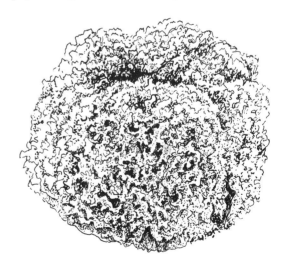

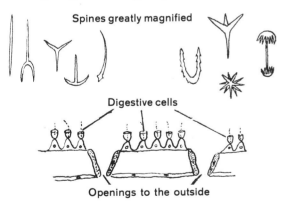

Many of the inside channels of a sponge are lined with these digestive cells. See the threads that draw water in through the pores. A microscope would be necessary to see these spines of a sponge's skeleton.

This bath sponge is the elastic skeleton of a sea animal. Unlike most sponges, the species of this family have no needlelike inside spines. Drying leaves a soft flexible shape, very pleasant to touch.

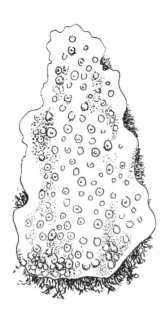

This bright-yellow sulphur sponge lives in shallow water from Cape Hatteras northward, being especially abundant along the New England coast. It measures up to 8 inches in diameter with tiny knobs. Sponges in this family apparently produce sulphuric acid that absorbs the shells and limestone fragments where the animals grow.

The glove sponge. This straw-yellow sponge is common along the northern Atlantic coast of the United States, Nova Scotia, and England. It grows a foot or more in height.

that combine and form larvae. These larvae swim rapidly, pulling themselves along by threads that whip about. The young pore-bearer soon descends to the lower layer of its shallow-water home and attaches itself. From then on its hardly visible motion is a slow swelling and shrinking as food-ladened currents enter through hosts of tiny mouths and are expelled through a larger vent.

Some sponges can be strained through a piece of cheesecloth and separated into multitudes of individual cells. If these cells are left together they will reunite and continue life as before.

The sponges of most families have elastic skeletons supported by masses of

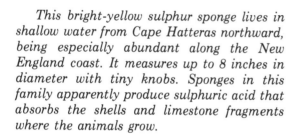

This fresh-water sponge is growing on a stick. Like salt-water sponges it is filled with tiny pores where water currents are drawn in to supply food to the patient animal.

In times of cold or drought, sponges die and fall apart. However, small cells with a resistant covering survive. Here winter cells from a fresh-water sponge wait for the warmth of spring. Then a new colony will begin to grow.

transparent spines. Each spine may be only $\frac{1}{25}$ inch in length or even smaller. The beautiful glass sponges of the tropics lack the horny tissues of their relatives and display shining frames of delicate interlocking needles.

Fresh-water sponges grow only in clean water. Often found on pipes at reservoirs or on water-soaked logs, they respond to sunlight by showing a pale-green color. In shaded places they will be yellowish or white. In July and August they are at the height of growth. By November, winter buds are present, the only parts of these little animals that live during cold weather.

Perhaps if you search carefully in clean clear water, you may find some tiny sponges quietly straining food from the current.

Sponges and mollusks have a charm all their own. A sharp-eyed observer will find them on ocean or fresh-water borders.

Class Project

Visit someone who has a collection of seashells and sponges. Point out the different classes of mollusks: the chitons, tooth shells, bivalves, and snails. Notice the varied shapes of the sponges and their many pores. What colors do you see?

Questions

1. What does the word *mollusk* mean?

2. Mollusks except octopuses and squids have three main body parts. They are (a holdfast by which the creature attaches itself permanently in one spot; a mass of soft inside organs; fins for swimming; a mantle or mantles, each with the valve it forms; a large fleshy foot; meat that no animal likes to eat [choose three]).

Match the sentence beginnings with the proper endings (a–d) below.

3. Most mollusks live ———.

4. Many mollusks live ———.

5. Some mollusks live ——— and
———.
   (a) in damp places
   (b) in salt water
   (c) in freshwater
   (d) in the desert

6. Mollusks are (very numerous—next to insects in numbers of species; fairly common—about one thousand species; rather rare—only a few dozen species).

7. A chiton has (one valve, two valves, three valves, four valves, eight overlapping valves [choose one]).

8. The tooth shells resemble (elephant

tusks, church steeples, straight-sided rods).

9. Squids and octopuses defend themselves by (squeezing enemies to death, lashing enemies with long arms, clouding water with ink and swimming away).

10. Which of the following enjoy eating the flesh of mollusks (choose four)? tigers, gulls, big fishes, bears, wolves, crabs, sea stars

11. Which of the following are true of octopuses and squids? (choose five)?
fast moving, slow moving, dim eyes that tell only light from dark, excellent vision from eyes much like human eyes, large shell covering outside, arms with one or two rows of suckers, smooth weak arms, swim forward with fins, swim backward with tail, swim backward by squirting water forward, never change color, can change color very quickly

12. Sponges are called pore-bearers because (their bodies are covered with many pores, water pours into the creature as it swims along, the solid body has a large pore in the center somewhat like a doughnut with its hole).

13. Sponges (never move, only swim around when they are young, only swim when they are adults, are continually floating about).

14. Sponges feed by (straining food particles from the water in which they live, enclosing fishes and other small sea creatures that swim too near, cleaning rocks and shells of algae that grow on them).

15. An outstanding characteristic of one sponge group is (ability to live in very deep water; long thin arms that trap food and draw it into their mouths; lack of horny parts and a display of delicate, shiny, glass-like skeletons).

"Sing unto him . . . : talk ye of all his wondrous works." Psalm 105:2

200

25. A Look at the Bivalves, the Ringed Worms, and the Comb Jellies

Most bivalves belong to the class of mollusks named for their hatchet-shaped foot. The two valves open and a hatchet-shaped foot slips out. The animal glides forward or digs down into the mud. At the hinge point is a thick hump called the beak.

Bivalves have no mouths or heads. On the back edge of the body are two openings called siphons. The lower siphon pulls in water and passes it over the gills. The gills strain out food and absorb oxygen. The water is then ejected through the upper siphon. Perhaps 3 quarts of water are filtered each hour by a medium-sized clam.

Some creatures in the hatchet-foot group spin a clump of strong threads. Fastening these to rocks they are secure against wave action. If they want to move, they cut the threads on one side and add new ones on the other.

The oyster is the bivalve most commonly eaten in this country. Naturally very plentiful along the Atlantic coast, it has been planted in the sea waters of California. Oysters of market size are from 3 to 6 inches long. Oysters to sell are raised in especially tended beds.

A full-grown female oyster may lay as many as 60 million eggs each year. Many of these wash out to sea. Crabs, fishes, and sea creatures of different kinds eagerly swallow them. Those that escape hatch into little top-shaped larvae. They attach themselves to one spot by cementing their left valves to solid objects. The right valve remains free and opens to admit oxygen and food.

An oyster that is not eaten may live for 10 years or more. It grows about an inch a year until it is 10 inches long.

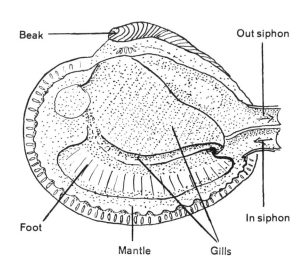

This clam is facing left. The left valve has been removed and the inner organs are visible.

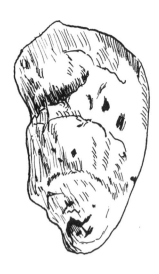

Oysters are a favorite food in this country. They are sold far inland as well as along the coasts where they live. Notice the heavy rough gray valves that grow up to 10 inches when undisturbed.

After this the shell increases in thickness and strength, but not in size. Oysters have rough, heavy, gray valves. An oyster lies on its left side and this valve is larger and more curved than the right.

Pearl oysters live in warm seas. Beautiful satiny material lines their valves. Buttons, knife handles, and other objects are cut from these shiny layers. If a grain of sand enters and lodges, it is slowly coated by the mantle. The covered speck becomes a pearl.

Pearl oysters are brought up by divers. For every good pearl found, about one thousand oysters are opened. A man from Japan learned how to catch an oyster and drop a tiny object into the mantle. These oysters were kept in a safe place for several years until the pearls had formed. Now pearls are much more plentiful than before.

Another hatchet-foot, or bivalve, is the clam. During the summer months when oysters are laying eggs and are not taken for food, the clams are harvested. The hard-shelled clam, or quahog ('kō-ˌhȯg), is the one caught and eaten most often. The quahog shell is white within. Purple borders the lower margin and deep violet blotches show where the clam's muscles pull the valves shut. Outside, the shell is a dull, grayish white. As the mantles add material to the valves, lines of growth etch both left and right surfaces.

Wampum was made by cutting flat round pieces from whelk shells and purple or blue ones from quahog valves. These were rubbed until the edges were gone and a smooth round bead was left. Strung on strips of buckskin they were called wampum and used for money by

Next to oysters, clams are the most popular food bivalve in North America. Here a clam glides along on its hatchet foot. Notice the siphons extended behind and the many fine lines of growth on its shell. This quahog may grow to a length of 6 inches. When young and tender it is called the cherrystone clam.

the North American Indians.

The largest clams are the giant clams of the Indian and the Pacific oceans. They may be 5 feet long and weigh 500 pounds. In sandy, fresh-water streams live tiny clams less than $\frac{1}{2}$ inch long.

Mussels are the most plentiful of the

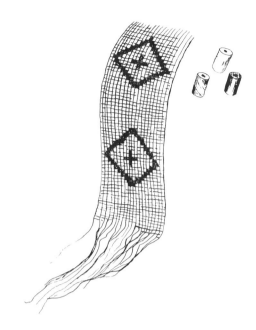

A wampum belt and beads. These beads are made from clam shells and are $\frac{1}{4}$ inch long. Purple and white are the main colors. Wampum was used for money by the North American Indians.

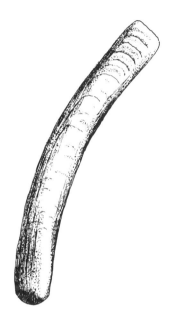

A razor clam. This yellowish or olive-green bivalve is a very speedy swimmer. It is found on sandy bottoms along the borders of nearly all seas. The hinge runs the length of the animal along the straighter edge. Razor clams can burrow into sand quicker than a man can follow with a spade. Length, 6 or 7 inches.

bivalves, living mostly in cool seas around the world. In Europe they are eaten by the ton for food, being cultivated there as oysters are in America. These delicious bivalves are blue with a horny black covering. They hold fast with spun thread to a solid

support instead of digging into mud as clams do.

The scallop is a very active mollusk. It darts about, clapping its valves and gliding swiftly through the water. By turning its siphons it quickly and easily propels itself in different directions. Zigzagging is a good way to escape

Mussels live on all the shores of the various oceans. They are raised for food in Europe and eaten by the ton. Blue-shelled with a horny black covering, they fasten themselves by coarse dark threads to the rocks where they live. They grow to a length of 3 inches.

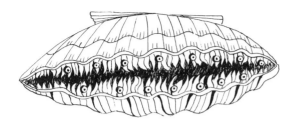

God has given scallops beautiful wavy-edged valves of white, brown, gray, or red that grow up to 3 inches in length. Here a mollusk swims by jet action as squids and cuttlefish do.

enemies. Sometimes the young spin coarse strings to hold on by, but the adults jump about, swimming by jet action as squids, octopuses, and cuttlefish do.

Scallops have beautiful, wavy-edged shells in different shades of gray, white, brown, and red with purplish color near the hinge. There are seventeen to twenty rounded ribs with wide shallow grooves between. Wings stand out on each side of the beak. Like oysters, clams, and mussels, these food animals are dredged out of bays and sold on the markets or canned.

Along the mantle of a scallop shine thirty to forty bright-blue eyes. Scallops, like oysters, lie on one side when at rest. The scallop lies on its right side and the right valve is smaller. Other mollusks live in an erect position on the edges of their twin-sized valves.

The wedge-shaped pen shells glide on a long foot. The foot spins powerful threads to anchor the mollusk. Fine scales project along the growth lines especially on the outer edges. Near the beak the scales may be missing altogether. The prickly pen shell is brown

and grows from 6 to 10 inches long. It has prickles instead of scales on its lower edge. One 6- to 10-inch animal in this family has delicious flesh and is sold on the markets as a large scallop.

In the Mediterranean Sea lives another pen shell, which spins a very fine silk fiber from its foot. Fabric woven of these threads has been sold as "tarentine" or cloth-of-gold. A pair of gloves made of this delicate silk can be fitted into a walnut shell. A shoulder cape will pass through a round ring an inch across.

Gleaming black pearls of great value are also taken from the pen shells.

Bivalves are most important as food. Millions of dollars are spent for clam chowder, oyster stew, scallop and

The giant Mediterranean pen shell. The bivalves of this family prefer warmer water. This species is larger than any other mollusk in the Mediterranean Sea, sometimes growing longer than 27 inches. Standing upright it attaches its many threads to individual grains of sand. Cloth-of-gold is woven from this marine silk. Black pearls of great value are found in its mantle.

mussel dishes that are eaten in many countries. Black pearls, white pearls, and the beautiful cloth-of-gold are other products from the bivalves.

Palolo (pə-'lō-lō) worms in the waters of the western Pacific Ocean also provide human food once a year. These animals are similar to earthworms in at least two ways. Both have segmented bodies with bristles on each segment. Every autumn the small sea creatures multiply their length by six or seven

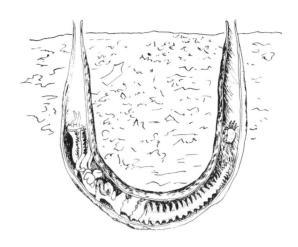

Parchment worms are tube builders that sometimes grow up to 18 inches long. Unless nosed out by a predator able to dig, this one will be safe in its U-shaped burrow. Plankton is its main food. Notice the small crab in the right arm of the burrow.

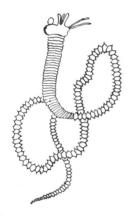

The palolo worm. This segmented worm provides a feast once a year for the peoples of the South Pacific Ocean. See the new tender part that is shed at dawn each year 1 week after the November full moon.

times, adding dozens of new differently shaped rings.

One week after the November full moon just at dawn the young tender parts of the palolo worms are shed. They swim to the surface of the water in countless millions, and men collect them in buckets for the annual feast.

However, most of the six thousand species of segmented worms are not eaten by man. They roam largely unnoticed in the oceans of the world.

The "fire worms" of Bermuda signal each other with greenish lights that can easily be seen on the beach. Each month, a few days after full moon, about an hour past sunset the fireworks begin. The worms circle

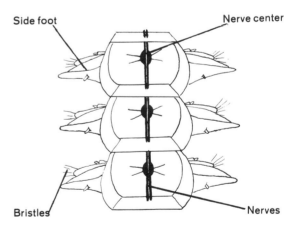

Side foot   Nerve center

Bristles   Nerves

Segmented worms were created by God according to this body plan. Digestive, reproductive, breathing, and sense organs are found in some segments in addition to the basic ones pictured here. Clamworms may have as many as two hundred segments.

and dart toward each other. Schools gather, swimming, blinking, and glowing. Lights flash and melt away.

Various clamworms of United States coastal waters shine dimly, but they do not herd together in large numbers as the "fire worms" do. Most of the time they live in U-shaped burrows formed of a sticky material from glands along their bodies. As this material hardens it picks up grains of sand and a flexible tube is formed. The worm lies concealed, drawing food and oxygen-ladened water into one arm of the tunnel and sending it out through the other. Clamworms may have as many as two hundred segments and commonly grow up to 8 inches or more. The male is a strong steel-blue color with touches of bright green. The female is dull green tinged with orange and red. Both have rainbow colors when the sunlight shines on them. Three species of clamworms are found from Labrador to South Carolina.

The plumed worm is one of the most beautiful of the ringed worms on the Atlantic coast. It may be 1 foot in

A sea gooseberry. This beautiful transparent orange-yellow comb jelly is $\frac{4}{5}$ inch long and $\frac{3}{5}$ inch across. It lives on the borders of all seas from the Arctic to the Antarctic oceans. The tentacles may stretch twenty times the length of the body. They resemble delicate plumes as all the branches grow out along one side.

length and $\frac{1}{2}$ inch in width. Its greenish iridescent body has bright-red plumed gills on the forward third which expand in rhythm as the creature breathes. Five golden tentacles adorn the head. It also builds an underground tube.

Leeches are segmented, too, but they belong to a different class, for they have no bristles. Living in freshwater, salt water, and also on land they usually have two suckers, one to hold by and the other to take in food. They grow up to 3 inches long and eat snails, fish, frogs, and turtles. Humans or warm-blooded mammals wading in streams or ponds may attract leeches and find them hanging fast, sucking blood like a mosquito.

When removing blood from sick people was a preferred treatment,

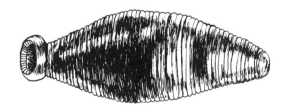

This leech is a segmented worm, related to the clamworms and the earthworms, but without bristles. See the large sucker that anchors the animal while it feeds from the smaller mouth at the other end of the body. It may grow to 4 inches long.

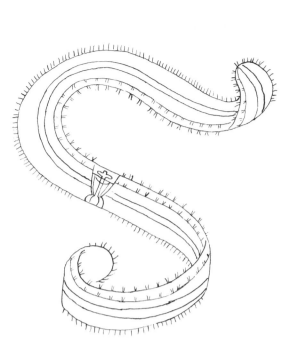

The Venus's-girdle living off the Atlantic coast continually rolls and unrolls as it swims near the surface of the sea. This very pale yellow comb jelly measures 6 inches in length by ⅜ inch in height. The stomach, the sense organ, and other structures are located in the center of the animal. Rainbow colors quiver along the margins of the creature as it loops about beaches and wharves, vibrating its combs.

doctors used leeches to take it painlessly from their patients.

Comb jellies, sometimes called sea gooseberries, are lovely transparent creatures that glide through both deep and shallow waters of various oceans. Ranging in size from less than 1 inch up to 4 inches, the ninety animals of this group are characterized by eight rows of comb plates.

Each comb plate is a clear, narrow strip hinged to the body on one edge and alive with short hairs on the other. The plates run from the balancing organ at the top to the mouth on the lower end. The combs, rippling from top to bottom, propel the small organism mouth first. To back away the animal reverses the motions of the hairs.

Some species have two tentacles that unwind through sheaths midway on the creature's body. Like fishing lines with hooks along their length, these tentacles float out on both sides as the comb jelly swims. Side branches trap plankton on their sticky cells. Occasionally the loaded threads are reeled in and food is wafted to the mouth. Then the lines may be let out again for another meal or else pulled completely inside the body.

Comb jellies without tentacles draw plankton directly into their stomachs.

Class Project

Visit your nearest fish market and see if it has any live oysters, scallops, or clams. Keep them in an aquarium with seawater and watch them for several days.

You may be able to dredge your own specimens from a bay, pond, or river. Fresh-water mollusks should be kept in a fresh-water aquarium.

Eggs enclosed in layers of gelatin float away from the parent. Some of these live to hatch, and the young emerge looking much like tiny adults.

The waters of our oceans are alive with beautiful forms and colors created by our loving heavenly Father. Let us not miss seeing them if we have the opportunity.

Questions

1. Bivalves, except scallops, have a (spade, hatchet, boat)-shaped foot.

2. Bivalves use their siphons by (drawing in food and oxygen-ladened water, spurting water out to propel themselves along, stretching out tentacles through the siphons, expanding their foot, ejecting used water [choose three]).

3. How does a bivalve use its gills?

4. Some bivalves hold fast to rocks during part of their lives. They do this by (growing a holdfast that penetrates the surface and provides an anchor, gluing one valve or the other to the rock, spinning strong threads and fastening them to the rock, using suction as chitons do [choose two]).

5. How are mollusks important to man?

6. How was wampum made?

Match the name of the mollusk with a description of its valves.
7. clam 8. mussel 9. oyster
10. pen 11. scallop
(a) blue; with a horny black covering
(b) gray, white, brown, or red; raised ribs divided by wide grooves
(c) dull grayish white; with many fine growth lines
(d) pink; smooth, bright, and shiny
(e) brown; wedge-shaped, fine scales or prickles projecting from the growth lines
(f) gray; very rough and heavy

12. Name two of the hatchet-foot class that are raised for food.

13. What bivalve good to eat has a wavy-edged shell?

14. What mollusk is eaten in this country during the months when oysters are not taken?

15. The pen shell family yields man three products. They are (ink, black pearls, silk thread, food, knife edges [choose three]).

16. I am a bivalve. I may be (an oyster, a lobster, a fish, a clam, a scallop, a sponge, a mussel, a comb jelly, a sea star, a clamworm [choose four]).

17. I am a bivalve. I have (two, three, four, five, six, seven, eight) valves.

18. I am a bivalve. I gather food in (a beak, a scoop, a saw, a strainer, my

teeth).

19. Man has discovered (six dozen, six hundred, six thousand) species of segmented worms created by God.

20. Name a segmented worm whose various species live in salt water, in freshwater, and in soil.

21. Some marine worms protect themselves by (building a tube to live in, clouding the water with ink to conceal themselves, tangling together in a clump too large to be swallowed, swimming faster than their enemies [choose one]).

22. Comb jellies are (small, $\frac{1}{2}$ to 4 inches across; medium, 6 to 12 inches long; large, more than 1 foot across).

23. The eight combs of a comb jelly (strain plankton from the water, propel the animal along, are used to dig into the sand).

24. (All, Some, No) comb jellies have tentacles.

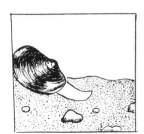

"Dost thou know . . . the wondrous works of him which is perfect in knowledge?" Job 37:16

26. Visiting With the Snails, the Slugs, and the Sea Jellies

Among the most beautiful of the mollusks are the univalves (one valve). Univalves also have a name meaning "stomach-foot," for their stomachs are in their large fleshy feet. Univalves are commonly called snails.

Let us visit first with the knobbed whelk, one of the largest snails along the northern Atlantic coast. This mollusk was also called the knobbed pear conch ('käŋk).

When young these little creatures have two heart chambers, gills, kidneys, a cap-shaped mantle, and a thin shell. As they grow, the shell turns halfway to the right, bringing the front and back ends of the body near each other. The shell continues to mature and turn. The right half becomes more and more crowded. When an adult, the whelk has only the left gill, heart chamber, and kidney. The matching one on the right side is gone. A few snails turn to the left and they lose the organs on the left side.

The whelk, like other univalves, has a head with a mouth and tentacles. The eyes are at the outside base of the tentacles. The tongue, like a very sharp hard file, is drawn back and forth over the food, rubbing off tiny pieces that are easily swallowed.

The upper back part of the foot carries a flat hard disk. When the whelk draws into its shell, this disk fits the

The knobbed whelk is yellowish gray with an interior of orange-red. The younger shells are occasionally streaked with purple. This mollusk lives from Cape Cod to Texas. Sometimes left-handed individuals are found. Length, 4 to 9 inches.

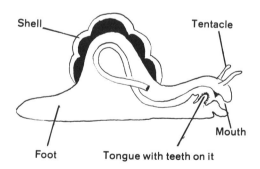

Shell   Tentacle

Foot   Tongue with teeth on it   Mouth

Here is the body plan of a univalve, or stomach-foot. The tongue can be extended through the mouth to file away hard substances, such as the valve of another mollusk that the snail will take for food.

opening like a door. It shuts out enemies.

This large snail feasts on clams and oysters. With its sharp tongue it rubs a round hole in each valve. Then it sucks out the soft body.

Another univalve is the periwinkle. This little mollusk happened to be brought from Europe, probably in egg

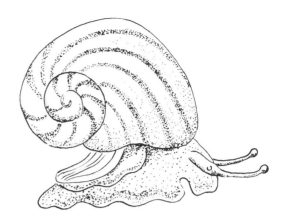

Snails do not depend upon water currents to bring in food. Many of them eat algae and seaweeds. Some are flesh eaters and feed on other mollusks.

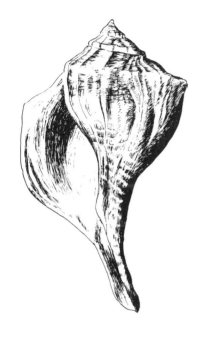

The lightning whelk is naturally left-handed. This fawn-colored animal is decorated with zigzag purplish-brown streaks that suggest lightning. It lives on the Atlantic coast south of Cape Hatteras. Length, up to 10 inches.

form. Its fat little round shell is as wide as it is long. Tons of winkles are sold in European and English markets, for they are very commonly eaten. Others are roasted and peddled from pushcarts on the city streets.

Periwinkles glide on a broad, square foot divided into a right and a left half.

These parts move one at a time like human feet, carrying the little creature forward. Periwinkles eat algae. Longer than their own bodies, their strap-shaped tongues are covered with several hundred rows of sharp teeth that eagerly scrape off the small green plants.

Two families of shells, the cowrie and the olive, employ their mantles differently than most univalves do. The last turn of the shell covers the older smaller turns so that the animal appears to be living in one chamber. The

This fat little periwinkle is only $\frac{1}{4}$ inch across. It is a very popular European food.

211

Watch a fresh-water snail feeding on the side of an aquarium. Use a magnifying glass to see the toothed tongue removing algae.

brightly tinted mantle extends from the opening and spreads on the outside of the shell. Only a thin line shows in the middle of the back where the two edges meet. Color and thickness are added from the outside. Olive and cowrie shells are always very shiny because the mantle protects from scratches and builds up gloss.

"A certain woman named Lydia, a seller of purple, . . . worshipped God . . . [and] attended unto the things which were spoken of Paul. And . . . she was baptized" (Acts 16:14, 15). The Bible writer Luke tells a short story of this godly woman whose home was near the Aegean Sea. On the shores of the Aegean lived many 3-inch, banded murex snails. These mollusks and other related species have a gland from which comes a brown fluid.

Murex shells furnished glorious red

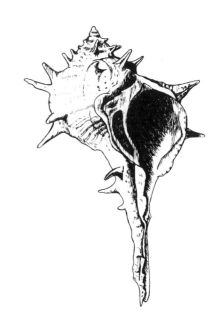

The dye murex shell reaches a length of nearly 3 inches. The island of Cyprus and the coasts and islands of the Aegean Sea are its home. Twelve thousand specimens produce only 1½ grams of the famous Tyrian purple dye. The prophet Ezekiel says in 27:7, 16, 24 about the city of Tyre: "Fine linen with broidered work from Egypt was that which thou spreadest forth to be thy sail; blue and purple from the isles of Elishah was that which covered thee. . . . They occupied in thy fairs with emeralds, purple, and broidered work, and fine linen. . . . These were thy merchants in all sorts of things, in blue clothes, and broidered work, and in chests of rich apparel."

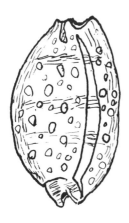

This purplish-brown measled cowrie has a high polish on its shell and round whitish spots. The spire is completely concealed by the last turn of the shell. Cowries were strung together and used for money in the past. The measled cowrie is found on the Atlantic coast from North Carolina south. Length, 3 to 4 inches.

Wentletrap is a Dutch word meaning "spiral staircase." Found along the Atlantic and Mediterranean shores, these graceful shells average about an inch in length.

and purple colors so costly that they were worn only by the kings of old. One such robe was thrown around Jesus by Roman soldiers (John 19:2). Twelve thousand shells yield only 1½ grams of dye.

For many years the dyers of purple kept their process a secret. They soaked the shells in salt water that was afterward boiled and strained to get a pale-green color. Wool dipped in the pale green and dried in the sun turned a muddy purple. Washed in lye the wool became a rich crimson or a beautiful reddish purple. Lydia made her living selling cloth dyed purple by the colors of the murex.

Like whelks the murex feed on bivalves, boring holes in the shells and eating the soft insides. Mollusks of a related family called the purple snails were used by the American Indians for red or purple dye.

Limpets are shaped like a top with a shallow peak. They grow to a length of 1 inch. In the adult form they do not have a twisted body as many other snails do. They live on the edges of the sea between the high tide and low tide mark. Only when water covers them do they leave home base. One species travels about 6 inches; another moves 6 feet. As the tide ebbs they return to the scar they have gouged out. They graze on algae. In one experiment the rock was chiseled between the limpet and its scar while it was absent. It could not find the way home.

More mollusks live in water than on land; but there are hundreds of land mollusks, too. They are found even in deserts. A desert snail is active only

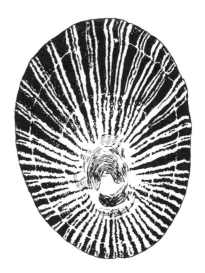

This Pacific coast limpet grows up to 4 inches long. Most limpets like the cooler waters. Some species have no hole at their peak.

when it rains or soon afterward. In dry times it waits quietly in its shell, with a thick film of mucus across the shell opening to keep moisture inside.

Many land mollusks have four tentacles, with eyes on the tips of the largest pair. Sea- and fresh-water univalves may have two or four tentacles. Their eyes are often at the base of their tentacles rather than on the tips.

Some species vary in appearance to match the most lately eaten food. Suppose that after eating only beets for several days you would find red color developing beneath your skin. After a week of spinach you would be green. At the end of 100 pounds of carrots you would be orange.

Stranger yet, the sea slugs do not digest the stinging cells of their prey animals. Instead they cover them with

A Real Visit

Watch a land snail gliding along. Does it leave anything behind? How many tentacles does it have? Do you see its eyes? Notice the pattern and the colors of the foot and the shell. What happens when it moves against something in its path? Give it a slice of apple, a bit of lettuce, a dab of butter, or some celery. What does it eat?

Another Real Visit

Look at a large garden slug. Notice the dark spots on a light background. See the mantle right behind the head. Find the breathing pore at the edge of the mantle. How many tentacles does it have? How many eyes? These creatures have good sight, smell, and hearing. Allow it to creep over a sharp razor blade. Is it injured?

Tiny mollusks without shells, living in salt water, are called sea slugs, a name that hardly fits brightly colored, graceful swimming creatures. Long fingerlike projections on the back are connected with its breathing system. Ocean animals with stinging cells and brilliant hues are its main diet. Often sea slugs glide about over rocks or sand in search of food.

mucus and stow them away in the projections on their backs. Fish tasting sea slugs, quickly learn to avoid the painful stinging cells. For some reason the bowhead whale does not mind and calmly swallows sea slugs in great quantities.

The polyps ('päl-əps) are an interesting group numbering more than nine thousand species. One of their names

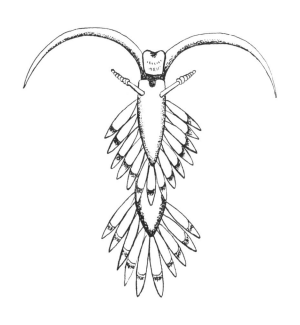

This plumed sea slug may be 4 inches in length when fully grown. It is orange or gray, spotted with green, white, or purple. If the slug eats algae it becomes green.

means "hollow intestine," for these highly colored animals have a tubelike body and a large mouth at one end. The mouth is surrounded with tentacles well supplied with stinging cells that aid the polyp in capturing food animals.

Sponges have a central cavity also and an opening at one end. But their body walls are not solid as are those of the polyps, nor is their large opening a mouth into which water flows. The countless small pores of a sponge are its mouths, and water *leaves* the sponge through the large opening.

Sponges and comb jellies absorb plankton and krill as clams, oysters, and other bivalves do. They have no stinging cells to help in food collecting.

Do you remember the zoospores of the algae that travel about? Each zoospore soon comes to rest, grows a holdfast, and lives the remainder of its days as an algal thread.

God has planned the polyps after a partly similar arrangement.

One class of polyps has species with permanently attached individuals. These always produce free-swimming creatures that move about. The free-swimming ones are not parents to other free-swimmers like themselves, but have young that are stationary. This design is called alternate generations.

A second class of polyps has some species without a stationary generation. Many large sea jellies, often called jellyfish, are in this group.

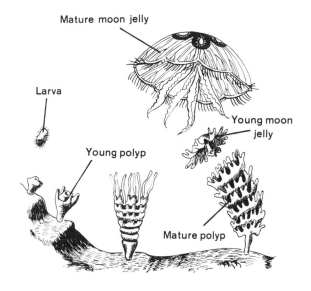

Alternate generations. The moon jelly pinches off from a stationary polyp. After it becomes mature it sheds reproductive cells. These cells combine with others to form larvae that settle to the ocean floor or wall. Gathering food by means of tentacles and stinging cells, the new generation goes on producing other sets of young moon jellies.

If you keep your eyes open you may see this tiny animal only ½ inch long hanging from the water surface, stretching from a water plant or swinging about. It is a hydra, a fresh-water polyp with a transparent body. Very rarely are free-swimming generations found.

A third class, including the corals and the sea anemones (ə-'nem-ə-nēz), has no free-swimming generation.

But every polyp, whether it moves or

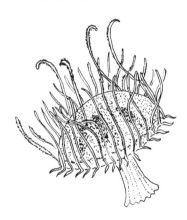

This little fresh-water jelly has been seen in a lake in Ohio, in Benson Creek, Kentucky, and in water lily tanks. The stationary generation of this little ½-inch umbrella is rarely noticed, but the jellies sometimes appear by the million.

not, has a tubelike body, without front or back, right or left, closed at one end and open at the other. Around the mouth are the tentacles armed with stinging cells.

Fresh-water polyps, called hydras, are most often observed as transparent individuals on the undersides of water lily leaves or the leaves of other aquatic plants. When fully contracted they seem to be tiny blobs of jelly about the size of pinheads. When stretched out in

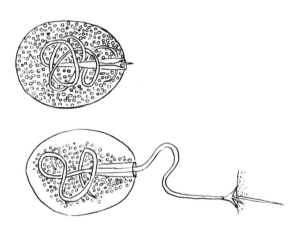

Here is a magnified stinging cell such as the polyps use to capture their food. See the trigger that is set off when the tip of the point is touched. The venom in the sack empties through the tube into the wound made by the spear.

search of food they may be ½ to 1 inch in length. Various species are gray, orange, or brownish. Some contain algal cells that lend a bright-green color.

Occasionally at long intervals little ½-inch umbrellas of at least one species are seen in large numbers in the waters of clean creeks.

Some sea jellies are large enough that contact with them is painful even to humans. Their food-catching cells are active as long as they are moist even after the animal is dead.

Should you be poisoned by a sea jelly, be careful not to rub the burning spot. To do so will trigger additional stingers that have not been set off yet. Alcohol of any kind stuns them. Pour it on quickly. Next best is to use a drying material. Talcum powder, fluffy dust, ashes, or fine sand can be sprinkled on without rubbing. When no dampness remains, pick off the threads.

Use caution with the polyps. Enjoy them without disturbing. Sometime you may meet a soft shining jelly with delicate veins and rainbow colors shimmering through crystal water with tentacles afloat.

Class Project

Visit a forest and look under leaf mold, logs, and rocks for snails. Keep them in a terrarium. See what food they eat. Watch for eggs and notice the young when they hatch.

Look for fresh-water snails on plants and rocks in shallow water less than 6 feet deep. Notice the round hard plate that closes the opening when the animal is inside. Mollusks with lungs do not have this door.

Questions

1. What does the word *univalve* mean?

2. What is a common name for a mollusk that is a univalve?

3. Most univalves (turn to the left, grow in a straight-sided cone, turn to the right).

4. Sea, land, and fresh-water snails eat with (a beak, a tongue with teeth on it, a pinchers, a strainer).

5. Most snails have (eyes, ears, head, arms, tentacles, tongue, teeth, mouth, foot, tail, legs, fur, hair, mantle, shell [choose nine]).

6. What does the knobbed whelk carry on the upper back part of its foot that adds to its safety when it is inside the shell?

7. What is the food of the knobbed whelk?

8. What good-tasting univalve is eaten by the tons in Europe?

9. Why are the shells of olive and cowrie always very bright and shiny?

10. The red and purple colors used in

the tabernacle, the high priest's clothing, Solomon's temple, and kings' clothing came from ———.

11. I am a univalve. I may be (an oyster, a whelk, a crab, a periwinkle, a sea star, a cowrie, a clam, a murex, a land snail, an olive shell, a comb jelly [choose six]).

12. I am a univalve. I am also called (hatchet-foot, head-foot, stomach-foot, spade-foot).

13. I am a sea slug. I am (beautiful, ugly, fast, slow, large—10 inches or more, small—$\frac{1}{2}$ to 5 inches, a mollusk, a sponge, a jelly, a worm [choose four]).

14. Alternation of generations means
(a) God's plan for the insects; each individual goes through three or four body forms very unlike each other: egg, larva, pupa, adult.
(b) God's plan for the mammals; each adult is a copy of its parents.
(c) God's plan for many polyps; each individual resembles its grandparents (not its parents) in being free-swimming or attached. Free-swimmers have stationary parents; stationary polyps have free-swimming parents.

15. Polyps have (mouths in their feet, porous bodies, hollow intestines, stinging cells, tentacles, scraper tongues, mantles [choose three]).

16. Sea jellies (have stiff glass skeletons, have transparent bodies, are usually fast swimmers, travel by means of fins, eat seaweeds [choose one]).

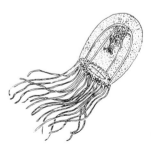

"Blessed be the Lord God, . . . who only doeth wondrous things." Psalm 72:18

4. Amphibians

Song at Dusk

Tiny toes touching the stem, you sing,
    "Come! Come! Come!"
Night is balmy in new-born spring.
    "Come! Come! Come!"
Are you a cricket in varnished coat?
Are you a warbler of silvery note?
No, you're a peeper with bubbled throat.
    "Come! Come! Come!"

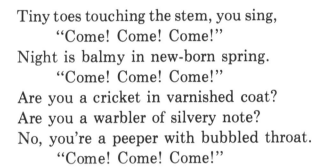

"God my maker . . . giveth
songs in the night." Job 35:10

27. Creatures of the Double Life

God has created most vertebrate animals in a wide variety of sizes. The tiniest bird is the 2¼-inch, dime-weight Cuban bee hummingbird. The biggest creature with feathers is the ostrich, weighing up to 345 pounds and standing up to 8 feet tall. Reptiles differ even more, for the smallest ones are 3-inch skinks and 7-inch earth snakes while the largest animal with scales is the huge leatherback sea turtle reaching 8 feet in length and sometimes 1,500 pounds. But the greatest extremes are in the mammal class. The least shrew weighs ¼ ounce and the blue whale sometimes more than 150 tons with a length up to 100 feet. Some fish are less than an inch long. The whale shark is a 45-ton giant growing up to 50 feet between nose and tail tip.

The Lord has designed only one class of backboned animals without sizable species. These are the amphibians (am-'fib-ē-əns). The goliath frog of west Africa is the largest frog. One 7-pound specimen with its hind legs extended stretched 32 inches from end to end while small relatives are only ½ inch long. The oak toad is a small 1-inch fellow. The giant toad grows to more than 9 inches long. The Japanese giant salamander measures 5 feet and is probably the largest amphibian.

Amphibian means "double life," for this group flourishes both in freshwater and on land. None inhabit the sea, and only a few species can survive in brackish water.

Amphibians are divided into three orders. Some tropical species called the caecilians (si-'sil-yəns) are burrowing and legless.

Two orders live in this country. The tailed amphibians are called salamanders and there are almost ninety species. Those without tails are known as frogs and toads. They number about seventy species.

Worldwide, God has made about four hundred species of salamanders, far outnumbered by His two thousand frog and toad creations.

Amphibians do not grow hair, fur, scales, or feathers. In many species the soft, tender skin acts like a lung, absorbing both moisture and air. Surface glands supply slime that prevents dryness. Amphibians often resemble earthworms in being damp, soft, sticky, and usually cool.

Parotoid (pə-'rō-toid) glands are found on the shoulders of many toads. Along with the smaller warts, these glands give out a thick, whitish liquid that burns the eyes and mouths of many animals that would like to eat the toads. When a young dog tries to chew one, the experience is very unpleasant.

Too weak to be harmful, the liquid is irritating.

Strong venom comes from several foreign frogs. Some South American people smear the tips of their hunting arrows with it. Food animals, when shot, die more surely and quickly. Several species are called arrow-poison frogs.

Amphibians are cold-blooded. Their body temperature is regulated by evaporation from their skins. Hot, dry weather sucks moisture from soil and animals. Death arrives if the creature cannot find shelter.

After rain falls in cool climates, evaporation is slow. In warm, wet areas the air is very humid. Frogs, toads, and salamanders enjoy both.

Insects experience metamorphosis (ˌmet-ə-ˈmȯr-fə-səs) as they develop from egg to adult. Within the secret darkness of the pupal case, the larva

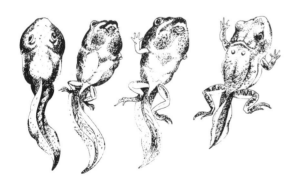

Here are four views of a developing toad. From left to right the tail becomes shorter and smaller. The eyes grow larger and bulge more. The mouth changes from a small, round algae-sucker to a wide opening able to swallow animal food. Legs grow from the body wall except for the left front leg which comes through the breathing pore as the animal shifts from gills to lungs.

transforms completely.

Amphibians metamorphose (ˌmet-ə-ˈmȯr-ˌfōz) also. When the eggs are laid in water, there is no need for protection against drying. Progress in shape, color, and movement can be easily observed.

Amphibians have good hearing. No outside ear openings are present, but the sound receivers, or eardrums, show plainly on the tailless amphibians. Round and flat, they usually cover the sides of the head behind the eyes.

The tropical legless burrowers, caecilians, have no voices. But the male frogs and toads have strong easily heard cries. Special pouches inflate and amplify the tones. Air is passed back and forth over the vocal chords between the lungs and the throat sac. The resulting sound may be a beautiful trill or a peeping or a bleating. It may be a snoring, a clicking, a croaking, a grunting, or even a loud bellow. Females do not call, but they occasionally squawk, especially when alarmed.

Digging amphibians loosen and shovel sand with the horny points on their back feet. Swimming amphibians sail along pushing water with the webs on their hind toes. Climbing members of the class cling with suction pads. Those living on the ground have neither horny points, webs, nor suction pads.

Both reptile and amphibian groups contain species without limbs. Snakes and legless lizards are reptiles. Most lizards and most salamanders have four legs. How are those animals with legs

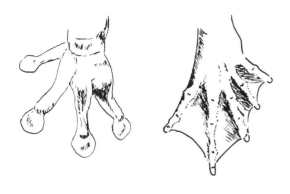

Here is the webbed hind foot of a water-dwelling bullfrog. With these paddles, it swims in long, strong strokes. This front foot of a spring peeper shows the suction pads used by the tree frog family in climbing.

told apart?

Each of a lizard's four feet has five toes. Every toe has a claw. Salamanders do not have claws. Their front feet have only four toes.

Lizards lack the vertical grooves on the sides of the body characteristic of most families of salamanders. Lizards usually have outside ear openings. Most reptiles have no voices. Gechos, crocodiles, and alligators are reptiles that squeak, grunt, or roar.

Dry scales cover the reptiles—the alligators, crocodiles, snakes, lizards, and turtles. Tender, clammy skin and sometimes warts are characteristic of the amphibians—the toads, frogs, and salamanders.

Reptiles emerge from eggs or are born alive looking much like adults. Most amphibians pass through metamorphosis. Some retain larval characteristics throughout life. A few are born alive.

All reptiles, including sea and river dwellers, nest on the shore. Some amphibians live entirely on land when grown. These, along with the aquatic salamanders and frogs, lay their eggs in water or wet places.

Before roads were paved, amphibians could more easily find water. Every horse-and-buggy path was full of holes. Spring rains filled them, and tailless amphibians were within easy hopping distance of a breeding spot. In some communities now there are neither streams, ponds, nor puddles. Toads and frogs are scarce.

One family of toads, however, can survive in surprisingly dry places. The spadefoot toad sometimes lives in deserts although it is very seldom seen.

Six species of these unusual creatures inhabit the United States. Four of them dig in Texas. A single black spade on each hind foot, and rather smooth skin are characteristic of the spadefoot toads. The pupils of their eyes, round in

This frog egg enclosed in its sac of jelly has divided into four parts. It will continue to multiply until it becomes a tadpole with breathing and digestive systems. Then it leaves the egg to gather its own food and to complete metamorphosis.

The plains spadefoot toad lives from Alberta and Saskatchewan south to Texas and Mexico. Eastern spadefoots range from New England west to Missouri and south through most of Louisiana and Florida. The western spadefoot inhabits the California coast and southern Colorado into the interior of Mexico. Mexico, Baja California, and the states bordering them are home to the Couch's spadefoot. Hurter's spadefoot toad digs in Oklahoma, Arkansas, Louisiana, and Texas.

darkness, contract in daylight to a vertical oval slit. Parotoid glands show faintly or not at all.

A spadefoot toad held on the palm of the hand will not leap away as another amphibian might do. Instead it will begin rocking backward, scratching with its little black spades in an attempt to dig in.

Sometimes as it burrows it will turn about as if screwing itself down. Very shortly it will have settled below without leaving a trace of its activity.

The plains spadefoot is found on the Alberta-Saskatchewan borders and south through Montana, Wyoming, and the Dakotas to the Chihuahuan Desert in Texas and Mexico. The little black spade on each hind foot is wedge-

shaped. A hard bump rises between the eyes. Males can be distinguished from females by three black pads on the three inner toes of each front foot. These pads show at egg-laying time. Four vague lighter lines often run down the back.

This small creature lives in open grasslands. Probably it eats insects and arachnids as it burrows deeper and deeper. Spadefoots have been found at a depth of 12 or more feet.

Weeks or months pass. The partly dormant creature is breathing through its skin. The plains spadefoot waits in the undried subsoil.

Sooner or later a heavy rain falls. Spadefoots spurt from the earth and gather by hundreds at wide shallow sheets of water. Their loud bleatings summon their fellows still below, and those struggle frantically to the surface. The sun has set. The air is cool and moist. The rain is deliciously fresh and wet. The delighted amphibians plunge in. The long-hoarded eggs drop by thousands into the water. Swelling in the liquid, they expand. In a day or two they hatch. If the weather stays cloudy and humid, the spadefoots frolic above ground, soaking, splashing, and eating worms, beetles, crickets, and spiders.

Hurter's spadefoot is recorded as once spending only 13 days from beginning to end of metamorphosis. This is a growth record, for other species require a little more time. If the puddle where the eggs are laid seeps away before that time, the tadpoles perish. Adults and young able to do so, burrow in again as the water evaporates. The earth dries; they tunnel deeper. If a second rain falls, they emerge again rejoicing. But until the next shower, they stay down. The soil chills; they retreat farther beyond the frost line. Hibernation begins.

Only one of the spadefoot toad family lives between the Mississippi River and the Atlantic Ocean. This is the eastern spadefoot with a sickle-shaped spade. It likes loose, sandy soil, too, and so avoids rocks and mountains. Brown, gray, or black, it has a distinct lyrelike design on its back. Two additional light lines adorn the sides. Males at egg-laying time have three black pads on three toes of each front foot.

Birds and insects are not the only animals that sing. Perhaps that

An alert little eastern spadefoot toad peers down from his perch. This small amphibian is grayish or blackish brown. Four light-yellow lines adorn its upper body, one on each side and two on the back beginning at the eyes and ending in a point at the tip of the spine. Size, $1\frac{3}{4}$-$2\frac{1}{4}$ inches.

chirping sound or that musical call you heard came from neither bird nor cricket, but from the throat bubble of a little amphibian.

Class Project

When daytime temperatures regularly rise above freezing, construct an amphibian breeding place in a low, partly sunny spot. Use a sheet of either black or clear plastic. Cover several square feet with water up to a depth of 6 inches. Build around the edges with rocks or bricks so that the water will be retained. Bring in loose soil or leaf litter and arrange a gradual ascent to the pool on all sides. Supply an inch or more of dead leaves on the bottom for tadpole food. Introduce a few minnows to dispose of mosquito larvae. A rock or piece of waterlogged wood will give shade for the minnows.

If no frogs or toads are noticed nearby, release amphibians picked up elsewhere in the community. If no natural cover is available for protection on cold nights, provide several decaying pieces of wood on the bank beneath which they can burrow. Watch for strings or clumps of eggs.

Questions

Write the letter of the correct sentence ending after the number of the backboned animal class it describes. Not all these characteristics belong to reptiles or amphibians.

1. Reptiles—
2. Amphibians—

(a) are covered with dry scales that retain moisture.

(b) are covered with tender skin supplied with slime glands or mild poison glands.

(c) with legs have five toes with claws on each foot.

(d) with legs have no claws. There are usually four toes on the front foot and five toes on the hind foot.

(e) lay eggs in water or in damp places.

(f) lay eggs on land.

(g) are usually small. A few individuals may reach the length of 5 feet.

(h) of the largest species weigh hundreds of pounds.

(i) are cold-blooded.

(j) are sometimes warm-blooded and sometimes cold-blooded.

(k) are warm-blooded.

(l) may have sharp, horny points or webs on their hind toes. Some have suction pads on all eighteen toes.

(m) often hatch from eggs. Some species are born alive.

(n) are always born alive.

(o) are always hatched from eggs.

(p) are found living in the sea.

(q) are never found in salt water.

(r) often have ear openings.

(s) have round, flat sound receivers on the outside of the head, but no outside ear openings.

(t) have no voices except for a few species.

(u) have many species with loud voices.

3. Spadefoot toads live in (very dry, very wet, sandy, stiff clay, rocky) soil (choose two).

4. Spadefoot toads can be seen (almost every day of the year, on very few days of the year, when the ground is wet, when the ground is dry, in freezing weather, at very high temperatures, when the air is warm and damp [choose three]).

5. Spadefoot toads (are very warty, are rather smooth, have thickly webbed toes, have sharp points on their hind feet for digging, have suction disks for climbing, have round pupils in daylight, have horizontal slit-shaped pupils, have vertical slit-shaped pupils in daylight, [choose three]).

"Stand still, and consider the wondrous works of God." Job 37:14

28. Hopping Insect Eaters

Br-r-r-r-r-r-r-r-r-r-r-r-r-r-r-r-r-rl.

A soft melodious trill ripples out on the quiet evening air. Long and peaceful, it sounds through the dusk of the spring night. Listen!

Br-r-r-r-r-r-r-r-r-r-r-r-r-r-r-r-r-rl.

One of the most beautiful sounds in God's creation on this planet is the call of the American toad. His voice often comes from the garden where he patrols bean rows and lettuce to capture an insect menu.

In Georgia, Alabama, and Mississippi he begins to sing as early as March. In the North or on high mountains he may call as late in the season as July.

By day the American toad looks through eyes as lovely as its voice. The velvety black pupils are surrounded by irises glinting gold within bright metallic rims. Sparkling and watchful, these keen organs observe every movement nearby; and the tongue is quick to connect with animal tidbits. Spadefoot toads have vertical pupils. Other toads have horizontal pupils. The skins of most toads gradually darken or lighten to match their surroundings.

The brightly colored Hudson Bay toad, much like its direct relative, the American toad, is found from the coast of Labrador to west of the James Bay in eastern Ontario. The reddish dwarf American toad lives from Indiana to northern Texas or Oklahoma. The trill of the dwarf American species is higher pitched than the other two, but all three have melodious voices.

A still higher tone comes from the throat of the southern toad, found from southeastern Virginia to the Mississippi River and throughout Florida. Usually

Among the most beautiful of animal sounds in North America is the call of this American toad. His throat bubble is almost as large as his head. Brown, gray, brick-red, or olive of skin, its light spots may be tan or yellow while its dark ones are brown or black. The one or two large warts in its dark spots are sometimes dark brown, red, orange, or yellow. The chest is usually spotted. Size, 2 to $3\frac{1}{4}$ inches. The Hudson Bay and the dwarf American toads are near relatives.

The American toad and its subspecies are found in the eastern part of North America from Newfoundland, Quebec, and Ontario south to Texas and the other Gulf states. The Canadian or Dakota toad lives from the Northwest Territories south to Montana, South Dakota, and Minnesota. Listen for a melodious trill. (Shaded—American toad range, lines—Canadian toad range.)

heard from March to October, he, too, purls a melodious trill, 2 to 8 seconds long, and an octave higher. The American toad sings 6 to 30 seconds without stopping.

A second trio of toads that resembles the American toad group is the Woodhouse's toad and its nearest relatives, the Fowler's toad and the southwestern Woodhouse's toad. All seven species so far mentioned have smooth, bulging parotoid glands on their shoulders. Toads other than spadefoot toads have two sharp points on each hind foot for digging.

The American toad trio have one or sometimes two warts in each dark blot on their sides and backs. Usually they have chest spots on creamy underparts. The Woodhouse's toad and its two nearest relatives have three or more warts in each dark spot and, in most

specimens, no markings on the undersides. These slight differences in appearance can be noticed by a keen observer.

But, alas, *any* listener can know the difference in the calls of the American toad group and the Woodhouse's group. Instead of a long liquid ripple, there is only a short coarse *wa-a-a* much like the bleating of a sheep, lasting 1 to 4 seconds.

Students of toads are also able to identify these warty animals by noticing the tiny ridges on their heads between their eyes and their parotoid glands. These ridges are shallow and scarcely thicker than a heavy sheet of

This Fowler's toad has three or more small warts in each of its dark spots. Usually the underparts are clear and unmarked. Woodhouse's and southwestern Woodhouse's toads have a similar appearance. Like the American toad they have a light line down the center of the back. Greenish, yellowish, brownish, and grayish with darker spots, the Woodhouse's toad group has a whitish or pale-yellow belly. Size, 2 to 3 inches.

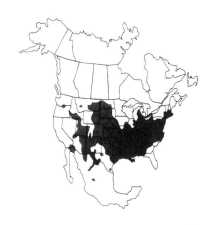

The Woodhouse's toad, the Fowler's toad, and the southwestern Woodhouse's toad are found in some areas of nearly every state except some of the New England states, Minnesota, Wisconsin, and Florida. Listen for a sheeplike wa-a-a.

paper. The ridges of the Fowler's toad touch the parotoid glands; the ridges of the American toad are partly or altogether separate from the glands. The southern toad has knobs on the rear tips of its ridges that extend far back onto its neck.

Found from southwestern Kansas to southern California and into Mexico is the red-spotted toad. It lives in dry country but chooses a home near a cattle watering tank, a pool, or a spring.

The red-spotted toad calls during April to September in a pleasing 4- to 10-second trill somewhat like the southern toad. This creature lays eggs singly instead of in strings as fellow amphibians do. When rains fall, it searches out a pool; then , climbing onto rocks at the water's edge, it warbles away.

After 40 to 60 days, the young are jumping out on shore. Newly metamorphosed red-spotted toads are $\frac{2}{3}$ inch long. Adults grow to 3 inches.

Along the rims of northern lakes lives the Canadian or Dakota toad. This 2- to 3-inch creature may be brownish, greenish, or reddish. The warts in the dark spots on its back are brown or rusty, and a light stripe runs along the spine. Altogether it is rather a handsome creature. Unlike most other toads, it has a large bump between the eyes; but its horizontal pupils and thick sprinkling of warts distinguish it from the plains spadefoot that also has a bump between the eyes.

The Canadian toad has a rather soft, low trill lasting up to 5 seconds and repeated two or three times a minute. Its air-filled vocal sac is round, as are the sacs of all the before-mentioned species. It takes to water like a frog, and may swim out away from the bank to

The red-spotted toad is a dry-country toad found near watering troughs, springs, and streams of the Southwest. Shades of brown, olive, or gray are its background colors; and the warts are tan or reddish sometimes set in small dark spots. There is no spinal stripe, and the parotoid glands are small and round. The voice is a beautiful musical trill of 4 to 10 seconds long heard from April to September on rainy days. Size, $1\frac{1}{2}$ to $2\frac{1}{2}$ inches.

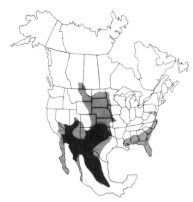

The oak toad occupies the Atlantic coastal and Gulf states from Virginia to Louisiana. The red-spotted toad lives from California to Kansas and far into Mexico. The great plains toad is the most northerly of the three although it likewise lives south into the interior of Mexico. (Shaded—great plains toad, vertical lines—oak toad, horizontal lines—red-spotted toad.)

avoid capture.

The great plains toad, also called western toad, is often found along irrigation ditches, in river bottoms, and in grasslands of the Middle West. It moves about only at night and is a great burrower. It has very large dark blotches on its back, each bordered by a light line and containing many warts. Its skin may be gray, brownish, yellowish, or greenish.

A male toad singing is a sight to see. The large sausage-shaped vocal sac puffs out until it is one-third the size of the animal itself. An earsplitting sound like a riveter at work rends the air. A call may last 30 seconds, and a chorus of these noisemakers can be heard for 4 miles.

The smallest toad living in this country is the oak toad, which varies in its colors from light gray to black. From a sausage-shaped vocal sac like that of

the great plains toad issues a loud peeping like a sadly lost baby chick. From April to October its calls are heard. It hunts food in the day, unlike most toads, which hunt at night. Warm, heavy rains trigger the oak toad's egg laying.

Toads, as other amphibians do, lay their eggs in water or in a damp place. The eggs are like long strands of jelly with round black dots spaced a fraction of an inch apart. Once laid, they absorb water and swell until they may occupy more space than the animal that laid them. Soil that clings and conceals is soon picked up.

In several days tiny creatures called tadpoles or polliwogs emerge. New tadpoles hang motionless by mouth suckers most of the day although they occasionally wiggle quickly to a new position an inch or so away.

The markings of an oak toad always appear in pairs on either side of a spinal stripe which is white to orange. The warts are red, orange, or brown. If the background color is dark brown or black, the stripe may be the only pattern because both spots and warts will be hidden. The voice of this small creature sounds like a lost baby chick. Size, $\frac{3}{4}$ to $1\frac{5}{16}$ inches.

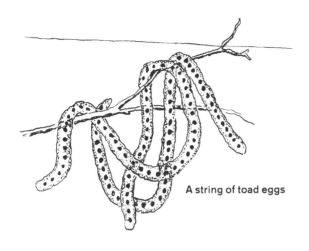

A string of toad eggs

The black specks are clumps of cells. Each will develop into a toad if not eaten first. The gelatin covering encloses the eggs until they hatch.

A polliwog draws water into its mouth, passes it over the gills, and through a hole in the left side of the body. Days pass. Hind legs appear. Front legs develop beneath the skin. Eyes bulge out. Eyelids grow. The head flattens, and the mouth widens. The front legs enlarge, the left one emerging from the breathing pore and filling it. Meanwhile lungs form to replace the gills when the toad lives on land. Tadpoles eat mostly vegetable food, such as algae; but toads enjoy a diet of insects, arachnids, and earthworms. The digestive system changes.

The tail is becoming smaller. The material in it supports the growth of the rest of the body. The creature begins to breathe near the top of the water. It raises its head above the surface more and more. One day it hops onto the bank. From then on, it breathes air altogether and can drown just as surely as any other lunged animal.

Toad eggs hatch soon, sometimes in 3 days or less. Two months later, metamorphosis is finished and the miniature adult is hunting food on land.

Possibly eight thousand eggs are laid by a single female, but very few survive. Crayfishes, water insects, snakes, turtles, and larger frogs all swallow eggs and small tadpoles. Toadlets are picked up by a host of other creatures. As they develop an unpleasant taste, enemies decrease; but hognosed snakes, skunks, crows, and hawks continue to eat even full-sized adults. Toads grow larger throughout life.

The tongue of a toad, fastened at the front of the mouth, is a long elastic organ covered with very sticky saliva. Toads eat only moving food. If an insect remains quiet within reach of a toad, it will not be swallowed so long as it is

This Gulf Coast toad is eating a meal worm by flipping out a sticky, limber tongue. Notice the dark side stripe bordered above by a light stripe extending back from a triangular parotoid gland. Its voice is a short, rather musical trill lasting from 2 to 6 seconds and repeated six or more times a minute. Size, 2 to 4 inches.

still. Only when it begins to move, will the mouth open, the tongue fly out and back, and the lips shut faster than our eyes can follow. As soon as the food animal is inside, the eyes close and become level with the outside of the body. They bulge into the mouth cavity, apparently helping to push the morsel down the throat.

Like insects and various others of God's animals that grow rapidly, the toads often shed their skins. They begin by yawning widely. They twist, stretch, and yawn again and again. They rub their sides with their toes, extend their legs, and arch their backs. The front feet scratch and pull. The skin remains attached at each side of the jaws while it is slowly loosened everywhere else. At last all is peeled off and stuffed into the

←——— 2¼ inches ———→

This walking toad's track was made on a dusty road. Notice how the feet dragged.

mouth. Several large gulps pull it inside. Now the amphibian is fresh and clean in a new skin.

Toads feast on thousands of insects and are important predators of many crop-eating beetles and bugs. It has been estimated that each animal devours several thousands of insects a month. Toads should never be killed, but be encouraged to live in gardens and around lawns and shrubbery.

The giant toad, a South and Central American species, has been brought into the United States to protect the sugar cane crop. Growing up to 8½ inches, not counting the legs, these warty amphibians devour large numbers of sugar cane beetles that would otherwise feed on the cane. Australia, Hawaii, and tropical cane-growing countries have welcomed the giant toad as a muncher of sugar beetles.

Toads are cold-blooded; so in winter they must seek shelter. They burrow into the ground below the frost line. Some crawl under deep piles of leaves which protect them from the cold and provide comfortable moisture. Digestion stops. Breathing and heartbeat slow. The toad sleeps.

The earth turns and whirls along its orbit. Sooner or later the small creature wakes to the warmth and activity of another spring.

The sun shines. Balmy airs float past. The toad digs out, then hops toward a sheet of shallow water. The throat bubble fills.

Br-r-r-r-r-r-r-r-r-r-r-r-r-r-r-rl.

Class Project

Using an amphibian guide, list the tailless amphibians that live in your area. Determine which species are heard at the present time of the year. Become familiar with their calls by listening to records or by reading voice descriptions.

During or after rain showers, linger near water and listen for their songs. Bring reports to class of any amphibians seen or heard.

Questions

1. Which of the following are correct (choose two)?
   (a) All toads have voices.
   (b) All toads have beautiful voices.
   (c) Some toads have lovely voices.
   (d) No toads have musical voices.

2. After toad eggs are laid (they remain the same size, they partly dissolve and become smaller, they absorb water and grow larger).

3. Which statement is correct?
   (a) Like insects emerging from pupa cases, toads are as large when they complete metamorphosis as they will ever be.
   (b) Unlike insects emerging from pupa cases, toads grow most after they complete metamorphosis.

Match the animals with their songs (a-f below).

4. American, Hudson Bay, and dwarf American toads
5. Woodhouse's, Fowler's, and southwestern Woodhouse's toads
6. Southern and red-spotted toads

7. Oak toad
8. Great plains toad, also called western toad
9. Canadian toad, also called Dakota toad
   (a) A loud, piercing sound like a riveting machine, lasting up to half a minute
   (b) a soft, low trill up to 5 seconds long and repeated 2 or 3 times a minute
   (c) a low, rich trill lasting up to half a minute
   (d) a sweet, very high-pitched trill up to 8 or 10 seconds long
   (e) a peeping like a lost baby chick
   (f) A short, coarse *wa-a-a* like the bleating of a sheep, lasting 1 to 4 seconds

10. Toads most often lay their eggs (in long strings, one at a time, in clumps, in sheets, in bands three or four eggs wide).

11. Which statement is true?
    (a) Toads lay eggs by the thousands. Most of them become full-sized adults.
    (b) Toads lay eggs by the dozens.

Most of them become full-sized adults.

(c) Toads lay one to twenty eggs. Most of them become adults.

(d) Toads lay eggs by the thousands. Few of them become full-sized adults.

(e) Toads lay eggs by the dozens. Few survive.

(f) Toads lay one to twenty eggs. All of them perish.

12. Toads (eat both vegetable and animal food throughout their lives, eat mostly vegetable food as tadpoles and animal food as adults, eat mostly animal food as tadpoles and vegetable food as adults, eat vegetable food almost entirely from hatching time on, eat animal food almost entirely from hatching time on).

13. Toads (die out over the winter but the eggs survive, migrate when cold weather comes, hibernate when cold weather comes, are active throughout the year both in warm and in cold climates).

14. The following animals eat toads even though the skin glands put out a burning liquid: (dogs, cats, rats, skunks, owls, hawks, crows, hog-nosed snakes).

15. Toads (are of no use to man one way or another, are valuable to man because they destroy many harmful insects, damage garden plants by chewing off tender shoots).

Divide male and female characteristics of toads. Some belong to both.

16. Male—

17. Female—

(a) two points on the sole of each hind foot for digging

(b) unspotted light throat without folds

(c) horizontal pupil

(d) parotoid glands

(e) black or dark throat sagging in folds

"Sing unto him . . . : talk ye of all his wondrous works." Psalm 105:2

29. Long-legged Leapers

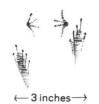

←—3 inches—→

One of the surest signs of winter's close is the call of the spring peeper. The air may be chill; unmelted snow can lie on the ground. But if warm rains fall or mild breezes blow, a sound like distant sleigh bells tinkles from woodland pools. The peepers call.

This tiny singer with the **X**-shaped mark on the back is welcome to all who know him. Clear pink underparts, bright eyes, and slender legs add to his delicate appearance. Rarely seen when silent, this small amphibian sounds its gay whistle at early dusk.

The chorus frogs are equally tiny. The western chorus frog with its near relatives—the New Jersey chorus frog, the upland chorus frog, and the boreal chorus frog—is characterized by dark side stripes. Each has a light line lying along the upper lip, and usually the back is striped with rows of dots or solid lines.

Spring peepers and chorus frogs belong to the tree frog family although they climb only into weeds and low bushes in search of insects. The females grow much larger than the males.

The four cricket frogs are tree frogs, too, but their lack of toe pads reveals that they live on the ground. Their calls sound like two pebbles being clicked together. When chased, they hop one way and then another just like a desperate cricket zigzagging to safety. A dark triangle between the eyes, webbed

In the north the spring peeper is heard from the first warm rain to as late as June. In the south this light-brown, gray, or olive amphibian begins singing in November and continues at various times until March. Size, $\frac{3}{4}$ to $1\frac{1}{4}$ inches.

From the southern shores of the Hudson Bay south to the Gulf of Mexico, the northern spring peeper lives and thrives. The southern spring peeper in Georgia and northern Florida is similar with dark spots below.

toes without pads, warty skins, and black stripes down the insides of the thighs distinguish these tiny $\frac{5}{8}$- to $1\frac{1}{4}$-inch frogs from the equally miniature chorus frogs. Chorus frogs frequently have a dark triangle between the eyes, too, and small pads on slightly webbed toes.

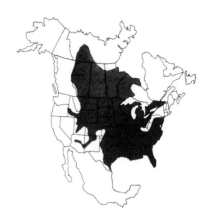

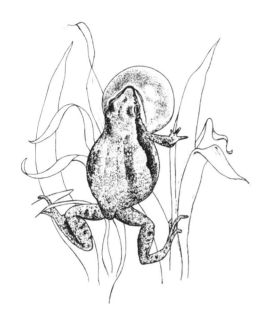

Chorus frogs call during cool rains. They live from near the Arctic Circle in the west south to Arizona and the Gulf of Mexico. In the east they range north to New York. Listen for them from February to June.

This western chorus frog as well as its nearest relatives has two dark stripes beginning at the tip of the nose, running through the eyes and along the sides to disappear where the hind legs join the body. If you take a good pocket comb and flip twenty of its small teeth with the tip of your thumb, you will hear a sound similar to the one being voiced here. Size, $\frac{3}{4}$ to $1\frac{1}{2}$ inches.

small beetles, and termites are its food for it has a small mouth. Sometimes it visits anthills after dark and eats its fill.

The eastern narrow-mouthed toad burrows beneath boards, logs, leaf mold, and sawdust piles near the borders of streams and ponds. The great plains species likes rocky, open-wooded slopes and marshy sloughs. It descends

Narrow-mouthed toads are extremely small and plump frogs. The fold of skin across the head can be rolled forward to wipe insects off the eyes.

A narrow-mouthed toad runs on short legs, hops an inch or so at a time, and then scuttles swiftly away. Ants,

The narrow-mouthed toad has a triangular body slanting from a slender, pointed snout to broad hips. The skin is smooth, glistening, and moist with a fold of skin crossing the head from side to side. Size, $\frac{7}{8}$ to $1\frac{1}{2}$ inches.

The wood frog ranges farther north than any other American reptile or amphibian. Labrador and Alaska are its home; and it lives, too, in high mountains farther south.

orphosis at the length of $\frac{1}{2}$ inch.

Slightly larger than these junior-sized amphibians is the wood frog, a beautiful black-masked copper, pink, or bronze inhabitant of the far North. Found in Labrador, most of Alaska, and south to northeastern Georgia, this lovely creature may be various shades of brown to nearly black. Sometimes it is two-toned with one color on the back and another on the sides. There may be a spinal stripe. There is always a white band below the black mask.

True to name, these amphibians prefer moist woodlands and do not live by ponds or streams as most frogs do. A shallow tundra pool may be all the water necessary to receive the greenish egg masses.

Male wood frogs at egg-laying time have enlarged front legs and inside toes. Their vocal sacs expand under the chin and over both shoulders as they voice a call like the sound of a wheel needing oil, *kraa-aarrak-kraakk*.

The eggs float in clumps of perhaps three thousand. They may be laid from

into cracks of drying mud and digs under stones. It also roams the Sonoran and Chihuahuan deserts. These odd-shaped amphibians share the burrows of the kangaroo rats and various reptiles. They have even been discovered as den mates with tarantulas, apparently quite at peace with the big, hairy spiders.

Probably the bad-tasting skin secretions of this small frog are a protection against snakes, lizards, and birds.

Narrow-mouthed toad males gather at shallow water pools, their front feet resting on leaves and stems, their bodies and hind legs floating free. Their dark throats blow out in a short whistle ending in a 1- to 4-second bleating buzz. The sound does not carry very far, but a listener near at hand hears a loud urgent chorus. If the water is deep with vegetation floating on it, the pale-throated female deposits her eggs on the wet mat. Tadpoles finish metam-

The wood frog may be buff, tan, pink, or bronze with a dark patch reaching back from the eye. Size, $1\frac{3}{8}$ to $2\frac{3}{4}$ inches.

From the eyes to the tip of the spine the pickerel frog has a double row of square dark spots. On the hidden surfaces of the hind legs are streaks of bright orange or yellow. Males call underwater as well as above water in a 1- to 2-second snore. Size, 1¾ to 3 inches.

mid-March to April while the snow is still on the ground and the water is cold. The 2- to 4-inch cluster is attached to vegetation near the edge. If this shallow border water freezes or evaporates, the eggs will die.

Some of the eggs often do hatch in 10 to 14 days; and the froglets that survive, metamorphose later at the length of ¾ inch.

While wood frogs vary a great deal from one location to another, the Pacific tree frog is very changeable as an individual. Furthermore, it can go through all its diverse colors and patterns in 10 minutes. Deep, even green with or without darker green markings, tan with brown patterns, gray shades, a spotted back, reddish color, a dark

triangle between the eyes, and a black eye stripe from nose to shoulder are some of its alterations.

The males are smaller than the females, and they have a dark throat. Calling in a reedy, swinging vibration the populations carry on egg laying from January to July.

Like the boreal chorus frog and the northern cricket frog that have shorter legs than their southern relatives, the individuals of the wood frog tribe that live in the far North have shorter legs than those of the same species farther south.

The pickerel frog has a light band running along the upper jaw and pale-yellow ridges extending from the eyes to the bases of the hind legs. Cool northern bogs and streams are its home although it does venture into fields to catch insects.

Like many toads, pickerel frogs have strong secretions from their skin glands that repel predators. These liquids can even cause the death of other species confined with them.

Similar in appearance to the pickerel frogs are the leopard frogs. Four species are found in North America. Their spots are rounded, sprinkled at random; and they have no bright colors on the hind legs as the pickerel frogs do. The dark spots of the northern leopard frog, like those of the great plains toad, have light borders. Leopard frogs have twin vocal sacs that swell out on their shoulders when inflated. Clucks and grunts are uttered with a 3-second hoarse snore.

Leopard frogs are common and widespread. The four species are shiny bronze or green with dark oval spots of various sizes. Raised light lines run from the eyes to the tip of the body along both sides. Underparts are whitish. Size, up to 4 inches.

The southern leopard frog often has a light spot on its eardrum. Its head is long and pointed. It has fewer spots on its sides than the northern leopard frog. Similar raised ridges extend back from the eyes. The voice is a quavering croaking. Males can be told by the vocal sacs that show even when collapsed.

Along the Pacific coast lives one of the most unusual frogs in the world. This is the tailed frog. It lives in cold, rushing mountain streams at 40 degrees or colder. Anyone wishing to take one home alive must keep it at a temperature lower than 40 degrees. Usually these little creatures do not leave the water unless the weather is cold and rainy. The skin is rough. The toes are webbed. The pupils of the eyes are vertical like those of the spadefoot toads

in daylight. But there is no sign of ears or voice. A distinct "tail," short and pointed, on the male, gives this creature the name of tailed frog. It lives from southern British Columbia along the coast to northwestern California and as far east as the Rocky Mountains of Montana.

The bullfrog lives throughout most of the United States. It grows to a length of 6 inches, and the flesh of its legs is often used for food. Bullfrogs, like the northern leopard frogs, do not show vocal sacs unless they are singing. However, sex can be told by observing the size of the eardrums. Males have eardrums larger than their eyes. Females have eardrums smaller than their eyes.

Mature bullfrogs are much larger than other frogs and can easily be distinguished from them by size alone. Young bullfrogs, as small as other species, can be identified because they have no ridges on the back as green

Leopard frogs are among the most common frogs of North America. These long-legged leapers are found in most of the United States and Canada except the West and Southwest.

frogs and bronze frogs have.

Bullfrogs are named for their deep bellowing voices much like that of a bull. They do not need to seek water at egg-laying time, for they always live in or near water. At the first sign of danger they leap in and dive to the bottom, disappearing into the mud. Most predators, especially land mammals and birds, will immediately give up the chase. Snakes and water mammals will probably not attempt to dig them out.

Bullfrogs eat small snakes, fishes, crayfishes, insects, water beetles, and even small ducklings. Their tadpoles may be more than 6 inches long and spend 2 years in metamorphosis. Bullfrogs lay their black and white eggs in thin sheets about 2 feet square on the water surface. At a length of $1\frac{1}{2}$ inches the young bullfrog hops out on land.

Frogs defend themselves in various ways. Sometimes they hide under boards, rocks, and vegetation. If surprised, they may sit so quietly that the enemy does not notice them. If discovered they leap toward the nearest water at top speed.

Frogs other than wood frogs and narrow-mouthed toads usually stay near water. Winters are spent hibernating in the mud on the bottom. Above a temperature of 40 degrees the frog needs more oxygen than he can obtain from the water. But at temperatures below 40 degrees a frog can draw the required oxygen from the water that surrounds it. The need for oxygen decreases in the cold.

Like all God's creatures, the amphibians have been created to thrive wherever He has designed them to be. Burrows, deserts, low vegetation, cold streams, warm ponds, the far north—all are the happy homes of the musical amphibians.

Class Project

Collect some frog or toad eggs. Place them in an aquarium with several gallons of the water in which they were found. Examine the eggs twice a day with a hand lens.

When they hatch, return all but four tadpoles to the spot where you collected the eggs. Notice the gills which show only briefly before they are covered with skin and become internal. Watch the growth of the tadpoles. A lettuce leaf on the water's surface, floating and rotting, will provide food for them. Release the adult toads or frogs when metamorphosis is complete.

1. Which statement is correct?
   (a) Like birds, frogs and toads are usually quite identical to others of the same species.
   (b) Like cows, frogs of the same species have permanent markings that vary from other individuals of the same species.
   (c) Unlike cows or birds, many frogs have colors and patterns that change from one hour to the next. Most frogs do not have entirely permanent colors.

2. In which of the following ways can male and female frogs or toads of the same species be told apart?
   (a) Males have webbed toes, females unwebbed.
   (b) Females have webbed toes, males have no webs.
   (c) Narrow-mouthed toad and wood frog males have dark throats, females light throats.
   (d) Narrow-mouthed toad and wood frog females have dark throats, males have light ones.
   (e) Males are larger than females.
   (f) Males are smaller than females.
   (g) Bullfrog males have eardrums larger than their eyes; females of the same species have eardrums smaller than their eyes.
   (h) Bullfrog females have eardrums larger than their eyes; males of the same species have eardrums smaller than their eyes.
   (i) Females have sagging skin on their throats because they sing with inflated vocal sacs. Males do not sing and have no throat folds.
   (j) Males have sagging skin on their throats because they sing with inflated vocal sacs. Females do not sing and have no throat folds.

3. The boreal chorus frog, the woodfrog in the far North, and the northern cricket frog have (larger ears, whiter skin, shorter hind legs, louder voices) than the same or similar species in the South.

4. Frogs can hibernate under water because (they need more oxygen at below 40 degrees than at warmer temperatures, they need less oxygen at below 40 degrees than at warmer temperatures, they draw oxygen through their skins from the water that surrounds them [choose two]).

5. Frogs benefit man by (eating injurious insects, destroying weeds).

6. Frogs finish metamorphosis and begin living on land when they are (much smaller than adults, adult size, much larger than adults).

7. Frogs and toads are never found in (the far North, deserts, rain forests, salt water, grasslands, mountains, ponds, underground burrows, streams [choose one]).

8. For their size, frogs have (quiet,

average-volume, very loud) voices.

9. Frogs with webbed toes are (burrowers, icebreakers, swimmers, climbers, fliers).

10. Frogs with suction pads on their toes are (burrowers, icebreakers, swimmers, climbers, fliers).

"O Lord, . . . I will shew forth all thy marvellous works." Psalm 9:1

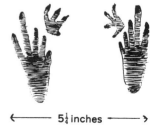

←—— 5¼ inches ——→

30. The Tailed Amphibians

Search a damp, ferny corner. Pull up several mossy rocks near a tinkling brook. Lift the wet leaf mold near that old decaying stump. Explore beside a gushing falls where cold water drips.

Tiny, timid amphibians called salamanders—of soft moist skin, big eyes, and fleshy widespread toes—live in these secret places. Many persons spend an entire lifetime without seeing them although the Americas have far more species than all the remainder of the world combined. Seven families live on this continent.

Most of the giant salamanders are not very attractive. Mud puppies, for example, are quite homely. They have tails wider than their bodies, tiny beadlike eyes near the tops of their heads, and insignificant legs. Their smooth skins may be grayish or rusty with faint blackish spots.

Dark red gills attach at the neck. In cold water rich in oxygen these gills are small tight fringes. If the home waters are muddy or warm with scant oxygen, the mud puppy's gills grow large and feathery. They wave continuously. Fishes, eggs of all kinds, insects, worms, and other water creatures are taken for food.

Mud puppies, unlike frogs and toads, never grow lungs and come out on land. They are permanent water dwellers. Catching sight of them in weedy or marshy places, one will probably think first of eels or water snakes. Southerners have named them water dogs. They may lie coiled like a snake and when disturbed, lash their bodies as a snake does in fleeing. Some giant salamanders have legs so tiny that the front pair is hidden by the gills.

Mole salamanders are another amphibian family. They spend most of their time underground. They have five toes on each hind foot and four toes on each front foot. The delicate skin of their sides is divided by grooves, numbering between one and two dozen.

A mud puppy, or water dog. This aquatic salamander is covered with blotched black and brown skin. It grows slightly more than a foot long and is found from Quebec and Manitoba south to Kansas, southern Missouri, and the Tennessee River. Water dogs live in larger rivers and lakes as well as in creeks. Fish and fish eggs, mollusks, and insects are its food.

The tiger salamander, numbering eight species, ranges through the greater part of the United States. Here are the easternmost areas where the blotched, the gray, the barred, and the eastern tiger salamanders are found.

Various species of the mole salamanders range from southeastern Alaska, Hudson Bay, and southern Labrador south throughout the Mexican plateau.

Sometimes if iodine is lacking in the water, mole salamanders continue in larval form. They breathe through gills until they are reproductive adults. Students formerly took these creatures to be a separate species, but more study showed them to be the same as others that had completed metamorphosis. Adding iodine to the water causes some of them to develop until they are able to live on land.

The tiger salamander, belonging to the mole salamander family, usually spends its adult life on land, living in burrows. Earthworms, insects, arachnids, and various creatures found underground are its food. Like other amphibians, it lays its eggs in water, often after early spring rains. In the

South, most egg laying takes place in winter. Rainy nights are frequently chosen for wandering. To see a salamander by day, one must look beneath rocks, boards, and leaf litter in damp places.

The skin of a newt is rougher and less slimy than that of a mole salamander. Newts lack the grooves on the sides between the front and hind legs. They have the burning skin secretions of various other amphibians and few predators will eat them. Newts spend most of their lives in water.

However, there is one species, the red-spotted newt, that changes its habitat twice. It begins life as an egg laid in water by the parent. After the egg hatches, the larva grows and develops. Finally the gills are replaced by lungs, and the young adult climbs out on land. It is now called an eft. Its smooth, clear skin is bright orange-red or maybe a dull orange. From 1 to 3 years the eft

Tiger salamanders most often have a dark brown or black ground color with yellowish markings. In the West, tiger salamanders often remain in larval form, breathing with gills throughout life and reaching a length of 13 inches. Adult specimens measure 6 to 8 inches long from tip of nose to base of tail.

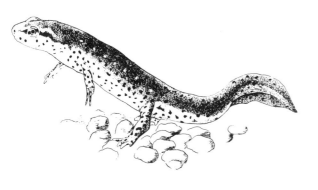

This red-spotted newt, like other newts, lacks the deep side grooves and the slippery skin of most other salamanders. It has red spots in all stages. At various times in its life it is yellow and tan with or without a high tail fin. The land form is all red, and the intermediate is a dark red-spotted olive above and a black-spotted yellow below. Head and body length, $2\frac{1}{8}$ to 4 inches.

lives in damp woods, hunting insects and hiding by day. At the end of this time, the eft once again returns to the water, where it lives permanently. The color of this species varies a great deal throughout its life, but it always carries red spots.

The red-spotted newt flourishes where water is clean. Lakes, quiet pools in streams, ponds, marshes, and ditches are its home. It is sometimes seen in winter, walking about on the bottom. After summer showers, the red efts often come out by dozens or even hundreds and travel over mossy banks during the day.

Especially on the eastern coastal plain, the red-spotted newt may have only two stages. It grows from a larva to a water-dwelling adult and does not become a land-roaming eft at all.

On the western coast live the Pacific newts, larger than the eastern ones and uniformly dark above. Their general habits are similar to those of their eastern relatives. Some species succeed in returning to the same pool even when taken a distance of five miles and released. Students surmise that they are guided by a sense of smell.

The largest family of tailed amphibians is the lungless salamander group. Almost two-thirds of the salamanders found throughout the world are lungless salamanders. In these species, oxygen is absorbed through the lining of the mouth and through the skin. There are no lungs.

The brook salamander, the dusky salamander, and the woodland salamander groups are lungless. They vary in appearance as much as the frogs do, and even more because the same individual changes as it becomes older. Many of these animals open their mouths by lifting the upper jaw rather than by dropping the lower one.

The brook salamanders live in small bodies of water where fish, their most likely predators, are scarce. Aquatic vegetation is a safe hiding place. Some species have short projections extending down from their nostrils.

Dusky salamanders are good jumpers and may leap several times the length of their own bodies. These delicate little creatures have four toes on each front foot and five toes on each hind foot as the mole salamanders have. Some dusky salamander females are said to protect their eggs by moving

The western red-backed salamander has a reddish, yellow, or tan stripe on its body and tail bordered by two dark lines. Bellies are spotted equally with black and white. This amphibian, one of the woodland salamanders, is found in southwestern Canada, Vancouver Island, western Washington, and western Oregon. Here a female coils protectingly about her eggs. The eye of the young shows plainly through the clear wall of the egg.

them to a damp hole during dry weather and returning them when the earth's surface is wet again. Woodland salamander larvae develop inside the eggs and emerge in adult state. They have no metamorphosis in water as most other amphibians do.

In limestone regions of the United States and in Europe are found the blind salamanders. These live in caves or other underground waters. Sometimes they are drawn up from deep wells. Pale and partly transparent, they often show internal organs and eggs through their pinkish skins.

The blind grotto salamander in the larval state is much like other tailed amphibians. It lives in mountain brooks and springs, eating animal food. When the grotto salamander matures, tail fins

and outer gills disappear, eyelids grow partly or altogether closed. The brown, gray, and yellow colors vanish. This now-blind creature finds an Ozark cave where it locates food by the sense of touch.

The climbing salamanders with their smooth skins and flat bodies, are found mostly on the Pacific Coast. The Lord has made them well able to climb sheer cliffs and to hide in their cracks. Clouds, fog, and showers dampen rocks sufficiently to keep them comfortable. The speckled black salamander of California is a climbing salamander found in forested areas and damp rockslides. When disturbed it jumps forward a few inches, springing with its hind feet and slapping its tail against the ground. This tail also coils and supports the weight of the body while the salamander climbs. An eastern mountain relative resembles a lichen in its color and skin pattern.

The Mount Lyell salamander in the Sierra Nevada lives near edges of melting snow sometimes at elevations of more than 10,000 feet. It is one of the web-toed salamanders; its webs act almost as suction cups while it climbs about over the nearly vertical rocks in search of beetles, flies, termites, spiders, and centipedes. The strong tail, curled under and forward, brakes the animal's descent as it is pressed into the ground. While the salamander climbs, the tail is extended and waved from side to side for balance.

More than half the year this small amphibian lies dormant beneath the frozen snowy ground.

The Siberian salamander, a chunky 4-inch creature, lives well north of the Arctic Circle. Hibernation brings the animal through the long, severe winters, but no one understands how it can dig below the frost line.

Occasionally these salamanders are found frozen in solid chunks of ice. When spring comes and the ice thaws, they continue their activities as before.

Professor Victor Twitty of this country studied salamanders for years. Finding 262 male salamanders of a land-dwelling species in a single pool at egg-laying time, he marked them and set them free. For 12 months the amphibians roamed the woods in search of food, hid underground in dry weather, then returned to the home pool for egg laying. Year after year a large number came back. Professor Twitty, after 7 years, continued to find and mark 32 percent of the original 262. A larger fraction of the 262 he discovered in other places.

Next he captured one thousand

A Siberian salamander. This shiny creature lives in very cold areas. It has even been found frozen solid in ice and has survived without apparent damage. It spends its winters hibernating below the frost line of its home range.

females, marked them, and took them 3 miles away across a 1,000-foot ridge. Within 3 years eighteen individuals had arrived at the starting point.

Salamanders unable to see can return to a known spot from a mile away. So sight was probably not a guide. Can it be that the Lord has provided these amphibians with ability to smell something distinctive about their own part of a brook from a distance of 3 miles? Or do they pick up other clues unknown to humans? How has the Lord made these animals able to navigate? Will we ever know?

Class Project

Search for salamanders in damp soil. Keep them in a moist terrarium and provide insects, pill bugs, or hamburger bits for food. Identify the species if possible. Release them while the weather is still warm.

Questions

1. Salamanders are (amphibians, reptiles, arachnids).

2. Salamanders are most closely related to (snakes and lizards, frogs

and toads, alligators).

3. Salamanders eat (animal food, plant food, about equal amounts of plant and animal food).

4. (Most people, Very few people) are familiar with salamanders.

5. Salamanders living in caves sometimes lack (legs, hearing, color, ability to smell, tails, sight [choose two]).

6. (Some, Every, No) species of salamanders can endure freezing cold.

7. Salamanders where winters are severe (die, migrate, hibernate, live over winter in egg form).

8. Salamanders do not live (choose three)
   (a) in desert dry places.
   (b) in and near ditches.
   (c) in swamps.
   (d) on the surfaces of permanent ice fields.
   (e) in springs.
   (f) in pools.
   (g) in salt water.
   (h) on wet soil near glaciers.
   (i) in and near ponds.
   (j) in sloughs.
   (k) on high, wet mountains.
   (l) in streams.
   (m) in the far North.
   (n) in rivers.
   (o) in woods.
   (p) in damp meadows and pastures.

Match the name of the salamander family with the letter of the correct description.

Family

9. Giant salamanders
10. Mole salamanders
11. Newts
12. Lungless salamanders

Description

(a) include two-thirds of the world's salamanders, among them the climbing, the dusky, the brook, the blind, the web-toed, the woodland, the red-backed salamanders, and others; absorb oxygen through the skin and the linings of the mouth and throat; have grooves on the sides of the body; lay eggs in water or damp places.

(b) spend their lives in water except for the species that lives on land from 1 to 3 years; have rough skin without slime or grooves on the sides of the body.

(c) include mud puppies and others; always live in water; are long, dark, slender, eel or snakelike.

(d) include tiger salamanders and others; live in burrows; lay eggs in water; have smooth, clammy skin and grooves on the sides of the body; sometimes fail to metamorphose.

"Dost thou know . . . the wondrous works of him which is perfect in knowledge?" Job 37:16

Glossary-Index

ə represents *a* in about, *e* in camel and farmer, *i* in coffin and fir, *o* in come and debtor, *u* in run and fur

a	cat, match	e met, cherry	ī time, five	yü cube, few	ȯi coin, boy
ā	ate, face	ē meat, relief	ō cone, oats	ü tube, soup	aū town, out
ä	father, not	i pin, sing	ȯ dog, claw	u̇ put, look	ŋ ring, ink

---

albino (al-'bī-nō), a person or animal deficient in pigment, usually with a milky or translucent skin, white or colorless hair, and eyes with pink irises and deep-red pupils; a plant that lacks coloring matter, 106

alga ('al-gə), one species of algae; a single plant of this group, 33

algae ('al-jē), seaweeds, pond scums, green slimes, thallophytes containing chlorophyll, 24-30, 32-33, 38, 47, 195, 211-213, 215, 231

algal ('al-gəl), pertaining to an alga, 33, 35, 215-216

Amanita (ˌam-ə-'nīd-ə), a mushroom group containing dangerously poisonous species that grow from a cup often concealed underground, 15-16

ambergris ('am-bər-ˌgris, 'am-bər-ˌgrēs), a waxy substance taken from the intestine of the sperm whale, used in the manufacture of perfumes, 137-138

amphibian (am-'fib-ē-ən), any animal able to live both in water or on land; example: a frog, 53-55, 221-225, 229-230, 232-233, 235, 237, 240, 243-244, 246-247

amplify ('am-plə-ˌfī), to make louder, 222

antibiotic (ˌan-tē-ˌbī-'ät-ik), a substance mostly produced by bacteria and fungi, used as a medicine, 40

antler ('ant-lər), a hard, bony, solid, branched growth, usually in pairs on the heads of bucks of the deer family (including elk, moose, and caribou) and on the heads of caribou does. These branched bony processes are dropped each year and new ones grow to replace them. 95-97

aquatic (ə-'kwät-ik), growing on, living in, or frequenting water, 170, 223

arachnid (ə-'rak-nəd), an invertebrate animal belonging to the group containing spiders, scorpions, mites, and ticks, 70, 179, 183, 224, 231, 244

Artist's fungus ('ärt-əsts 'fəŋ-gəs), a species of pore mushroom growing as a bracket on oak or beech trees, 18-19

bacteria (bak-'tir-ē-ə), the simplest of colorless plants, usually microscopic, 35, 40-41, 46-48

Baja California ('bä-hä ˌkal-ə-'fȯr-nyə), the lower California Peninsula between the Pacific Ocean and the Gulf of California, 146, 180

baleen (bə-'lēn), the whalebone of the mouths of the toothless whales, 135-137, 141, 189-190

beak ('bēk), 1. the thick place or hump at the hinge of a bivalve on both sides. These humps are the earliest part of the shell. 2. any of various rigid, projecting mouth structures, 195-196, 201, 204

beluga (bə-'lü-gə), the white whale, from 10 to 20 feet long, 188

bird ('bərd), a feathered warm-blooded vertebrate, 39, 53-56, 66, 102, 104, 109, 111-112, 120, 123, 128, 161-162, 166, 178, 182, 221, 225, 240

bivalve ('bī-ˌvalv), an animal (as a clam) with a two-valved shell, 194, 199, 201-205, 213, 215

blowhole ('blō-ˌhōl), 1. a nostril in the top of the head of a whale or other cetacean. 2. a hole in the ice to which aquatic mammals (as seals) come to breathe, 135, 138, 188

blubber ('bləb-ər), the fat of whales and other large marine mammals, 146

boreal ('bō-rē-əl), of, relating to, or located in northern regions, 235, 238

brackish ('brak-ish), water that is somewhat salty, 221

burrow ('bər-ˌō), a hole in the ground made by an animal (as a ground hog) for shelter and habitation, 64, 73, 75, 78, 109, 114, 121, 123, 128, 153-156, 158-161, 170, 173, 181, 183, 186, 224, 232, 236-237, 240

caecilians (si-'sil-yəns), burrowing, legless amphibians, 221-222

candelabra plant (ˌkan-də-'lä-brə 'plant), algae of the group called stonewort, 27

canine ('kā-ˌnīn), relating to dogs, wolves, jackals, and foxes, 109-110, 112-114

carbon dioxide ('kär-bən dī-'äk-ˌsīd), a heavy colorless gas, CO_2, formed by the combustion and decomposition of organic substances; it is absorbed from the air by plants in photosynthesis, 25, 39-40, 44

Carnivora (kär-'niv-ə-rə), an order of flesh-eating mammals, 149

carnivore ('kär-nə-ˌvȯr), any of an order of flesh-eating mammals; a flesh-eating animal; a plant that eats insects, 120, 123, 129

carrion ('kar-ē-ən), dead and putrefying flesh, 102, 109, 112, 115, 122-123, 129

cell ('sel), a small mass of the living substance that is the basis of all plant and animal life, with its surrounding walls; the least structural unit of living matter capable of functioning independently, 11, 24-27, 33, 41, 45, 196-198, 207, 214-216

Cetacea (sē-'tā-shē-ə), the mammal group including whales, porpoises, and dolphins, 134

cetacean (sē-'tā-shən), relating to the mammal group Cetacea; a member of this group, 134-135, 138-139

Chihuahuan Desert (chə-'wä-ˌwän 'dez-ərt), a desert lying in Mexico, New Mexico, and Texas, taking its name from the Mexican state of Chihuahua, 224, 237

chiton (ˌkī-tən), any of the mollusks having an upper shell of hard plates, 194-195, 199

chlorella (klə-'rel-ə), any of a group of single-celled green algae, some species of which contain large amounts of proteins, fats, and carbohydrates suitable for use as human food, 30

chlorophyll ('klȯr-ə-ˌfil), the green color of some plants, 25, 28, 30, 33, 38

conch ('käŋk), a spiral univalve with a large heavy shell and thick expanded lip. It lives in warm seas north to Florida. Some whelks are called conchs. 210

coney ('kō-nē), the European hyrax, a hoofed mammal mentioned in the Bible. Its size, color, shape, and habits resemble the American cony, usually called pika. 77

cony ('kō-nē, 'kun-ē), the little chief hare, or pika; also spelled coney, 77

coral ('kȯr-əl), a stony substance composed of the skeletons of polyps; the sea animal whose skeleton becomes coral, 216

coypu ('kȯi-pü), a South American water rodent introduced into the United States on the Gulf Coast and in the Pacific Northwest, 173, 176

desmids ('dez-məds), one-celled, green fresh-water algae, 25-26

diatoms ('di-ə-ˌtämz), one-celled, golden-brown fresh- or salt-water algae, 27

dormant ('dȯr-mənt), asleep, inactive, 54, 73, 130, 162, 181, 224, 246

echolocation ('ek-ō-lō-'kā-shən), a process used by bats and cetaceans for locating distant or invisible objects by means of sound waves reflected back to the emitter (that is, to the bat or whale) by the object, 84-85, 134-135, 145, 148

elliptical (i-'lip-tə-kəl), of, relating to, or shaped like an ellipse. The pupil of a cat's eye is elliptical in shape. 107

estivate ('es-tə-ˌvāt), to pass the summer in a dormant state, 181

estivation (ˌes-tə-'vā-shən), the state of an animal that estivates, 181

extinct (ik-'stiŋt), no longer existing, 93, 132, 137, 149, 189, 190

feline ('fē-ˌlīn), belonging to the cat family; catlike; a feline animal, 101, 110

ferment (ˌfər-'ment), to cause or undergo fermentation, 40-41

fermentation (ˌfər-mən-'tā-shən), a change such as occurs when yeast makes sugar into carbon dioxide and alcohol, 40-41

filament ('fil-ə-mənt), a very fine threadlike structure, sometimes microscopic, 26-27

fish ('fish), a strictly aquatic, cold-blooded vertebrate, having fins instead of limbs, and having gills to get oxygen from the water, 30, 53, 55, 104, 120, 134, 139, 145, 170, 173, 188, 190, 240, 245

fixation (fik-'sā-shən) of nitrogen, the act of changing nitrogen into a solid form that can be used by plants, 48

flank ('flank), the side of an animal between the ribs and the hip, 173

flukes ('flüks), the parts or lobes of a whale's tail, 134

food chain ('füd 'chän), the relationship of an animal to its food items and to its predators, 39

form ('form), the resting place of a rabbit or a hare, 78-80, 171

freezing ('frēz-iŋ), to become motionless (as a rabbit) to elude an enemy, 79-80

fruiting bodies ('früt-iŋ 'bäd-ēz), spores and the plant parts that hold them; for example, mushrooms, 27, 33-34

fungal ('fəŋ-gəl), pertaining to a fungus, 33, 39

fungi ('fən-ˌjī), more than one fungus, 32, 38-42, 44-45, 47-48

fungus ('fəŋ-gəs), a plant such as the mushroom or mold that grows on other plants or on decaying matter and has no green coloring, 21-22, 32-33, 35, 38, 44

game ('gām), wild animals hunted for sport or food, 109

genus ('jē-nəs), a group of plants or animals ranking next above the species and next below the family. The dog family is composed of several genera (plural of *genus*). One genus contains the gray wolf, red wolf, and the coyote. Another genus has the kit fox and the red fox as members. The arctic fox and the gray fox are in separate genera. Animals in each genus have characteristics in common. (Compare with "order")

gilled mushroom ('gild 'məsh-ˌrüm), mushrooms with radiating plates forming the undersurface of the cap, 13-14, 16, 44

gills ('gils), 1. breathing organs used underwater. 2. the radiating plates forming the under-surface of the cap of a mushroom, 13-14, 18, 21, 194, 201, 206, 210, 231, 240, 243-244, 246

gram ('gram), a metric unit of weight; 0.035 ounce, 213

guano ('gwä-ˌnō), the droppings of bats or sea birds, used as a fertilizer, 88

habitat ('hab-ə-ˌtat), the place where a plant or an animal grows or lives naturally, 56, 59, 120, 244

halibut ('hal-ə-bət), a marine food fish, 188

hare ('har), various swift, timid, long-eared mammals (as the jack rabbit) having a divided upper lip, long hind legs, and a short tail. The young are

252

open-eyed and furred at birth. 79-82, 103, 114, 172, 186, 190

hibernate ('hī-bər-ˌnāt), to pass the winter in a torpid or resting state, 69-71, 73-74, 85-86, 88, 124, 130, 157-158, 164, 187, 225, 240, 247

hispid ('his-pəd), covered with bristles, stiff hairs, or minute spines, 64, 66

horn ('hȯrn), (on mammals) a hard, bonelike, permanent growth composed of material similar to hoofs, occuring in pairs on the heads of adult (both sexes) mountain goats, bighorn sheep, musk oxen, bison, and domestic cattle. Pronghorns are the exception with one prong on each horn and a central bony core that is retained each year when the outer covering is shed. 91,

host ('hōst), any living animal or plant which provides food or lodging for a parasite, 44

Hydnum repandum ('hid-nəm ri-ˈpand-um), an edible, whitish mushroom with toothlike structures hanging from the cap, 19-20

hydra (hī-drə), any of numerous small tubular fresh-water polyps having at one end a mouth surrounded by tentacles, 216

hypha ('hī-fə), a thread growing from a spore; a strand of the mycelium, 11

hyphae ('hī-fē), plural of *hypha*, 11-12

incisor (in-ˈsī-zər), any of the cutting teeth in the center top and bottom of the jaw, 61, 66, 80, 82, 155, 174

insect ('in-ˌsekt), an invertebrate animal that has three pairs of jointed legs, a body formed of three parts, one pair of antennae, and one or two pairs of wings, 54-55, 64, 66, 69-71, 74, 85, 87-88, 104, 110, 115, 120-121, 127, 154-156, 159, 162, 169-170, 179, 186, 194, 222, 224-225, 231-232, 235-236, 238, 240, 244-245, 247

iris ('ī-rəs), the colored part around the pupil of an eye, 101, 227

javelin ('jav-ə-lən), a light spear thrown as a weapon or in hunting, 182

javelina (ˌhä-və-ˈlē-nə), a peccary, 182-183

kelp ('kelp), any of various large brown seaweeds, 28, 149

kit ('kit), a young or undersized fur-bearing animal, 105, 121, 176

krill ('kril), small weakly swimming creatures, usually crustaceans (lobsters, crabs, and shrimps), eaten by baleen whales and other animals, 189, 190, 215

Lactarius (lak-ˈtā-rē-əs), a large genus of white-spored fungus, 13-14

larva ('lär-və), the early form of an animal (as a frog) that at birth or hatching is unlike its parent and must metamorphose before assuming the adult features, 222, 244-245

mycelia (mī-'sē-lē-ə), plural of *mycelium,* 12, 33

mycelium (mī-'sē-lē-əm), rootlike threads which develop when a spore germinates, 11-12

nitrogen ('nī-trə-jən), a colorless, tasteless, odorless, gaseous element that constitutes 78 percent of the atmosphere by volume and is a part of all living tissues, 46-48

nodule ('näj-ˌül), a small round lump; a swelling on a root that contains symbiotic bacteria, 47-48

nutria ('nü-trē-ə), the coypu or its fur, 173-174

order ('òr-dər), a grouping of plants or animals ranking next below the class and next above the family. The order of even-toed hoofed mammals is composed of four families: (1) peccaries, (2) the pronghorn, (3) deer, elk, caribou, and moose, (4) wild cattle—bison, bighorn sheep, mountain goat, and musk ox. Animals in each order have characteristics in common. 78, 185, 221

organism ('òr-gə-ˌniz-əm), a living being, 40

oxygen ('äk-sə-jən), a colorless, tasteless, odorless gaseous element that constitutes 21 percent of the atmosphere by volume and is essential to life, 41, 47, 138, 180, 194, 201, 206, 240, 245

palolo (pə-'lō-lō), a segmented worm found in great abundance near the coral reefs of the Samoan islands in the southwest Pacific, 205

parasite ('par-ə-ˌsīt), a plant or an animal that lives in or on another living creature, hindering it by taking food or shelter or both, 44, 145

parasitic (ˌpar-ə-'sit-ik), pertaining to an animal or a plant that is a parasite, 44

parotoid gland (pə-'rō-toid 'gland), a large gland behind the eye and sometimes above the ear in various toads and frogs, 221, 224, 228-229

peccary (pek-ə-rē), a small piglike American mammal found from Texas south to Paraguay; a javelina, 182-183

pemmican ('pem-ə-kən), a concentrated food composed mostly of dried meat, fat, and berries and used by North American Indians, 93

penicillin (ˌpen-ə-'sil-ən), a substance taken from a green mold and used to keep bacteria from multiplying as in treating an infected wound, 40

Phenacomys (fə-'nak-ə-ˌmis), rare volelike rodents living in cold forest regions of Canada and in the high mountains of the western United States, 161

photosynthesis (ˌfōd-ō-'sin-thə-səs), the food-making process of chlorophyll in the presence of light, 25, 38-39

pika ('pē-kə, 'pī-kə), a small mammal of the hare family living in the high mountains of North America; little chief hare also called cony, 77-79, 81-82, 92

Pinnipedia (ˌpin-ə-ˈpē-dē-ə), an order (or suborder according to some systems of classification) of aquatic carnivorous mammals including the seals and the walrus, 144

piñon (ˈpin-ˌyən), a group of dwarf pine trees whose seeds are called "nuts", 161

plankton (ˈplaŋk-tən), the passively floating sometimes-minute animal and plant life of a body of water, 190, 194, 207, 215

pod (ˈpäd), a whale or seal family group, 135, 137, 145

polyp (ˈpäl-əp), a water animal with a hollow tubelike body, closed and attached at one end and opening at the other by a central mouth, surrounded by tentacles armed with stinging cells. Some polyps are not attached, but are free-swimming. 214-217

polypore (ˈpäl-ē-ˌpōr), a pore fungus, 18

pore (ˈpōr), a minute opening in an animal or a plant, 18-19, 21, 199, 215, 231

pore-bearer (ˈpōr ˈbar-ər), the literal meaning of Porifera (pə-ˈrif-ər-ə), the name applied to sponges, 198

precocious (pri-ˈkō-shəs), capable of a high degree of independent activity from birth, 98

predator (ˈpred-ət-ər), one that preys, destroys, or devours; an animal that lives by predation, 39, 64, 74, 79-80, 98, 115-116, 120, 122-123, 125, 157, 165-166, 171-172, 175, 232, 238, 240, 244-245

pronghorn (ˈpròŋ ˌhòrn), a ruminant mammal of western North America that sheds its horns (not antlers) each year, 90-91, 93

pruning balm (ˈprün-iŋ ˈbäm), a substance smeared on wounds or cuts to aid the healing of living trees, 12

punk (ˈpəŋk), a dry spongy substance prepared from fungi and used to ignite fires, 19

pupa (ˈpyü-pə), an intermediate stage of a metamorphic insect, 222

pupil (ˈpyü-pəl), the dark center in the iris of the eye which expands and contracts, 101, 107, 144, 223, 227, 229, 239

quahog (ˈkō-ˌhòg), a round thick-shelled American clam whose purple and white valves were used along with whelk shells in making beads for wampum. It is a very important food clam. 202

rabbit (ˈrab-ət), a small long-eared mammal that is related to the ordinary hares but differs from them in producing naked young and in its burrowing habits, 39, 57, 78-82, 102, 104, 109-111, 122-123, 167, 171, 178, 181

reptile (ˈrep-təl), any of a class (Reptilia) of air-breathing vertebrates that include the alligators and crocodiles, lizards, snakes, and turtles, 53-55, 111, 120, 178-179, 182-183, 221-223,

rodent ('rōd-ənt), a mammal with long, sharp, continually growing front teeth used for cutting or gnawing, 61, 64, 71-75, 81-82, 86, 102, 109-110, 114-115, 155-157, 161, 163-165, 174-176, 179-181, 183, 185-186

ruminant ('rü-mə-nənt), characteristically cud-chewing; a cud-chewing animal, 91, 92, 95-98, 182

saprophyte ('sap-rə-ˌfīt), a fungus which may be a bacterium, or any other plant that lives upon dead plant or animal matter, 39, 44

saprophytic (ˌsap-rə-'fid-ik), pertaining to a saprophyte, 39

Sargasso Sea (sär-'gas-ō 'sē), an elliptical, relatively still tract in the North Atlantic Ocean strewn with free-floating seaweed called sargassum, 29

sargassum (sär-'gas-əm), a brown seaweed growing abundantly in warm tropical water, 28

scavenger ('skav-ən-jər), an organism that feeds habitually on refuse or carrion, 39

scent post ('sent 'pōst), a mat of cut stems, leaves, and mud topped with a few drops from the musk glands of the muskrat; other animals make scent posts of other descriptions, 172

scull ('skəl), to propel forward through water with a crosswise motion, 144

scum ('skəm), a coating of algae, 25

sea anemone ('sē ə-'nem-ə-nē), a polyp with bright colors, and many tentacles around its mouth. It resembles a flower. 216

segment ('seg-ˌment), any of the parts into which a thing is divided or naturally separates, 21, 205-206

sepia ('sē-pē-ə), 1. a genus comprising the cuttlefish. 2. a brown color prepared from cuttlefish secretions, 197

siphon ('sī-fən), an organ through which water is drawn into or expelled from the body of an aquatic animal such as a mollusk, 201

smut ('smət), a parasitic fungi growing on cereal grasses and marked by transformation of plant organs into dark masses of spores, 44-45

Sonoran Desert (sə-'nō-rən 'dez-ərt), a desert lying in Mexico, California, and Arizona, taking its name from the Mexican state of Sonora, 237

species ('spē-shēz), a category of biological classification ranking immediately below genus, 13-16, 19-21, 24-25, 27, 32-33, 36, 44, 55, 58-59, 61, 63-66, 69, 75, 78-80, 86-87, 90, 95, 109-110, 122-123, 128, 137, 140-141, 144, 147-148, 159, 165, 167, 171, 173-174, 178-181, 185, 190, 194, 205-207, 213, 216, 221-224, 227-229, 232, 236, 238, 243-245

specimen ('spes-ə-mən), a plant or animal, entire or in part, prepared and kept as an example to illustrate a species or variety, 18, 66, 149, 221, 228

spermaceti (ˌspər-mə-ˈset-ē, ˌspər-mə-ˈsēt-ē), a white waxy solid separated from the oil of the sperm whale, 137

spore (ˈspōr), an extremely small reproductive cell, 11-15, 18-21, 27, 33, 40, 45

symbiosis (ˌsim-bī-ˈō-səs), two species living together in a relationship helpful to both (such as the yucca moth and yucca plant or the algae and fungi together in a lichen), 32

symbiotic (ˌsim-bī-ˈät-ik), pertaining to symbiosis, 32, 47

tadpole (ˈtad-ˌpōl), a larval amphibian, 224, 230, 237, 240

tarantula (tə-ˈranch-ə-lə), any of various large hairy spiders of the southwest United States and Europe, 237

teat (ˈtēt), a nipple through which milk is drawn from the mammary gland, 72

tentacle (ˈten-tə-kəl), a long, thin, flexible projection from the head or mouth of an animal used for feeling, grasping, or sometimes for moving, 154, 206-207, 210, 214-217

thallophyte (ˈthal-ə-ˈfīt), a plant without true roots, stems, or leaves; algae, fungi, bacteria, and lichens, 24-25, 32-33, 44

thallus (ˈthal-əs), the body of a thallophyte, 33-34, 36

univalve (ˈyü-ni-ˈvalv), a mollusk shell of only one piece, 194, 210-211, 214

valve (ˈvalv), one of the distinct pieces of the shell of a mollusk, 194-195, 201-203, 210-211

veil (ˈvāl), a membrane covering the gills of a fungus; this is broken as the cap of a mushroom opens, leaving a ring on the stem, 13, 15

venom (ˈven-əm), poisonous matter secreted by some kinds of animals and transmitted to prey or an enemy, 183, 222

vertebrate (ˈvər-tə-brət, ˈvər-tə-brāt), having a spinal column, or backbone, 53-55, 101, 134, 221

vocal sac (ˈvō-kəl ˈsak), inflatable resonating sacs in the mouth of various frogs and toads, 229-230, 237-239

volva (ˈväl-və), a membranous sac or cup about the base of the stem in many gill fungi. Remants of this volva also remain in the form of warts on the surface of the cap of some species. 13

wart (ˈwȯrt), a horny projection on the skin or a hardened protuberance on a plant, 15, 21, 221, 223, 228, 232

whelk (ˈhwelk, ˈwelk), a large spiral-shelled sea snail, one kind of which is used in Europe for food. Whelks have short spires, large body whorls, and long front canals. 210, 213

yeast (ˈyēst), a minute fungus, 40-42

yucca (ˈyək-ə), plants of the lily family, 32

zoospore (ˈzō-ə-ˌspōr), a spore, produced among some algae and fungi, that is provided with tiny hairs by means of which it can move about; a similar body among some microscopic animals, 26-27, 215